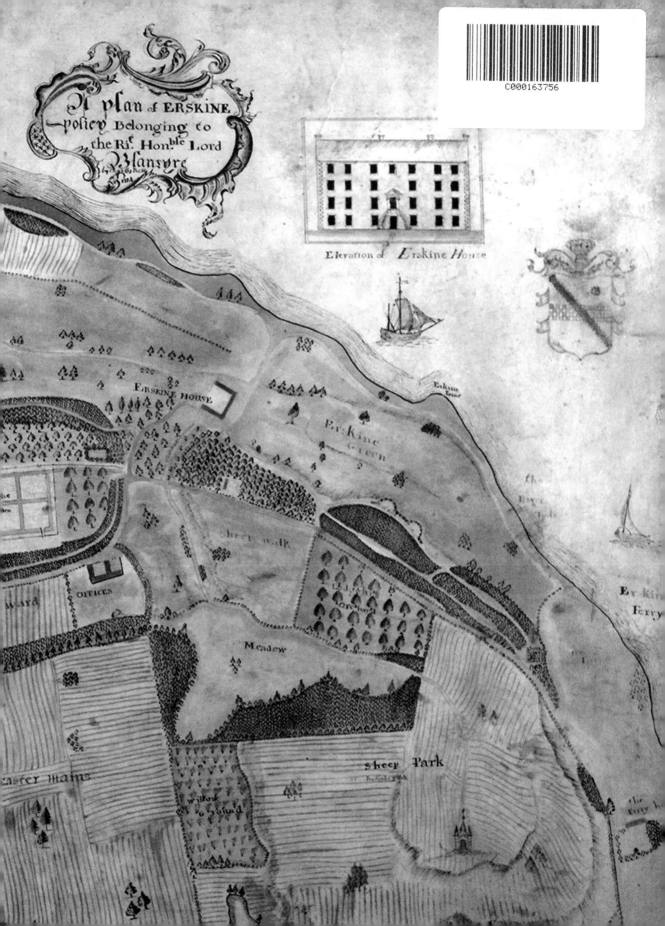

A plan of ERSKINE posses Belonging to the R.t Hon.ble Lord Blantyre

Elevation of Erskine House

ERSKINE HOUSE

Erskine Green

Erskine Ferry

sheep walk

Orchard

Meadow

OFFICES

Sheep Park

aster Mains

willow ground

The Scottish Countryside

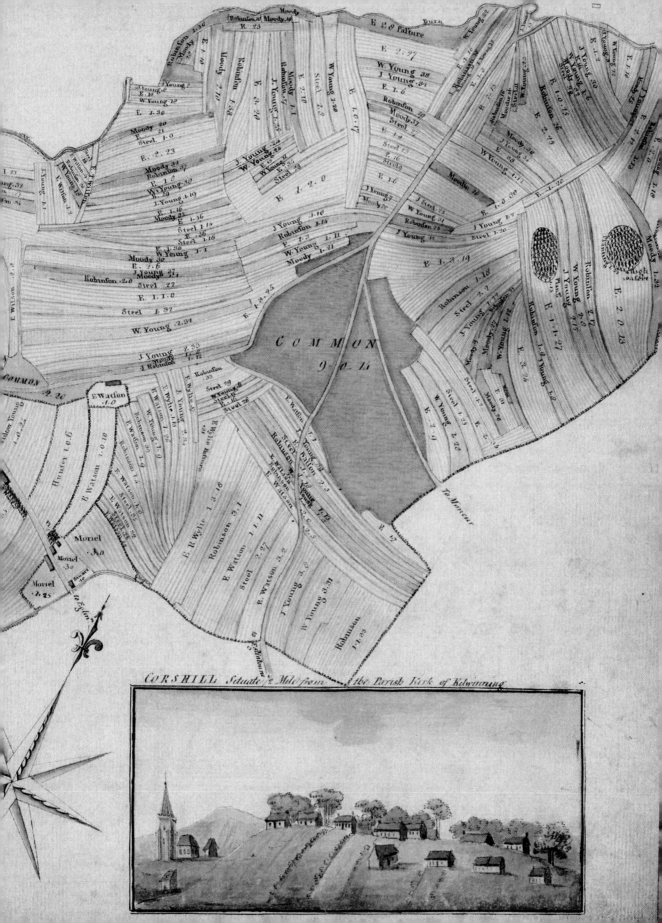

CORSHILL: Situate ½ Mile from the Parish Kirk of Kilwinning

ROSEMARY GIBSON

The Scottish Countryside

Its Changing Face, 1700–2000

IN ASSOCIATION WITH
THE NATIONAL ARCHIVES
OF SCOTLAND

JOHN DONALD

First published in Great Britain in 2007 by
John Donald, an imprint of Birlinn Ltd

West Newington House
10 Newington Road
Edinburgh
EH9 1QS

www.birlinn.co.uk

ISBN 10: 0 85976 686 1
ISBN 13: 978 0 85976 686 9

The publishers gratefully acknowledge subsidy from
the Scotland Inheritance Fund.

The publishers thank those who gave permission for copyright
material to be reproduced. Information on copyright holders
(other than NAS) has been given in the captions in the main text.
Every effort has been made to trace copyright holders. If there
are any omissions, the publishers will rectify these at the first
available opportunity.

This publication is value added. If you wish to re-use, please
apply for a Click-User Licence for value added material at
www.opsi.gov.uk. Alternatively, applications can be sent to:

Office of Public Sector Information
Information Policy Team
St Clements House
2–16 Colegate
Norwich
NR3 1BQ

Fax: 01603 723000

British Library Cataloguing-in-Publication Data
A catalogue record for this book is available on request from
the British Library

Printed and bound in Slovenia by Associated Agencies Ltd, Oxford

Contents

Abbreviations

APS	*The Acts of the Parliaments of Scotland*, 12 vols. in 13 (1814–75)
General Report	J. Sinclair, ed., *General Report of the Agricultural State and Political Circumstances of Scotland* (Edinburgh, 1814)
NSA	*New Statistical Account of Scotland*
OSA	*Old Statistical Account of Scotland*
SGM	*Scottish Geographical Magazine*
SHS	Scottish History Society

All document references are to material in the National Archives of Scotland (formerly the Scottish Record Office).

Illustrations

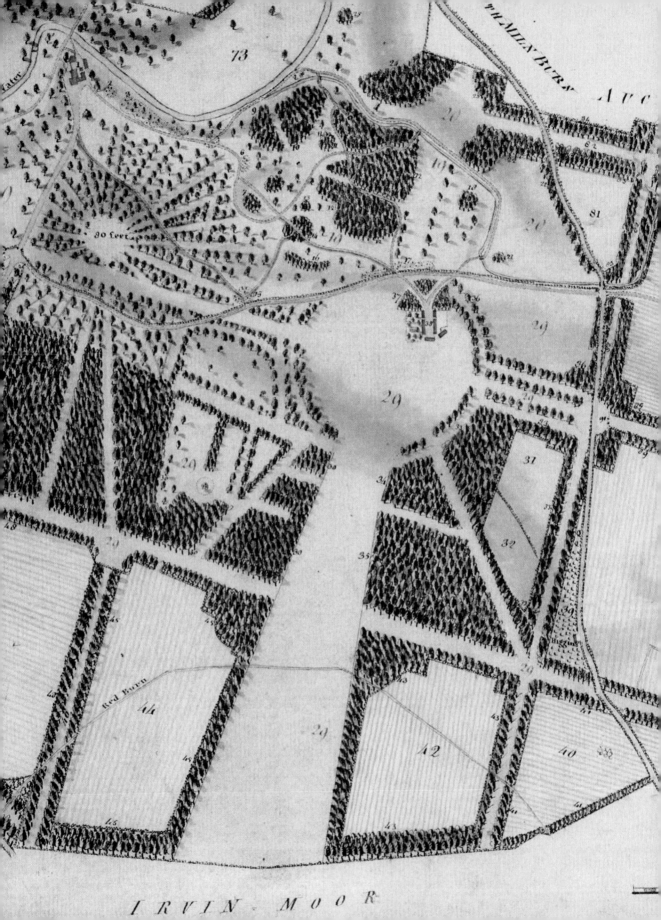

Acknowledgements

I am grateful to the following owners for permission to use plans and photographs from their collections: the countess of Airlie; the duke of Buccleuch and Queensberry KT; Sir Robert Clerk of Penicuik; the earl of Dalhousie; Mr W.G. Drummond Moray; the earl of Eglinton; the duke of Roxburghe; the earl of Seafield; Brodies WS; Dundas & Wilson CS; Garden Haig solicitors; the National Railway Museum; the National Trust for Scotland; and New Lanark Conservation Trust. Thanks are also due to Professor Sandy Fenton and to the many colleagues in the National Archives of Scotland who have assisted with this publication.

Rosemary Gibson
National Archives of Scotland

The Moor abo...

of Grafs-Shot Law

Back of Lilliards Edge

e Rigg

Back of Grafs-Shot Law

F

Quarry

MOOR

ll Top

Quarry

White Side

G

Low House

Galla-Rigg Moor

Fore side of Grafs-Shot Law

F

Bite-about

Fore side Moor

Miekle Galla-Rig

Little Galla-Rig

of Dods

F

Moss and Pafture

MOSS and MOOR

Black Dean

Weft Mofs-end

D

Mofs Rigg

Black Dean Moor

Eaſt Mofs-end

Whale Stones

Moor

G

Buttons Dales

Black Ditch

Windy Edge

High Wudy Edge

Sandy Ford Park

Middle Rigg

Wet Ditch

F

Low Windy Edge

Low Windy Edge

Hard Rig

Fan Knows

oſed Situation for a House

ugh Park

Weft Windy Edge

Meadow

Whinny Ditch

OX Road Head

Sangh Shot

Scaw Roods

Back Side

North Broad Shot

Moor

Keſting Know

Scaw Hill

Fore Side

Miekle Ditch

Trow Penny

ALE WATER

Beans Acre

South Broad Shot

ow Hauc

Scaw

Scaw Park

Broad Law Park

D

Townhead Park

Provoſt's Park

Ancrum Kirk

Trow Penny

Caſtle Hill or Little Park

Moor

Moor Park

Trow Penny

G

Park

Garden

Trow Penny

Eaſt Field

Quarry Park

Weſt Field

Introduction

THE rural landscape we see today is largely a man-made creation. The Scottish countryside looked very different 300 years ago. Then the landscape had a fragmented appearance, with numerous clusters of small farms scattered throughout. These were surrounded by narrow strips of cultivated ground in an otherwise bare landscape. Trees and hedges were scarce, but large areas of moorland and bog covered the countryside. There were few roads: many areas had only muddy tracks as a means of communication. But in the eighteenth and nineteenth centuries the appearance of the landscape changed dramatically. This was a time when agriculture developed from subsistence level to a commercial scale, when land ceased to be a symbol of power and became a source of income. New methods of agriculture, the enthusiasm of improving landowners and tenants, the development of rural industries and a revolution in transport all combined to bring about 'a great change upon the face of the country'.

These are the words of John Forbes, factor on the Lovat estate in the 1760s. He was predicting how the landscape would be transformed when the old system of runrig cultivation ended. At the time 'a barren muir of great extent' had just been enclosed on the estate and was about to be planted with 200,000 fir trees. In Forbes's opinion these would ensure 'a thriving Plantation, which will much beautify the Country, and turn out at last a great advantage to the Estate, & be a supply of wood & firing'.[1]

Forbes's views on the aesthetic and commercial advantages of enclosing land and planting trees were widely shared by landowners throughout Scotland. In the eighteenth and early nineteenth centuries, armies of labourers drained, enclosed and planted on estates across the country. The waving rigs and furrows of the old runrig cultivation vanished. So too did the clusters of buildings comprising the fermtoun, the centre of the jointly run small farms that formed the backbone of the old system of agriculture. Architects constructed magnificent new homes for Scotland's elites, and gardeners laid out elegant designed landscapes around them.

The transformation of Scotland's landscape did not occur overnight. Although the peak of improving activity, the agricultural revolution, took place in the sixty years from 1760 to 1820, change was under way from the later seventeenth century. Landowners began to experiment with their estates, mostly by planting trees around the house and in the enclosed ground known as policies, though sometimes, as at Yester in East Lothian, on a massive scale.

The basis for much later work was laid by several acts of the Scottish parliament in the period 1661–95 which encouraged enclosure and the division of commonties and runrig lands. Even by 1700, multiple tenant farms were reducing in numbers, written leases were becoming more common and rents formerly paid in kind were starting to be commuted to money payments. In the years after the Union of Parliaments in 1707, the movement of Scottish elites to London required their estates to provide them with higher incomes. In many cases the need for higher rents drove the process of improvement. In 1723 the Society of Improvers was founded in Edinburgh to provide a method of disseminating information to landowners keen to modernise their estates. Improvement was very much part of the Scottish Enlightenment. Landowners were no longer content to accept what nature provided. In the interests of aesthetics and efficiency, barren landscapes should be both beautified and made productive.

The pace of agricultural change varied widely across Scotland. The south-east led the way, with the seeds of the agricultural revolution being sown there in the second half of the seventeenth century. Much depended on the income of the landowner, as improvement was an expensive business. The fertility of the land and an estate's proximity to markets provided by large population centres such as Glasgow and Edinburgh were also crucial factors. As a result, modernising of estates in the Highlands did not take place until the nineteenth century, and then with social upheavals largely avoided in the Lowlands. Even with committed owners, improving an estate often took decades and could result in bankruptcy.

The whole process of development was encouraged by Montgomery's Act of 1770, which allowed owners of entailed estates to borrow a proportion of the cost of improvements against the estate. Estates were entailed to protect them from being sold or from passing to another family through marriage. The succession to such estates was restricted to certain heirs, and the owner could not burden the estate with debt. At least a third of the estates in Scotland were entailed at this time, so the loosening of restrictions had a substantial effect on the scale of improvements as owners borrowed funds to build new houses, enclose and drain fields, and plant trees. The Napoleonic Wars were an important external factor in the impetus for commercialisation, providing as they did increased demand and improved prices.

By 1850 or so, much of the Scottish lowland landscape had an ordered appearance. Larger farms had replaced the multiplicity of small units, and sizeable fields were enclosed by hedges or dykes. Shelter belts of trees and plantations were growing and softening the contours of the landscape. Marshes had been drained and turned into productive land. New villages were springing up to provide employment and accommodation for workers who had become surplus to the requirements of the new system of agriculture. Improvements in rural housing had removed some of the blots on the landscape caused by old-style cottages. Mining and textiles industries were now operating on a major scale and added some unsightly contributions to the new face of the country. Communications had improved with the building of a proper road system, and by the end of the nineteenth century a network of canals, roads and railways criss-crossed the country. In the space of less than a century Lowland Scotland had developed from a rural society based on subsistence agriculture into an industrialised and urbanised economy.

Huge changes in the social and economic structure of the Highlands left their mark on the area, first with the clearance of townships to form sheep farms, then with the growth of sporting estates. By the late nineteenth century these attempts to make Highland estates economic had led to acute shortages of land in many crofting areas. A period of unrest and protest led to government intervention, first with the Crofters Act of 1886, which provided security of tenure, and then in the late nineteenth and early twentieth centuries with land settlement programmes, which created new crofts in the Highlands and smallholdings in the Lowlands.

In the later nineteenth and into the twentieth centuries, the provision of piped water supplies and the advent of electricity brought great alterations to the landscape, both in the Highlands and the Lowlands. Reservoirs, power stations, pylons and hydro-electric dams made their appearance in previously undisturbed parts of the countryside. Though electricity brought immeasurable benefits to Scottish citizens, its physical manifestations caused great concern when they first appeared, and continue to do so. Another twentieth-century development which has not been universally welcomed is the blanket conifer cover which post-war forestry brought to many parts of Scotland.

Landscape change is a continuous process and now, early in the twenty-first century and with enormous pressures on the countryside, a highly contentious subject. The eighteenth- and nineteenth-century improvers fashioned new landscapes without let or hindrance, but now any proposal to change the face of the country must be submitted to planning authorities, who have the unenviable task of juggling the competing claims of local communities, developers, visitors and conservationists. Developments such as new roads, superquarries, fish farms and wind farms are hotly debated and often vigorously opposed. It is changed days from the 1840s, when Lord Cockburn, a high court judge, found himself ridiculed for protesting against the destruction of the countryside that railways brought: 'shares are actually up for a railway through Killiecrankie, and by Dalwhinnie and Aviemore! And any one who puts in a word for the preservation of scenery, or relics, or sacred haunts, is set down as a beast, hostile to the "poor man's rights", or "modern improvement", and the "march of intellect".[2]

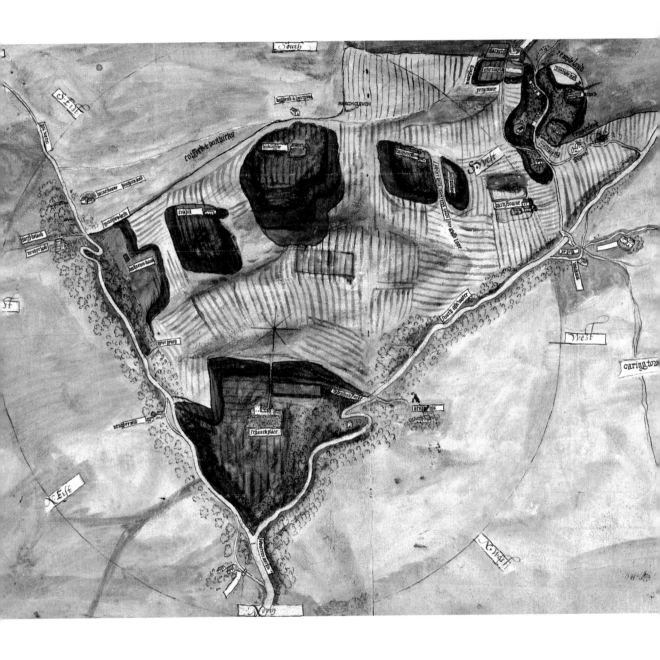

This book has its origins in an exhibition in 1997 to publicise the unique plans collection of the National Archives of Scotland (formerly the Scottish Record Office). This remarkable resource has been used to illustrate the transformation of the Scottish landscape between the eighteenth and the twentieth centuries. There are over 100,000 plans in the collection, relating to estates, buildings, industry and transport in all areas of Scotland. These plans, many of them magnificently illustrated, give a unique picture of Scotland's past, providing snapshots of the Scottish countryside through almost 300 years of change.

1. (*Opposite*) **The lands of Arniston, 1586** (RHP 82800).

This plan gives a picture of the Midlothian landscape of the late sixteenth century. Arniston, spelled 'Harnstoune', on the right of the plan, is simply a farm among other farms, long before the days of the elegant Adam mansion house. The cultivated land around the farm is divided into strips. The estate of Shank, however, had a small manor house, shown on the plan as 'schanck place'. Trees line the banks of the river South Esk on the right and the Gore Water on the left, but the rest of the landscape is bare.

The map is the reverse of the layout we are accustomed to see: here south is shown at the top of the plan. Maps of this date are rare in Scotland. This one was drawn for a court case over boundaries in dispute between George Dundas of Dundas, who had bought the estate of Arniston in 1571, and Nicol Elphinstone of Shank.

The Old Face of the Countryside

At that time there was not one acre upon the whole esteat inclosed, nor any timber upon it but a few elm, cycamore, and ash, about a small kitchen garden adjoining to the house . . . All the farmes ill disposed and mixed, different persons having alternate ridges; not one wheel carriage on the esteat. Nor indeed any one road that would alow it . . . The whole land raised and uneven, and full of stones . . . and all the ridges crooked in shape of an S, and very high, and full of noxious weeds and poor, being worn out by culture, without proper manure or tillage.[1]

Sir Archibald Grant of Monymusk (1696–1778), one of the best-known improvers of his time, left this vivid description of the condition of his estate in the early eighteenth century, before he embarked on its modernisation. Even allowing for the bias of the committed moderniser, the disadvantages of the old ways of working the land are clear from his account.

Before the agricultural revolution, farming in Scotland was very much a communal affair. The traditional farming structure was a small farm held jointly by a group of tenants, anything between two and eight families. The size of farms varied hugely across the country, but the proportion of farmers with substantial holdings was very small. In Lothian, the Borders and Fife, joint farms could be over 400 acres, while in Angus and the north-east, under 300 acres was the norm. As these were multiple-tenant holdings, some families had as little as 20 acres to live on. According to the improvers, 100 acres was the minimum necessary to form a viable unit. Although by the late seventeenth century the south-east, which led the way in commercial farming, housed some tenants who had achieved individual holdings of this size, most farmers in Scotland existed on fewer than 40 acres.[2] For tenants with holdings of this size, the type of agriculture practised in Scotland before the agricultural revolution was very much on a subsistence level.

Houses and outbuildings in such farms were clustered together in fermtouns. Settlements grew up near churches, castles and mills, and their echoes can be seen in the common place-names Kirkton, Castleton and Milton. The fermtoun also housed cottars, who had a cottage and a few acres of ground in return for working on the farm. Cottars were often tradesmen such as shoemakers, masons or weavers, so the fermtoun resembled a small self-contained village.

Before the changes of the eighteenth century, land was cultivated on the infield/outfield system, an open-field method of farming in common use in northern Europe. Infield was the more fertile land near the farm settlement. In less fertile areas it might account for only about a quarter of the farm's acreage. It was kept in constant cultivation, usually with bere (a hardy form of barley) and oats, Scotland's main food crop. In more fertile areas of the Lowlands and the Black Isle, wheat, which was less hardy, might be sown on the infield in addition. Outfield, the poorer outlying ground, grew only oats. Crop yields were often at subsistence level, with the outfield providing a return of only three times the grain sown, giving just sufficient grain to sow, to eat and to pay the rent, or 'ane to saw, ane to gnaw and ane to pay the laird with a'', according to the old saying. Crop returns from the infield were generally four- to fivefold, but in more favoured areas, with the use of fertiliser such as seaweed, yields could be much higher.

The arable lands of the infield and outfield were divided from the pasture on the surrounding moorland by a dyke made of stone or turf – the head dyke. In upland areas this common pasture made up the bulk of the farm's acreage. Cattle were sent out beyond the head dyke in spring and in some areas in summer would go to the furthest grazings – the summer shielings. The level at which cultivation was practical varied widely across Scotland. In drier, more fertile areas in the Grampians, head dykes can be found at up to 1,000 feet above sea level, while in the poorer soils of the west Highlands and islands, cultivation levels did not reach more than 100 feet.

Arable land was cultivated in small strips – the runrig system. Under this method, which ensured that everyone had a share of the good and bad land, each farmer had fragmented holdings scattered throughout the farm. The land could be divided into sunny and shadow shares, or by allocating strips sequentially, e.g. every third strip, or by drawing lots. Originally these parcels of land were reallocated period-ically, but by the seventeenth century many holdings were fixed. The runrig system required tenants to follow a communal approach to ploughing, harvesting and crop rotation. Tenants shared equipment and pooled their labour. There would be only one or two ploughs in a fermtoun. All the livestock was herded together. Proper herding of animals was vital when there were few hedges or fences to keep them away from growing crops.

The plans shown here illustrate how the arable land belonging to a farm did not form one contiguous block of cultivation – it was dispersed across the more fertile and better-drained parts of the holding. Such islands of cultivation were separated by boggy areas and rough pasture. Also clear is the ridge and furrow pattern of cultivation. The land was ploughed into ridges, separated by baulks or furrows, which assisted drainage. Rigs could be anything from three to eleven metres wide and up to a metre high. This system of cultivation was suited to the hand sowing of seed. The waving S shapes of the ridges were caused by the unwieldy old Scots plough, which had to be pulled by eight oxen and took so long to turn that the ploughman would begin turning the animals before the end of the ridge. Where they have not been destroyed by modern cultivation, these ridges can still be seen in the landscape, often on moorland or pasture.

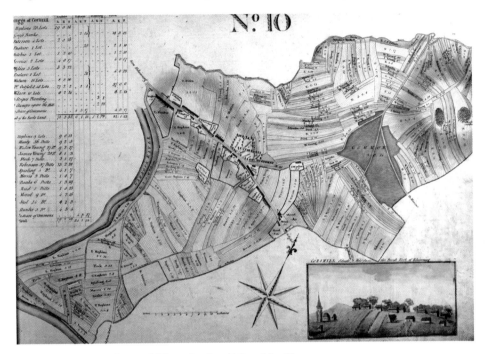

2. The runrigs of Corshill, 1789, by John Ainslie
(RHP 3, p57: courtesy of the earl of Eglinton). See also detail on p. ii.

In 1789 the earl of Eglinton, an enthusiastic improver, had his estate surveyed by John Ainslie, a noted surveyor of the time, with a view to modernisation. This plan provides a vivid picture of the existing runrig system of cultivation around an Ayrshire village. The strips of ground are all shapes and sizes, and run in all directions. The surveyor has recorded the tenants' names and the size of the holdings: they range from just over an acre to thirty-seven acres.

The houses of the village are strung out along the road leading from Kilwinning to Eglinton Castle. The settlement is illustrated in the vignette. The common pasture can be seen on the right of the plan, criss-crossed by tracks. Even in the late eighteenth century the landscape is mostly bare. There are only a few trees near the village and two small plantations to the right of the common.

The land around Corshill was divided into that owned by the earl of Eglinton and leased out to tenants and that owned by other proprietors. These were probably descendants of those who got feus (leases in perpetuity) of the land when the estates around Kilwinning Abbey were broken up in the sixteenth century.

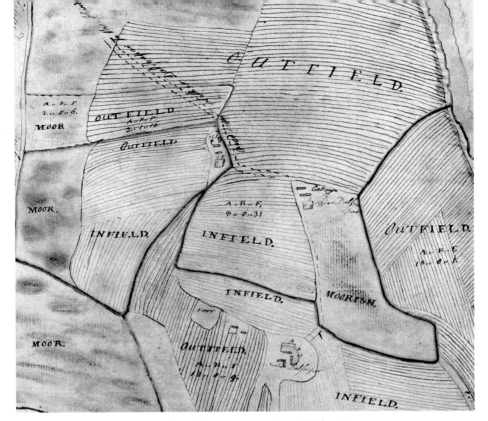

3. Braehead and surrounding farms, 1766, by William Panton
(RHP 1665/2: courtesy of Dundas & Wilson CS).

A plan of farms of the earl of Panmure's estate in Angus illustrates the infield/outfield system. The movement of cattle was a vital element in this form of cultivation as their manure was often the only form of fertiliser available. The infield received most of the manure from the farm to allow it to be cropped continuously. After harvest, the cattle were turned onto the stubble, and the infield also received manure from beasts kept in the byre during the winter.

The outfield, the larger portion of a farm's lands, would be cropped with oats for about three years until exhausted, then used as pasture for a few years to recover. In spring, cattle were brought in at night from the common pasture to temporary enclosures on parts of the outfield which were about to be cultivated. Uncultivated areas of the outfield served as common grazings and were also an important source of turf for dyke building and roofing.

Nether Dalsoupar, the farm towards the foot of the plan, had nineteen acres of infield and thirty-nine of outfield. Beyond the outfield is the barren moorland, which provided rough grazing for stock. This farm's pasture and moorland accounted for another nineteen acres, giving a total holding of seventy-seven acres to support several families. Various areas of ground are described as 'boggy pasture'. Upper Dalsoupar has a 'Cottoun', i.e. the cottars' dwellings. The track through the fields is the road to the church.

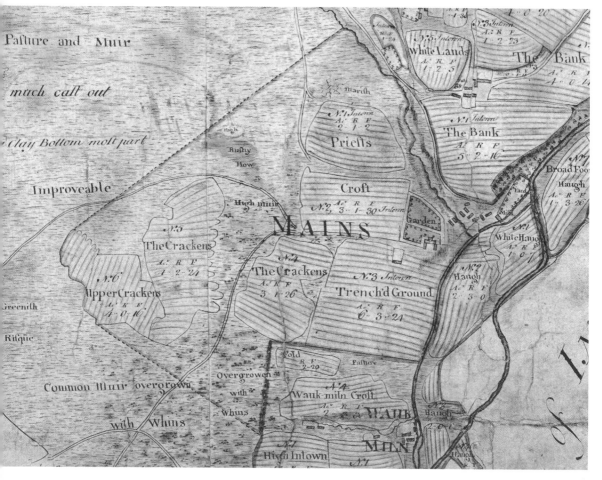

4–5. The lands of Haddo, 1766, by John Home (RHP 11776 and 11777).

These two plans illustrate the effect of improvement on the landscape. The first plan shows the lands of Haddo in Forgue parish, Aberdeenshire (not to be confused with the Adam mansion in Methlick parish), as they were, with small unenclosed fields and virtually no trees. The lands were divided into the Mains farm of fifty-two acres and four other holdings of between twenty-six and sixty-three acres. Some areas of the pasture and moorland are marked 'improveable', but one area of moor towards the bottom of the plan is described as 'overgrown with whins' (gorse).

    The second plan shows the surveyor's view of what the estate should look like. He has laid the grid pattern of improvement across the landscape. Haddo Mains is to be enclosed with larger regular fields, surrounded by plantations. A new mansion-house is to be built near the river, with a winding drive leading up to it and extensive gardens. The size of the mains farm has doubled to 108 acres. The rest of the estate is to be

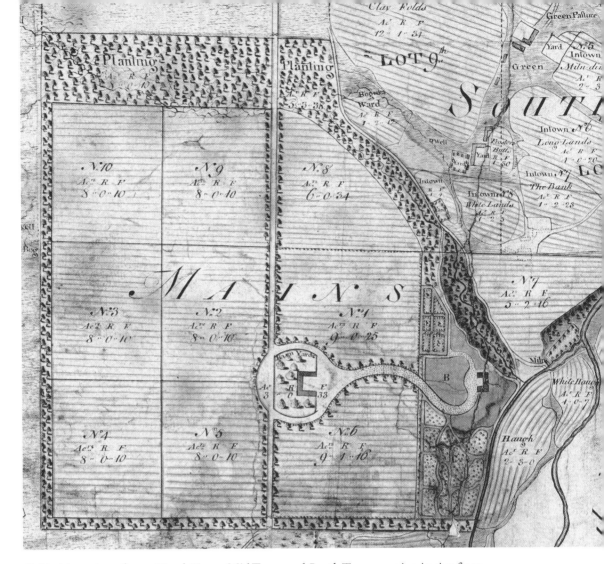

divided into three farms, North Town, Mid Town and South Town, ranging in size from 71 to 105 acres.

Thirty years later the local minister commented on the improvements which had taken place on the estate:

> We must not pass by the improvements and plantations of Captain George Morison, late of Haddo. Haddo lies on the N.W. side of the burn of Forgue . . . The house stands on a gradual sloping bank, a few yards from the burn, built after the modern taste, and affords genteel accommodation for a large family. On the haugh between the rivulet and water course to the mill, lies the garden, fenced with a high stone wall, and well stored with a great variety of fruit trees and bushes. At no great distance from the house, there are several patches of thriving plantations of fir, alder, birch &c. The fields are well cultivated and yield good crops. Taking the whole in one view, Haddo is one of the most pleasant situations in this or the neighbouring country.[3]

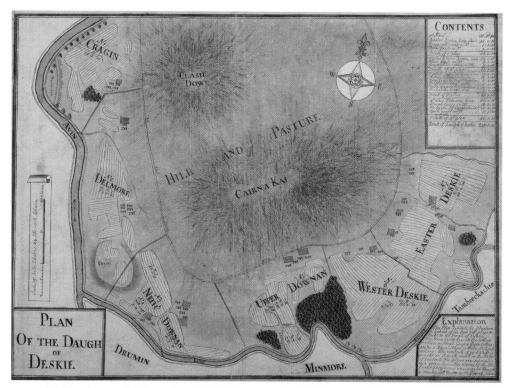

6. The farms of Daugh of Deskie, 1761, by William Anderson (RHP 2487).

In 1761 a survey was made of the duke of Gordon's lands in Glenlivet, Banffshire. One of the plans illustrates the fermtoun, an irregular cluster of cottages, byres and kailyards. The drawings of cottages show the simplicity of rural housing of the mid-eighteenth century. If the surveyor's drawing of the cottages is a true reflection of the number of people on the farms, Easter Deskie's fifty-six acres supported thirteen families. These would include the tenants themselves, cottars and landless labourers.

All six farms are clustered between the rivers Avon and Livet and the hills behind, which provided rough pasture for their stock. In his accompanying report the surveyor outlined the possibilities for improving the arable or corn lands of Easter Deskie, and described the common casting of peat and pasturing of cattle:

> There is on the East side of the Corn Lands of the Easter Deskie a Large Field of Improveable Ground call'd the Greens of Deskie about Fifty Acres of it would Improve for Corn Land. The most part of it appears to be on a Clay bottom. There is no more improveable ground on any of the Possessions in the Daugh . . .
>
> All the Possessions of the Daugh of Deskie cast their Peats in the Moss of Cairn a kay . . . and Pasture promiscuously over From Balendallas March at the North and East and all North from the Waters of Fervie and Livett without any Interuption.

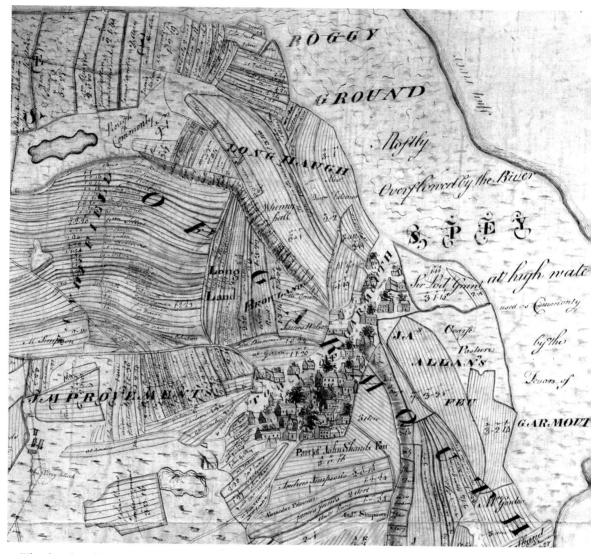

7. The lands of Garmouth, 1772–3, by George Taylor
(RHP 1423: courtesy of Brodies WS).

The village of Garmouth at the mouth of the Spey had runrig lands stretching out behind the settlement in long, thin curves. There are more trees in the village than there are in the surrounding countryside. Behind the cultivated ground is marshland and on the right boggy ground which was overflowed by the Spey at high tide. The surveyor, who recorded the tenants' names on the rigs, commented on the disadvantages of scattered holdings and the possibilities for improving the moorland. He felt it was too poor for cultivation, but would be suitable for tree planting:

The Lands of Garmouth are very good, not owing so much to the soil, which is but sandy, as to the Dung they Gather in their Streets. All the Feus are very Confused and Discontigous, one perhaps having his land in Ten or Twelve different places as may be seen on the above . . . Some parts of Garmouth presently suffer pretty much by the Spey but they are using every endeavour to prevent the same. There are a great Deal of Fine level moor on the Estate which w'd answer the purpose of Planting much better than Improving as it is extraordinary thin.[4]

At this time Garmouth was part of the estates of the second earl of Fife, a great improver, or as the French described him, *un grand agronome*. He planted trees on over 14,000 acres of moorland. The village was a major port, mainly due to the timber industry of the Spey. Logs were floated down the river from Strathspey to Garmouth, where there was also a shipbuilding industry. About twenty years after this plan was drawn, the local minister noted that several of the feuars of Garmouth were in opulent circumstances and that one owned a carriage.[5]

8. The village of Garmouth, 2004 (NAS. Crown copyright).

While it is difficult now to envisage its industrial past, the old part of the village today provides a good example of a settlement from pre-improvement times. In contrast with the planned villages of the eighteenth and nineteenth centuries, it is an intriguing jumble of narrow streets and haphazardly placed houses.

9a & b. Vignettes of ploughing, 1772, from a plan by William Aberdeen
(RHP 1220: courtesy of Brodies WS).

Details from a plan of the estate of Castlehill in Caithness show the lighter version of the old Scots plough still used at this period in the Highlands. The old ploughs were labour-intensive. This type required four animals to pull it, either horses or oxen, and two men to control it. When the new ploughs came into operation, they needed only two horses guided by one man.

These drawings show both oxen and horses being used for ploughing. The oxen are yoked abreast, while the horses are harnessed in couples as a 'long team'. The driver walks backwards guiding the animals. The man guiding the horses is wearing Highland dress.

2

Homes and Gardens

The Scotch Nobility, who were thus frequently led abroad, must have early become acquainted with the improved state of horticulture in some parts of the Continent; and this, when contrasted with the barrenness and wildness of their native seats, must have made a deep impression on their minds and produced a desire to make horticultural improvements. [1]

THE transformation of the countryside began at home and, as the quotation above shows, was often inspired by foreign travel. Most landowners started work on their estates by improving their house and its immediate surroundings. Although most levels of Scottish society had kitchen or cottage gardens to supply vegetables and herbs, it was originally only royal palaces and monasteries which had ornamental gardens as well. In the sixteenth century Scottish nobles started to create gardens for pleasure as well as to supply food, and from the early seventeenth century this trend became more common. Formal walled gardens began to appear around existing castles. The best-preserved example can be seen at Edzell Castle in Angus, created by Sir David Lindsay in 1604.

By this time the need for fortified houses was lessening and the aristocracy began to build homes for comfort and style, rather than tower-houses or castles for defence. As the quotation implies, Scottish elites were well travelled in Europe and, after the Union of the Crowns in 1603, increasingly so in England also. Their familiarity with European and English fashions encouraged a trend towards conspicuous consumption. Many estate owners could not afford to build new houses from scratch, and others were keen to maintain their castles and towers as a symbol of their families' antiquity and status. This led to the existence of many 'castle wise' houses which are a hybrid of older tower-houses and seventeenth- or eighteenth-century wings, such as Traquair in Peeblesshire.

In the more peaceful times after the Restoration of 1660, the classical country house began to make its appearance in Scotland. A succession of distinguished Scottish architects, including Sir William Bruce, James Smith and the Adam family, built stately homes such as Hopetoun House near Edinburgh and Duff House in Banffshire, or remodelled existing castles such as Thirlestane and Drumlanrig into up-to-date mansion houses.

Owners had extensive ornamental gardens and policies laid out to show their new or renovated houses to their greatest advantage. Orchards and kitchen gardens were planted to supply the household with fresh fruit and vegetables. Gardeners grew a huge variety of fruit, including peaches, apricots and figs, in greenhouses and on hot walls. Formal walled gardens near the house provided shelter for flowers and shrubs. Designers laid out avenues, terraces, knot gardens, parterres (formal flower beds) and borders for aesthetic appeal and for recreation. Water features were very popular and existing watercourses were turned into ponds, cascades, canals and fountains. Statues, sundials and pavilions were essential for any fashionable garden. Some of the grander gardens boasted mazes or labyrinths which were positioned so that they could be admired from the house.

Parks for cattle and deer were enclosed and protected with trees or walls. The planting of trees both beautified the policies and provided timber for sale. Trees were used to create walks and rides and to direct the eye to distant vistas. Bruce was one of the first to use landscape features as a focus for his designs. At his home of Balcaskie in Fife, he used the Bass Rock as the main feature for views from both house and garden. Such extensive and elaborate designs reflected the status of the families who created them. Around some of the large country houses, such as Drumlanrig, Taymouth and Yester, entire new landscapes were created.

In the later seventeenth and first part of the eighteenth centuries, French influences on garden design were marked. Estate owners used their experiences of European travel to plan improvements to their policies, and also kept a close eye on what their friends and neighbours were doing. Those who could afford it employed designers such as William Boutcher or Thomas Winter to create their new gardens and policies. Others used publications such as *The Scots Gard'ner* by John Reid for guidance in designing improvements. This book, which appeared in 1683, was the first gardening publication specifically aimed at Scottish conditions. Reid was gardener to Sir George MacKenzie of Rosehaugh at Shank (see Fig. 1). His advice on laying out a garden epitomises the formal approach of the period, which aimed at controlling nature:

> *Pleasure Gardens useth to be divided into walkes and plots, with a Bordure round each plot, and at the corner of each, may a holly or some such train'd up, some Pyramidal, others Spherical, the Trees and Shrubs at the Wall well plyed and prun'd, the Green thereon cut in several Figures, the walkes layed with Gravel, and the plots within with Grass, (in several places whereof may be Flower pots) the Bordures boxed, and planted with variety of Fine Flowers orderly Intermixt, Weeded, Mow'd, Rolled and kept all clean and handsome.*[2]

The second half of the eighteenth century saw a change from these formal designs to a more naturalistic style of landscape gardening. Late in the century, romantic and picturesque gardens, which tried to imitate rather than control nature, became popular. Scotland became famous for her horticulturalists, and by the early nineteenth century many of the stately homes of England had Scottish head-gardeners.

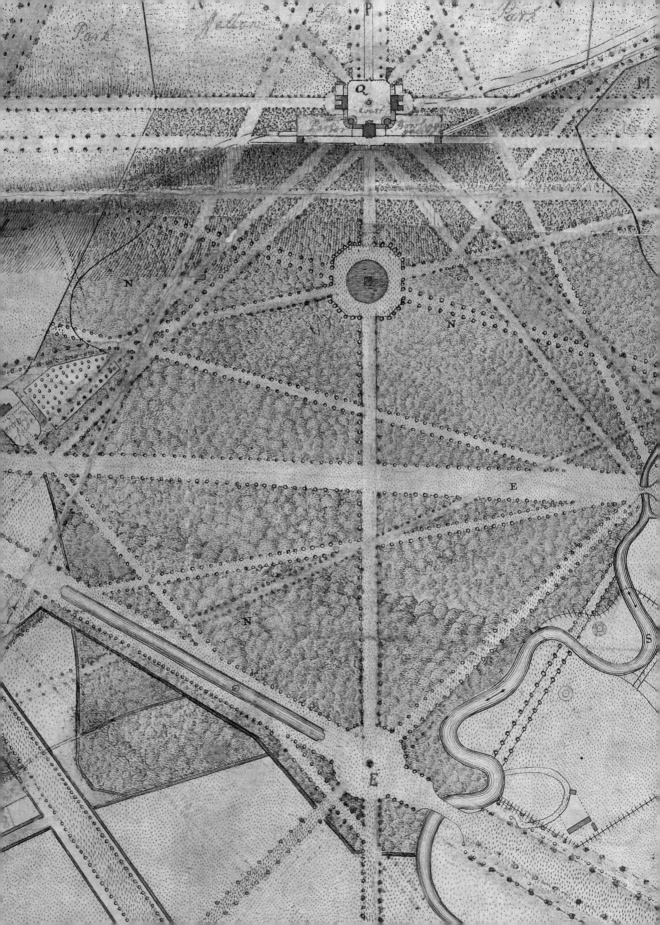

10. (*Previous page*) **The estate and town of Alloa, 1710 and 1728** (RHP 13258/1a).

At this time Alloa was owned by John, sixth earl of Mar. Although he is better known for leading the 1715 Jacobite rising, Mar was an improver of vision and a noted gentleman architect. In the early eighteenth century he remodelled not only the family home and policies, but also the adjoining town of Alloa. He laid the basis of a thriving manufacturing town and trading port by building a water supply to provide power for the mills and drainage for the coal mines. This survives today as the Gartmorn Dam, now a country park and reservoir. He also improved the harbour, and facilitated communications between it and the town by laying out the elegant lime-tree walk which can still be seen today. In Mar's plans for Alloa, economic and aesthetic improvements went hand in hand. One writer has summed up his achievement as 'a unique creation: a Scottish historical landscape garden with an industrial base'.[3]

When laying out the landscape around Alloa House, Mar blended his antiquarian interests with his experience of French gardens, gained on a grand tour of Europe and later in exile. Parts of his design were inspired by the gardens at Versailles. In accordance with garden design of the period, many historical sites in the area became the subject of vistas from the avenues in the gardens: for example, the avenue marked 'E' on the plan gave a view of Stirling Castle.

The grounds at Alloa were on a huge scale, covering four square miles, and considerable work was required to get the desired effects. In 1706 William Hutton, the manager of the mines at Alloa, who was also working on the policies, wrote to Mar about progress in laying out some of the avenues. He suggested cutting back some trees and levelling parts of the ground to achieve the view: 'The Bridge bewest the Inch is fixed And a passage for a Coach will be easily prepared as your Lordship commands, only from the round fold to the Bridge at Parkmiln it will not be got to keep the Vista, the Horse pool and other uneven ground being in the way: but a little to the Eastward can be got with cutting and pruning very few Trees and levelling some places.'[4]

All the work paid off. The new landscape included water features, flower borders, wildernesses and a bowling green. Visitors made favourable comments, some describing the gardens as the finest in Scotland, though one group did remark on the 'filthy naked statues'.[5] John Macky, who visited in the 1720s, praised the numerous vistas: 'To the South of the House is the Parterre, spacious and finely adorn'd with Statues and Vases; and from this Parterre to the River Forth, runs a fine Terras, or Avenue; from whence you have Thirty Two different Vistoes, each ending on some remarkable Seat or Mountain, at some miles Distance.'[6]

11. Alloa House, 1727, by John, sixth earl of Mar
(RHP 13258/13a).

After the failure of the 1715 rising, Mar continued to plan improvements to his estate while in exile in France. There had been a fortified house on the site since the early fourteenth century, and by the time of this plan Alloa House consisted of a fifteenth-century tower to which had been added a seventeenth-century mansion house. Mar wanted to unify the two and produce a modern home of classical appearance. He felt the tower was worth preserving because of its antiquity: 'There is something in the old Tower, espetially if made conform to the new designe, which is venerable for its antiquity and makes not a bad appearance, and would make one regrait being oblig'd to pull it down.'[7]

  The tower is on the left of the illustration. It is all that remains of the house, as the mansion house burned down in 1800. It was succeeded by a classical mansion, which was demolished in 1959. The tower stood empty for many years until in 1988 the thirteenth earl of Mar gifted the building to the Alloa Tower Building Preservation Trust. It has been restored and is now open to the public under the management of the National Trust for Scotland. Most of the former gardens are now covered by a housing estate, but a few acres remaining around the tower are being restored.

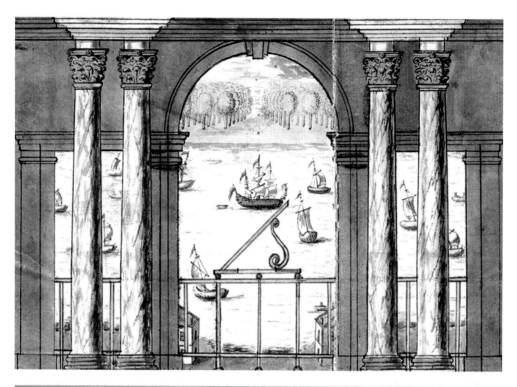

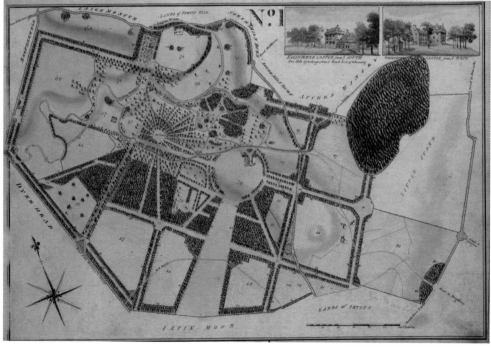

12. (*Opposite top*) **View from Alloa House towards the garden, 1731** (RHP 13258/11).

This stylised view is what Mar envisaged should be seen from the windows in the centre of the house.

13. (*Opposite bottom*) **The pleasure grounds of Eglinton, 1790, by John Ainslie** (RHP 3, p. 25: courtesy of the earl of Eglinton). See also detail on p. x.

The earls of Eglinton were among Ayrshire's foremost improvers. Even in the early seventeenth century, Eglinton Castle boasted gardens, parks and orchards. Throughout the following century the family introduced new farming methods, planted trees and developed these impressive pleasure grounds around the castle. The tenth earl brought in farmers experienced in modern agriculture and established an agricultural society to encourage his tenants to try new practices.

Another plan from Ainslie's survey of the estate shows the design of the gardens, along with vignettes of the castle shortly before it was rebuilt. The grounds show the beginnings of a move away from the formal geometric garden design towards the more natural landscape fashion of the later eighteenth century. Features of the estate include enclosed fields, parks surrounded by plantations, walks and a belvedere, or viewpoint. By the early nineteenth century the grounds had greenhouses containing 'a choice collection of upwards of 1400 rare and valuable plants', a kitchen garden stretching to five acres and an acre devoted to flowers.[8]

The twelfth earl's enthusiasm for improvements led to such expensive schemes as the development of the town and harbour of Ardrossan to allow the shipment of coal from the estate, and the start of the Glasgow, Paisley and Ardrossan canal. A further drain on the family's finances was the Eglinton Tournament, a mock medieval display held at the castle in 1839.

The family moved out of Eglinton in 1927, and in 1978 the park was gifted to Irvine Development Corporation. The grounds now form Eglinton Country Park and some of its features are being restored. Belvedere Hill and the woodland walks radiating from it can still be seen today. The park continues the centuries-old tradition of pleasure grounds.

14. (*Overleaf*) **Erskine House and grounds, 1774, by Charles Ross** (RHP 1043).

Erskine House in Renfrewshire was the home of Lord Blantyre. Tree planting had been going on at Erskine since at least the 1720s. The 1770s were also a time of great improvements. The plan shows orchards, meadows, sheep parks, plantations, river walks and a formal garden around the mansion house. The tenth Lord Blantyre, who

Clyde

Waterside park

Freeland holm

Freeland hill park

sandy park

kirkton park

wester mains

By a Scale of Chains

A plan of ERSKINE policy Belonging to the Rt. Honble Lord Blantyre

Elevation of Erskine House

ERSKINE HOUSE

Erskine Green

Erskine point

kitchen walk

OFFICES

Meadow

Easter Mains

willow ground

Sheep Park

Erskine Ferry

succeeded to the estate two years after this plan was made, extended the improvements from the policies to the whole estate and in 1778 enlarged the house.

In 1782 a local historian described the results of Blantyre's work and marvelled at the water supply he installed in the house:

> *The whole estate of Erskine has been very much improved within these few years by being wholly inclosed and numerous plantings, with beautiful avenues regularly planted and delectable beltings, broad and large, about the inclosures . . . Upon the west side of the gravel walk . . . down a gentle declivity toward the house, are planted a great many different kinds of trees, into various kinds of serpentine wyndings; at the west side thereof is newly made a large orchard and garden, around which is built a high brick wall, having a green-house and a pleasure-house within . . . About three or four years ago, a large addition was built to the west side [of the house] by the present lord Blantyre, which has made the house in the form of a square court . . . The water is conveyed by leaden pipes to any room in the house.*[9]

In the grounds there are two buildings, one like a pagoda on the right of the plan. All the best gardens had pavilions like these. They were intended to provide shelter, a resting place from which to enjoy the view and an opportunity to take refreshments. The gardens at Erskine were famous in the nineteenth century for their fruit trees and specimen trees, including the largest magnolia in Scotland.[10]

Lord Blantyre owned the Erskine ferry shown on the right of the plan: it crossed the Clyde to Old Kilpatrick. It was replaced in the 1970s by the Erskine Bridge. The house illustrated here was replaced in 1828 by a mansion house, designed by Sir Robert Smirke. In 1916 the house was turned into a hospital for limbless soldiers and sailors, and since then has served as Erskine Hospital for former servicemen and servicewomen.

15. (*Opposite*) **The orchard at Edgerston, 1728** (RHP 22228).

This delightful drawing is from a book of plans of the estate of Edgerston near Jedburgh, owned by Sir John Rutherford of that ilk. The existing house partly dates from the 1720s, and it seems from these plans that the whole estate was being modernised at that time. An accompanying description indicates that the grounds to the south of the house had a flower garden, grass and gravel walks, an orchard and a summerhouse:

> *This being the figure of the South Garden or orcheard lying South Next the South Court of the Main house, first a border of flowers goes round to the foot of the said garden. Next a grass walk, and over against the Middle of the House a gravel walk goes down the Middle of the garden and ends att the closing of the green walk where there are to be built a Summer House upon a little green Hill among a bush of Trees.*

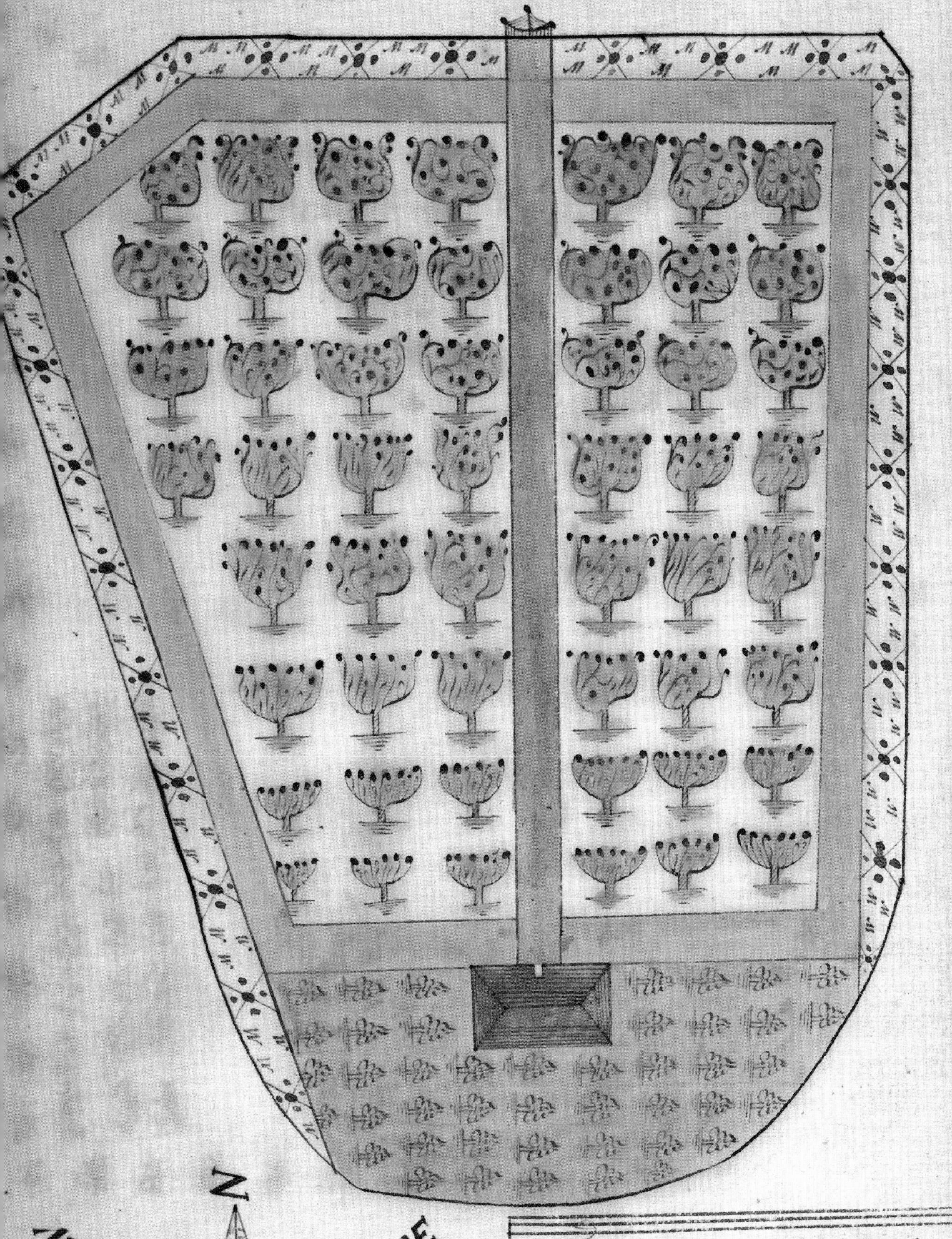

N

NE

This being the figure of ye

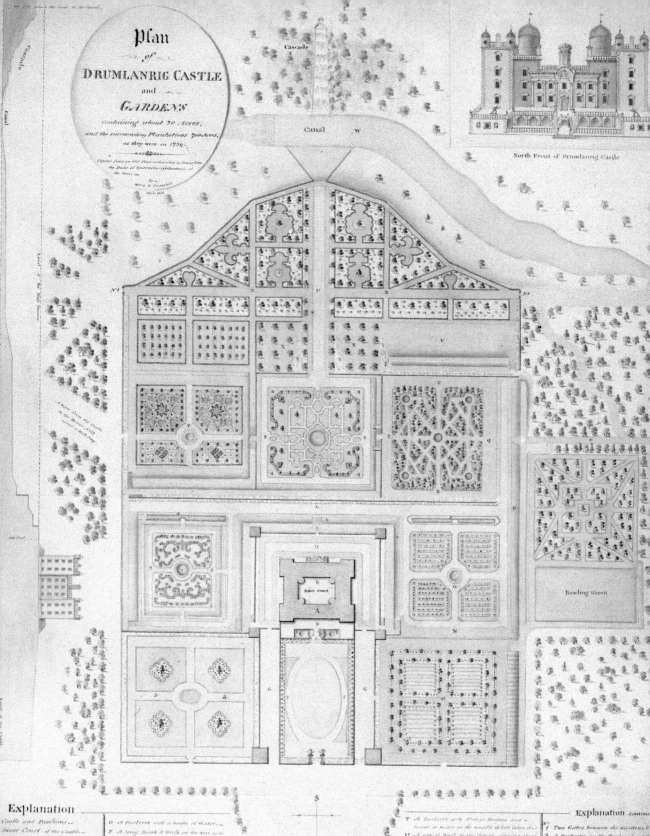

Plan
of
DRUMLANRIG CASTLE
and
GARDENS

Containing about 20 Acres,
and the surrounding Plantations 700 Acres,
as they were in 1739.

Copied from an old Plan exhibiting by David Low
to the Duke of Queensberry's Gardener at
the time,

By
Wm & D. Crawford
April 1816

Cascade

Canal

North Front of Drumlanrig Castle

Canal

Bowling Green

Inner Court

North Avenue

16. (*Opposite*) **Drumlanrig Castle and gardens, 1739**
(RHP 9459: courtesy of the duke of Buccleuch and Queensberry KT).

This plan shows the gardens at Drumlanrig as they were in 1739. It was compiled by David Low, who was gardener there for over thirty years. The grounds were of a fitting standard to match the magnificent castle built for the duke of Queensberry in the late seventeenth century, which is illustrated on the plan. The castle was modelled on Heriot's Hospital in Edinburgh and was referred to by one writer as 'a princely and pleasant Habitation'.[11]

Work on the grounds had been going on since the late seventeenth century and the gardens illustrated are the epitome of the Scottish formal garden of the period. They provide a good example of the use of water, an asset that no proper garden of the time would be without – a cascade and canal appear at the top of the plan. The gardens also had terraces, gravel walks, groves of trees, flower borders, parterres, a wilderness and a bowling green. This magnificent landscape was achieved by major engineering works to cut through the rocky slopes surrounding the castle and form the land into the elaborate patterns seen here.

Daniel Defoe was very impressed by Drumlanrig during his tour of Britain in the 1720s:

a palace so glorious, gardens so fine, and everything so truly magnificent, and all in a wild, mountainous country . . . nothing can be better designed, or indeed, better perform'd than the gardens are, which take up the south and west sides of the house . . . At the extent of the gardens there are pavilions and banqueting-houses, exactly answering to one another, and the greens trimm'd, spaliers and hedges are in perfection.[12]

The gardens changed considerably over the centuries, but are now being restored to their eighteenth-century glory. Some of these parterres can be seen at Drumlanrig today, replanted according to this scheme.

17. Drumlanrig Castle and gardens, *c.*1996
(By kind permission of the duke of Buccleuch and Queensberry KT).

3

Division of Commonty

There were several farms in this district run-rig, and large tracts of waste common moors, not long ago, but these are all now exchanged and divided, which may be considered the happy prelude of future improvements.[1]

LANDOWNERS' work on their houses and policies resulted in patches of improvement among the muddle of the surrounding farmland. The next stage of estate modernisation was generally the consolidation and enclosure of holdings, and this required the division of common lands. A commonty was an area owned by a number of proprietors and used by their tenants for a variety of purposes. These lands took up large areas of the pre-improvement landscape and could comprise anything up to several thousand acres of land.

As the minister of Doune implied in the 1790s, improving landowners regarded commonties as barren wastes and a hindrance to progress. To tenants, however, they were a vital element of Scotland's subsistence agriculture, and the resources they provided played a crucial part in the economic life of a township. Commonties were located on the periphery of the community, beyond the outfield and head dyke, and their main function was to provide rough grazing for livestock. In addition they supplied free fuel and building materials. From the commonty tenants could get peat and whins for their fires, stone and turf for building their houses, and heather, rushes or bracken for thatching them.

Commonties were also important to Scotland's cattle trade, in providing drovers with areas to rest their herds overnight on the way from the Highlands and islands to cattle trysts in the Lowlands or England. In addition they could be used as a reserve of arable land. Under pressure of population expansion, parts of the commonty might be taken into cultivation. They could also be used for industrial purposes: some commonties provided space for bleachfields.

Each tenant was allowed to graze a set number of animals on the commonty, decided in proportion to the size of his holding. This process was known as 'souming' and served as a control on overgrazing. Everyone's cattle intermingled on the commonty under the care of a common herdsman, a system which made improvement of stock by selective breeding impossible. Modernising landowners were keen to have commonties divided so that they could consolidate their holdings, try out new methods of agriculture and improve their stock. A favourite toast of Sir John Sinclair of Ulbster, one of Scotland's most enthusiastic improvers, was 'May a common become an uncommon spectacle in Caithness.'[2]

The Scottish parliament provided the legislative framework for dividing commonties in the seventeenth century. An act of 1647, which applied to the southern counties of Scotland, allowed commonty land which was underused as pasture to be converted into 'gude corne land'.[3] This limited act was followed in 1695 by 'An Act concerning the dividing of commonties'[4] which applied to the whole country. This act provided a simple method of dividing commonties by allowing one landowner to start a process of division without requiring the consent of the other landowners involved. Application was made to the Court of Session, and all landowners claiming a share of the commonty had to produce their title deeds to the land. The court then appointed a local official to carry out the division. Each proprietor received a share of the commonty in proportion to the size of his landholding, calculated on the valued rent of his property.

Many divisions were arranged by mutual consent to save the owners the expense of going to court. Division of commonty followed the geographical pattern of other agricultural improvements, spreading from the south of Scotland northwards, with divisions taking place in Shetland in the second half of the nineteenth century. Although a handful of commonties were divided in the seventeenth century, like other aspects of the agricultural revolution it was the mid-eighteenth century before the process gathered steam. From 3 divisions of commonty in the 1700s, the figure rose to 10 in the 1740s, then increased rapidly to 26 in the 1750s and 31 in the 1760s, to a peak of 55 in the 1770s. Thereafter divisions ran at between 21 and 34 a decade until the 1880s when they fell to 13, and thereafter to 2 in the last decade of the nineteenth century.[5]

It has been estimated that half a million acres of commonties were divided between 1695 and 1900,[6] and by the end of the twentieth century Scotland had very few commonties left. This contrasts with the position in England where, under the Enclosure Acts, parliamentary approval was required to divide common land. England still has in the region of half a million hectares of commons.[7]

The disappearance of commonties had a major effect on the landscape. The tracts of bare moorland complained of by travellers disappeared. Fields appeared in their place, surrounded by hedges. The maze of tracks across commonties also vanished, to be replaced by a more regular road layout. The disappearance of the commonty also had a profound effect on rural society. Tenants lost grazings and their source of free fuel and building materials. In the marginal agriculture practised in many parts of Scotland, this represented a substantial loss, particularly to the cottar class. Division of commonty was an important step in the process which ultimately led to the loss of small tenants and cottars from rural areas.

18. (*Previous page*) **The Haughs of Airth, 1784, by Robert Sconce**
(RHP 80865/1).

This plan of the runrig and commonty lands beside the river Forth at Airth, Stirlingshire, was prepared during a process of division started by Sir Lawrence Dundas of Kerse 'in order that each person's property might be Laid together and more contiguous'. The intermingled nature of the possessions is obvious on the plan. The runrig lands of the Haughs (riverside lands) are those coloured blue and yellow, while the commonty of the sea greens (so-called because they were covered by the sea at high tide) is the strip on the right beside the river. The mansion house of Powfoulis is at the bottom right, and farmhouses, coloured red, are scattered over the landscape.

The division of this commonty took over eighteen years to achieve. It started in Stirling Sheriff Court in 1771 and was remitted to the Court of Session ten years later as the landowners could not agree. It was sent back to the sheriff court in 1789 to proceed with the division. Evidence from witnesses in the action shows that at least one landowner, James Bruce of Powfoulis, had already enclosed some of the land without waiting for the official division. According to Alexander Cochrane, aged sixty, who was born and raised in the area: 'betwixt the foresaid march of Sir Laurence Dundas' part of the greens to the Pow upon the north side of the Powfoulis inclosure was esteemed to belong to Powfoulis and was pastured by his cattle and the deponent does not remember that he saw any other cattle pasture thereon and it is about seven or eight years since he banked and inclosed the west part of the said greens'.[8]

19. (*Opposite*) **The scattalds of North Cunningsburgh, Fladdabister and Clift Hills, 1881–2, by James Hepburn** (RHP 3962).

In Shetland commonties were known as scattalds, from *skattr*, the Old Norse for tax. Tenants paid rent for their land and 'scat' for their share in the privileges of the scattald. They too could be divided under the 1695 act. However, division of commonties came later to Shetland than to the mainland, and most scattalds were divided between 1825 and 1880.

The later move towards division was partly due to the importance of fishing to the Shetland economy: fishing and subsistence agriculture coexisted well together. However, in the nineteenth century Shetland landowners began to see the commercial possibilities of sheep farming. Clearances to make way for sheep started in the 1820s and gathered pace from the late 1860s, when improvements in shipping services to the northern isles and a rise in wool and mutton prices made this type of farming very attractive to estate owners. By the 1880s the home fishing industry was declining, and the combination of fishing and the old methods of agriculture was no longer commercially viable.

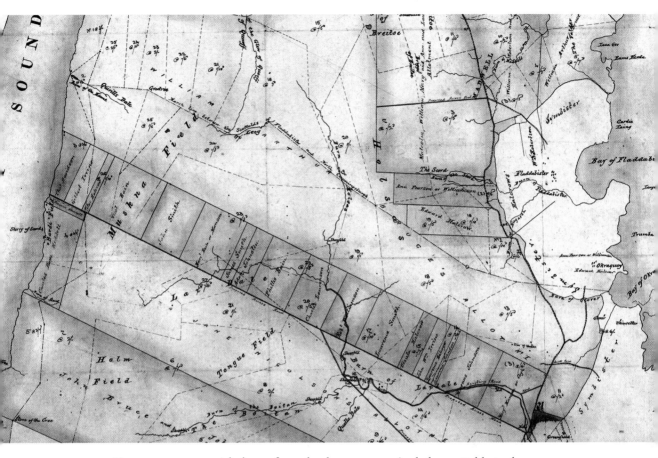

To run a commercial sheep farm, landowners required the scattalds to be divided so that they could fence off and manage their own land and stock. The plan shows the scale of some of Shetland's common lands: in this case four scattalds amounting to 4,000 acres were being divided. As late as 1969 there were still ninety-three scattalds in Shetland, and a few still remain undivided today.

4

Enclosure

On some farms, trees are planted in hedges. It is much to be regretted that this mode of inclosing was not more generally practised. These hedge rows, besides the warmth and shelter which they afford, embellish and enrich to a very great degree, the whole face of the country. Whatever reluctance and aversion, from ignorance or prejudice, the farmers might at first discover to inclosing, they now feel and acknowledge its advantages, and consequently are universally fond of it.[1]

THIS is the minister of Kilwinning in the 1790s, describing how enclosure affected the landscape. He observed that, while some farmers had initially been slow to accept the change, they had come to recognise its benefits.

Parliament had encouraged enclosures from the time of the Restoration. An act of 1661 enjoined owners whose lands were worth £1,000 Scots in annual rent to enclose four acres a year.[2] Freedom from taxation for nineteen years for land enclosed under the act was included as an incentive. In 1685 an 'Act in favour of Planters and Inclosers of Ground' renewed these provisions and extended the tax holiday for another nineteen years.[3] Ten years later an 'Act Anent Lands Lying Runrig' allowed a single landowner to apply to have runrig lands consolidated and divided among the proprietors.[4] Along with an act of 1669 which allowed neighbouring landowners to exchange pieces of ground in order to straighten the boundaries of their properties, these acts were used in the late seventeenth century by owners taking the first tentative steps towards modernising their estates. This legislation formed the basis for the outburst of enclosing activity which swept across eighteenth-century Scotland.

Once a landowner had the runrig and commonty lands divided and his own holdings consolidated, he was free to arrange them into fields and enclose them. Enclosure above all else transformed the face of the country. In place of the waving pattern of rigs in a bare landscape, there appeared geometric fields surrounded by stone dykes or hedges and ditches. The hedges were generally of hawthorn, and the dykes were built from the stones cleared from the fields.

Enclosure was the crucial factor in the development from the open-field system to the self-contained farm. It also underpinned the changes in the structure of rural society, marking as it did the move away from a communal to an individual approach to agriculture. A farmer was no longer obliged to sow and harvest the same crops as his neighbours at the same time. Nor did he have to send his cattle to the common pasture along with the other beasts from the fermtoun. With self-contained holdings, he could enclose his arable land to keep stock out and experiment with new crop rotations and fertilisers. He could fence off his pasture to keep stock in and improve the quality of his cattle by selective stock-breeding.

Enclosures on an estate started with the area around the mansion house. Tree-lined parks and avenues ornamented the house policies, provided an oasis of improvement in an otherwise treeless landscape and set an example for tenants to follow. They also had the very practical purpose of providing shelter belts for the new fields, and consequently better grazing for livestock and protection for crops. After the policies and the mains farm, a landowner would embark on the rest of his estate. The more general process of enclosure began in the south of Scotland in the late seventeenth century, particularly in Galloway and Wigtownshire, where the growth of the cattle trade with England led to the enclosing of large areas to hold the cattle.

The scale of these works was substantial. One Wigtownshire landowner, Sir David Dunbar, enclosed a park two and a half miles long and one and a half miles broad, which could winter 1,000 cattle.[5] Enclosures on such a scale required the eviction of hundreds of tenants, and in 1724 local people broke out in revolt at their removal from their holdings. Thousands of 'Levellers' threw down dykes across the south-west. In one incident a gang of 2,000 demolished seven miles of dyke in three hours.[6] It required the intervention of the army to quell the revolt.

Enclosure in the rest of the Lowlands proceeded peaceably. East Lothian and Midlothian saw many areas enclosed by the 1720s, but for the rest of the country the peak of enclosing activity was the second half of the eighteenth century. Although the landowners bore much of the cost of what was an expensive process, tenants would also take on some of the financial burden if they were granted an improving lease. As leases on jointly held farms came up for renewal, holdings were amalgamated into single-tenant farms and let on longer leases to farmers willing to carry out new methods of cultivation.

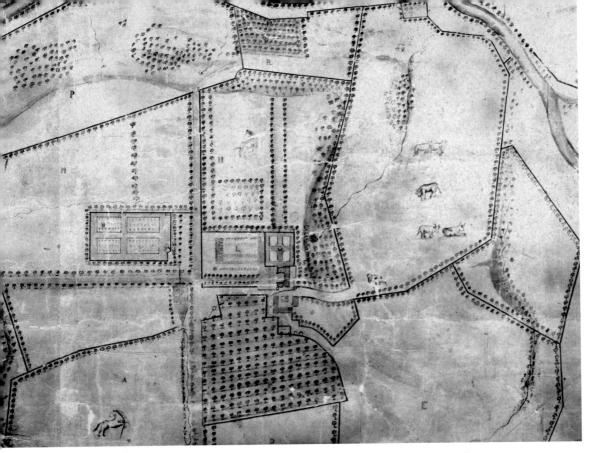

20. Enclosures at Penicuik House, 1712, by Mr Whitehead
(RHP 9373: courtesy of Sir John Clerk of Penicuik).

The estate of Penicuik in Midlothian was enclosed early. Sir John Clerk of Penicuik (1676–1755) was a respected improver, as well as a lawyer, antiquarian and musician. Although he did not succeed to the estate until his father's death in 1722, Sir John started improving it at the beginning of the eighteenth century and carried on for the next fifty years. He continued the work his father started in enclosing and planting around Penicuik House, went on to build a new mansion house at Mavisbank in the 1720s and started a factory village at Penicuik.

Sir John travelled extensively on the continent and visited famous gardens in England and Scotland. He used all this experience to advantage when designing the landscape of his estate and in his writings on improvements. This plan, which has been illustrated with cows, sheep and horses, shows extensive planting at the house and around the fields. Sir John regarded enclosing as the most important aspect of improvement: 'Inclosing by Hedges and Ditches is the main Improvement Which any of these Lands or indeed any other in this part of the Island can receive, because this may be laid down as a maxim, that if ground was never so good in itself, yet if it be not drain'd from too much moisture, & sheltered by trees or Hedges, it Will never be good for any thing.'[7]

21. Enclosures at Pitkellony, 1753, by William Winter (RHP 3485).

This plan provides a dramatic illustration of the effect of enclosures on the look of the countryside. The four parks to be enclosed stand out in their regular grid pattern against the unimproved landscape. The estate of Pitkellony near Crieff was owned by Captain David Drummond. It was bounded by the Perth estate, which had been forfeited to the Crown after the 1745 Jacobite rising, and was being run by the Forfeited Estates Commissioners.

In June 1753 Captain Drummond was planning to enclose his lands and asked to have the boundaries between the two estates straightened so that he could proceed with his improvements. He was frustrated by delays in obtaining the consent of all parties. It is clear from his extravagant claims that he was well aware of the effect his efforts would have on the appearance of the area. He reckoned his enclosures would be seen from the Grampians to the Ochils:

> as It is in the Intrest of boath, for Ease in Incloseing. Had it not been that Hindrance, I wou'd have Inclosed four Parks e'er now, two of them on the King's road, which wou'd both Beautify it, & the Countrie. One of them Incloses 84 Acres of Ground for Planting, on the top of a moor, which will make a fine Appearance from The Grampion to the Ochill Hills, and down the Strath of Earn, the lenth of Abernathie.[8]

5

Drainage

Nothing can be more unpropitious to improvement, than the appearance of an unenclosed tract, totally undrained, situated in a weeping climate . . . where enormous masses of peat stretch over a great tract of country, covered only with stunted heath, or the most miserable herbage. Notwithstanding these unfavourable appearances, such lands are susceptible of improvement; and when improved; what sight can be more delightful to the diligent cultivator, than to perceive that he has been the means of converting lands, of no value in their natural state, into one more fertile or of trans-forming a barren wilderness into a fruitful field?[1]

AS is clear from this extract, boggy wasteland was an affront to improvers. In the spirit of the Enlightenment, landowners were prepared to go to considerable lengths to change the natural environment into something more productive and more aestheti-cally pleasing. Across Scotland, marshlands and mosses were drained to bring more ground into cultivation. In the north-east some landowners settled displaced cottars on smallholdings on the periphery of new farms and encouraged them to reclaim the surrounding moor and moss land.

The most ambitious reclamation project was the drainage of Blair Drummond Moss on the carse of Stirling, which turned a large area of wasteland into fruitful fields. Some drained not only marshes but lochs as well in order to expand their acreage of arable land. In Moray the Loch of Spynie was drained over a number of years from a lake covering over 2,000 acres to a marsh of about 100 acres, surrounded by cultivated land. A further benefit of the draining of boggy areas was an improvement in the health of the inhabitants. On alluvial ground, river-beds were deepened and banks built up to prevent damaging floods.

Drainage and enclosure frequently went hand in hand. Ditches were dug to improve drainage to new fields, and hedges were planted on the earth thrown up from them. Box drains (see Fig. 24) and stone drains were also dug to improve the run-off of water. While these early drains and ditches provided some improvement, it was not until the 1820s that the real breakthrough came in field drainage. James Smith, a farmer at Deanston near Doune, invented a system for ploughing subsoil. His plough broke up the hard earth beneath the surface to a depth of sixteen inches and allowed water to drain through. This plough was one of the most important tools of the new agriculture. Around the same time, underground tile drains were developed. Together, subsoil ploughing and tile drains could transform boggy wastes into fertile earth. Land which was formerly overgrown with rushes bore crops instead.

Drainage programmes were encouraged by the rapid spread of drain-tile manufacture. The first tile-works in Scotland started at Cessnock in Ayrshire in 1826, and by the 1840s the county had ten tile-producers.[2] The Drainage Acts of the 1840s, which offered loans at low interest for draining land, resulted in a great deal of activity in the mid-nineteenth century. It was these new drainage methods which resulted in the flattening of the old ridges and gave fields the level appearance so familiar today. In turn the new flat surface of the fields allowed the introduction of new equipment such as reaping machines.

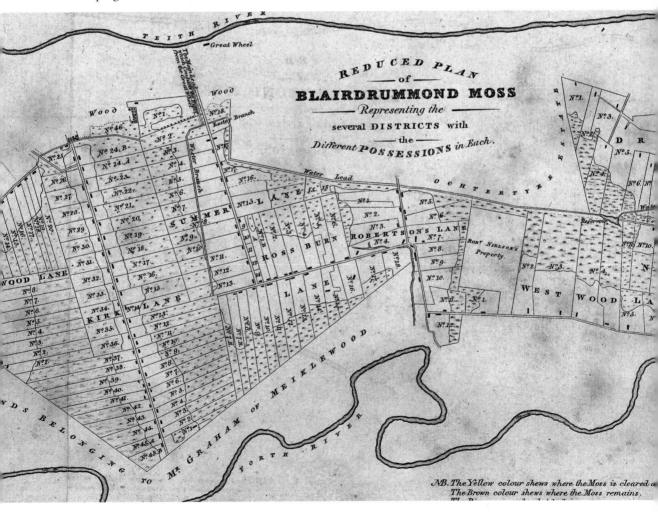

22. (*Previous page*) **Blair Drummond Moss, 1817, by John Legate from a previous plan** (RHP 4067: courtesy of Mr W.G. Drummond Moray).

Blair Drummond Moss formed part of the estate of Lord Kames, a vigorous improver who was also a judge, a philosopher and a pillar of the Scottish Enlightenment. He was a member of two bodies which did much to encourage Scotland's agriculture and economy in the eighteenth century – the Board of Trustees for Fisheries and Manufactures, and the Forfeited Estates Commissioners. His work on the Blair Drummond estate transformed the landscape of the carse of Stirling.

The carse was covered in peat bog stretching twelve miles north-west beside the river Forth. Peat lay up to twenty feet deep, but below this was fertile alluvial ground. Piecemeal efforts had been made to clear the moss since the early eighteenth century, and credit for the idea of floating the moss off may lie with a Dutch painter who was working on the house of a local laird, Mr Wright of Pearsie, early in the eighteenth century.[3] However, from 1767 Lord Kames reclaimed the moss on a grand scale by leasing eight- to ten-acre sections out to tenants, rent-free for the first seven years, in return for clearing the peat. Trenches were dug down as far as the clay, then the peat was stripped off the surrounding area and floated away in the trenches so that it drained into the river. In 1787 a waterwheel was built to give the required pressure of water in the ditches.

The plan shows the small plots of land laid out in a grid pattern. The 'Great Wheel' is on the top left of the plan, drawing water from the river Teith. The progress of clearance can be seen on the plots: the white parts are reclaimed ground, and the shaded parts are the remaining moss. The cottages of the smallholders, which were originally made of turf, are marked alongside the roads.

Possessors	Present Possessors	ages	Childrens names	ages	males	females	Total	Persons Deceased	age years	year died in	of what Diseases	males	females deceased	Total	number of Leases	Where they from
Brook	Duncan Gray	50	Duncan Gray	18												
	May McLean	50	Daniel	16												
			Peter	14	5	2	7								7	44	Comu
			Jean	10												
			William	9												
d McIntyre	John McIntyre	64	Mary McIntyre	11				Mary Wright	70	1799	Old age					
	Jean McKerracher	32	Daniel	7	4	3	7	Christian Wright	31	1810	Consumption	1	2	10	29	Balquhi
	Donald his father	79	Catherine	5				Daniel McIntyre	1mo	1804	Sickness					
			Charles	3												
Monteath	John Clark	52	James Clark	20												
	Janet Brown	42	John	19												
			William	17												
			Janet	15												
			Robert	14	7	6	13							13	3	Kilma
			Jean	12												
			Alexander	10												
			Hellen	8												
			Andrew	5												
			Kate	4												
			Mar													

23. Census of the inhabitants of Blair Drummond Moss, 1811 (GD 1/321/1).

Many of the 'moss lairds', as they were known, came from the Perthshire Highlands, anxious to have the opportunity of some land even if it meant years of back-breaking work to turn it into something profitable. First they had to dig up the moss and cast it into the drainage channels to float away. Then they had to remove ancient tree-roots from the clay, and plough the land. After being left to dry out for a month, the ground was ready for planting and gave very good results. The first tenants got a tack (lease) for thirty-eight years, rent-free for the first seven, with the rent gradually increasing thereafter.

These families had cleared two or three acres of their seven- or eight-acre plots. They all kept cows, poultry and cats. The census recorded 186 families, numbering 886 people, living on the moss. By the time the last leases ran out in the mid-nineteenth century, 1,700 acres had been cleared. The success of the scheme was such that the plots were eagerly snapped up by surrounding farmers or joined together into larger holdings. The contrast between the fertile land of the carse and the remaining part of the moss can still be seen today at Flanders Moss a few miles to the west.

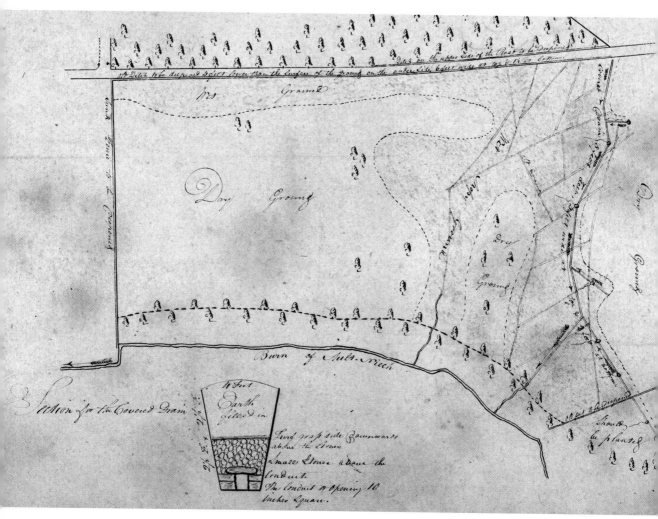

24. Plan for draining Coulchastle Park, 1802
(RHP 8977: courtesy of the earl of Seafield).

This plan and section illustrate drainage methods to be used on an estate in Morayshire at the beginning of the nineteenth century. Alongside the plantation at the top of the plan are ditches on either side of the road, which are to be deepened, as is a sunk fence on the left. The line on the right is a covered drain five feet deep, four feet wide at the top and two feet wide at the bottom. This is a box drain: the conduit at the bottom of the drain to carry the water off is covered by small stones with earth on top.

Tree Planting

No person acquainted with the naturally bleak, moist and ungenial climate of Scotland can refuse to acknowledge the great improvement it has received from plantations.[1]

FROM the sixteenth century the Scottish parliament had encouraged landowners to plant trees in an effort to overcome timber shortages caused by over-exploitation of woodlands. It has recently been estimated that in prehistoric times 50 per cent of Scotland's landscape was covered in trees. By the eighteenth century this had been reduced to as little as 4 per cent.[2] Scotland's inhabitants had made extensive use of her woodlands since time immemorial. They cleared forests to create farms, to graze livestock, to build houses and ships, to make furniture and utensils and to provide fuel. The devastating effects of this are clear from travellers' descriptions of Lowland Scotland, which frequently comment on the lack of trees in the landscape. Dr Johnston's famous remark 'a tree in Scotland is as rare as a horse in Venice' may be considered a witty piece of hyperbole, but he had a point. Before the work of eighteenth-century tree-planters took root, Scotland was not renowned for leafy glades.

Tree planting in Scotland started in the seventeenth century, when many estate owners began planting around their houses to enhance their appearance. This trend quickened after the Restoration, possibly encouraged by the enclosure act of 1661. However, it was not until the eighteenth century that tree planting moved out of the policies, and large plantations made their appearance in the countryside.

Improving landowners planted trees round their newly enclosed fields to provide shelter and 'warm' the land. In the spirit of the age, landowners planted for profit as well as pleasure. Timber was a vital commodity. The best wood was sold for house-, bridge- and shipbuilding. Trunks were used to make masts for ships and crucks, or frames, for houses, while smaller parts were used for roof timbers and floors. Wood was also required for furniture, domestic utensils, agricultural implements and carts. Barrels were needed in the fishing industry, in brewing and distilling, and for storing food. Bark was sold to tanneries for curing leather and was also used to make dyes. Charcoal was required for Scotland's developing industries, such as iron founding. In Argyll, for example, the Bonawe ironworks on Loch Etive created a considerable demand for timber in the area, using the produce of around seventy-four acres of woodland a year.[3]

Timber thus provided a very important supplement to the incomes of impecunious Scottish landowners, particularly those involved in the expensive business of improvement. Even as early as the 1680s, the earl of Panmure calculated that the value of his timber was equal to the annual rental of his estate.[4] Until the end of the Napoleonic Wars, Highland estate owners regarded the British navy's insatiable demand for timber as the answer to their prayers.

Landowners planted huge numbers of native trees, such as Scots pine, ash, elm, alder, birch and oak. Non-native species such as larch and beech were also tried. Pine grew quickly and provided a quick return on investment. Ash was used in the manufacture of ploughs and other implements, and birch was used for pit props and railway sleepers.[5] Alder provided roof timbers, while willow and hazel wands were used to make baskets and hurdles. The fourth duke of Atholl (1755–1830) was a great admirer of the larch, introduced to the estate by his grandfather in 1738. He clothed the hillsides of Atholl with the species, which was valuable for building houses and ships. Such was his enthusiasm for trees, he was known as 'Planter John'. He and other landowners planted millions of trees. Sir Archibald Grant of Monymusk is said to have held the record at over 48 million trees. It has been estimated that in the period 1750 to 1850 about half a million acres of trees were planted.[6] Sir Walter Scott, an enthusiastic planter himself, summed up the attitude of tree-planting landowners in *The Heart of Midlothian*, when Lord Dumbiedykes encourages his son from his deathbed: 'Jock, when ye hae naething else to do, ye may aye be sticking in a tree: it will be growing Jock when ye're sleeping.'

Early forestry not only changed the face of the country through extensive planting, but commercial timber operations brought other changes to the landscape as well. Dykes were built to protect growing woodlands from animals, new roads were constructed to allow timber to be transported and river beds were altered to permit the floating of logs from remote areas.

25. (*Overleaf*) **Glenmore and wood, 1762, by William Anderson**
(RHP 2504).

This attractive illustration shows Glenmore wood beside Loch Morlich, the property of the duke of Gordon. In a letter to the duke on the reverse of the plan, William Bell, his factor, says of Glenmore 'it is without doubt one of the prettiest places in Brittain'.

Commercial forestry, usually undertaken by English adventurers, began on Speyside in the seventeenth century. The industry got going on a large scale in the 1720s, when the York Buildings Company began to fell trees in Sir James Grant's Abernethy forests. The neighbouring Glenmore timber was reckoned to be the best fir-wood in Scotland,[7] and from the 1760s approaches were made to the duke of Gordon by people wishing to exploit the forest. In 1771 one hopeful outlined to the duke the commercial possibilities of Glenmore:

> *Since I saw & examined that wood, I cannot help frequently regretting that it is not manufactur'd, when it would be so very advantageous to the proprietor, & to the country, & I think I may add, such an advantage to the nation. I have before hinted to you, that many thousand masts, beams, & the finest plank of any lengths for Ship building can be had there, & as good in size & quality as the best imported from abroad . . . The timber that would not answer for masts, beams & the finest plank, would do very well for the House wright & the Joiner, to whom it would sell well, being of so good a quality.[8]*

The duke eventually sold much of the Glenmore timber in 1784 for £10,000 to Messrs Dodsworth and Osbourne, merchants in Hull, for use by the navy. The resin in the pinewood gave it waterproofing qualities which made it particularly suitable for shipbuilding. To facilitate access to the woods, a road was built from Loch Morlich to the Spey, and the bed of its tributary, the Luineag, was altered so that logs could be floated down to the sea at Garmouth (see Fig. 7) and Kingston, the adjoining village set up by the merchants for the building of ships.[9] A dam and sluice were built at the end of the loch to provide sufficient water power to float the logs. This was the traditional method of transporting Strathspey timber to the Moray Firth. Elizabeth Grant of Rothiemurchus vividly describes the process in the early nineteenth century in her autobiography, *Memoirs of a Highland Lady*.[10]

At Garmouth, the duke of Gordon's timber supplied a shipbuilding industry. In 1798 a navy frigate was named *Glenmore* to mark the connection. It was one of forty-seven ships built by the company from Strathspey pine.[11] This period of intensive felling did great damage to the landscape of Glenmore, and visitors commented on the destruction left by the exploitation of the forest. Subsequent replanting and natural regeneration have healed most of the scars. The wood was bought in 1923 by the Forestry Commission.

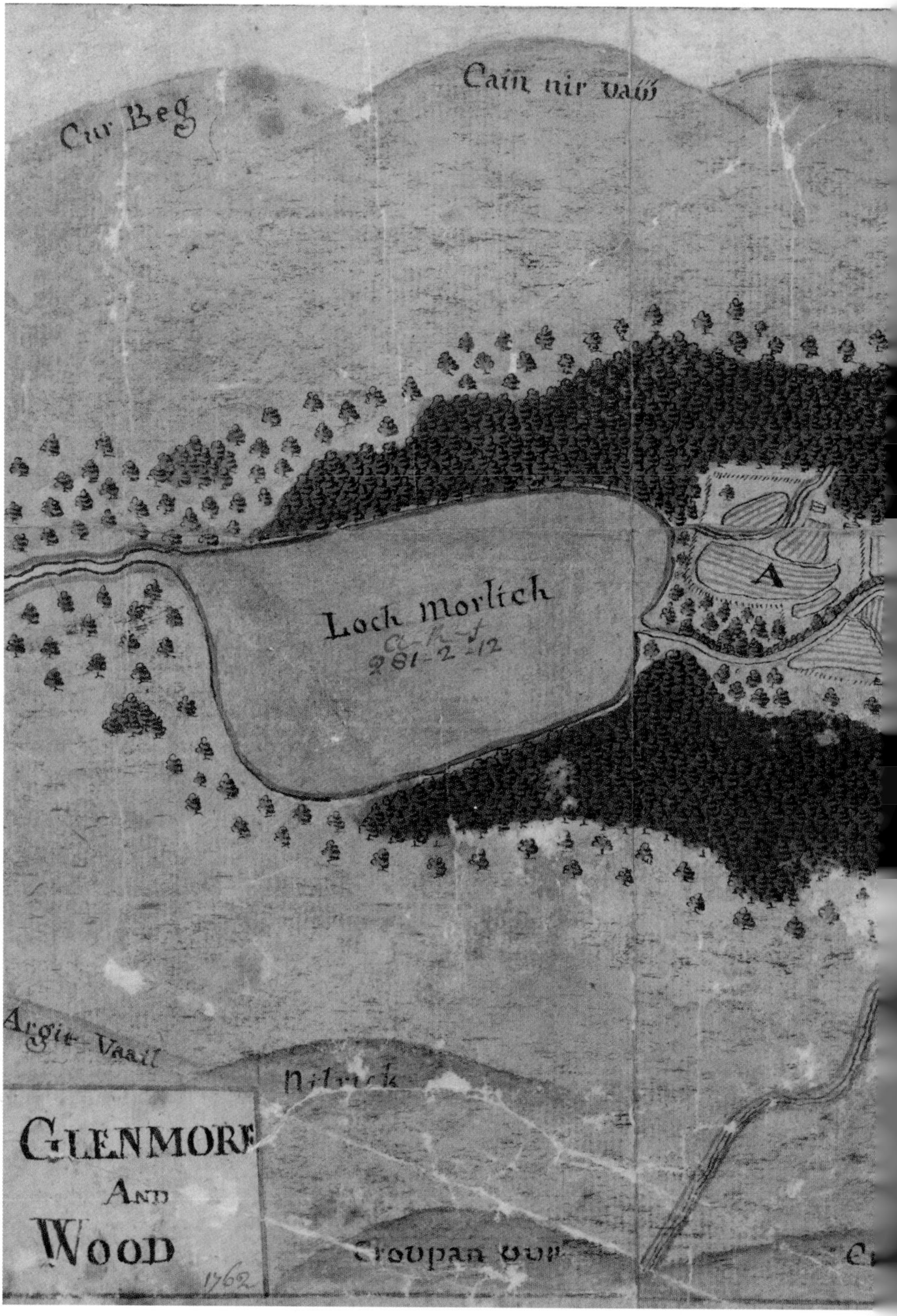

Cur Beg

Cain nir vaw

Loch Morlich
a-R-t
281-2-12

A

Argie Vaail

Nilnick

GLENMORE
AND
WOOD

1762

Croupan vuw

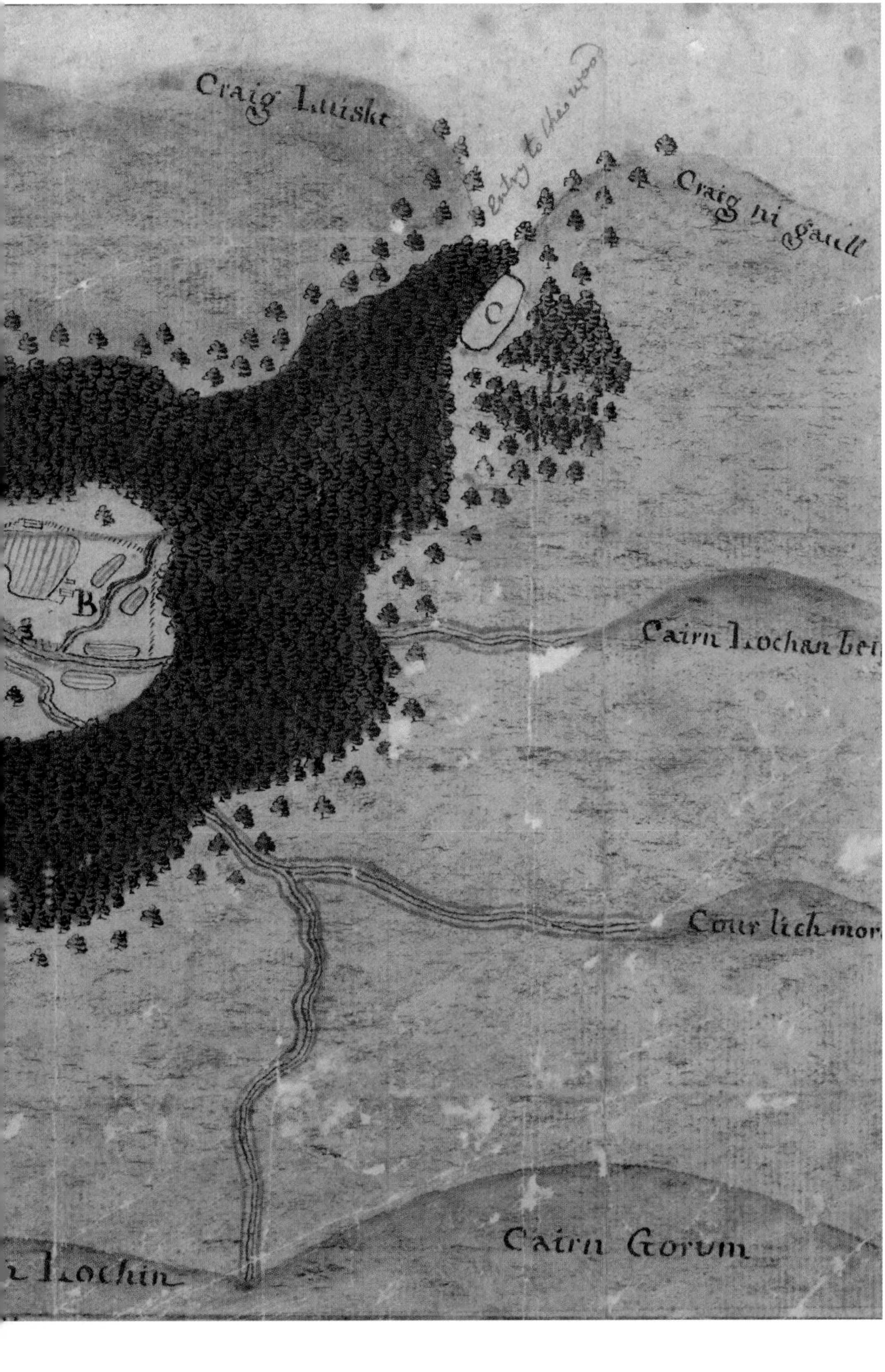

Craig Luiske

Entry to the wood

Craig ni gaull

C

B

Cairn Lochan beig

Cour lich mor

i Lochin

Cairn Gorum

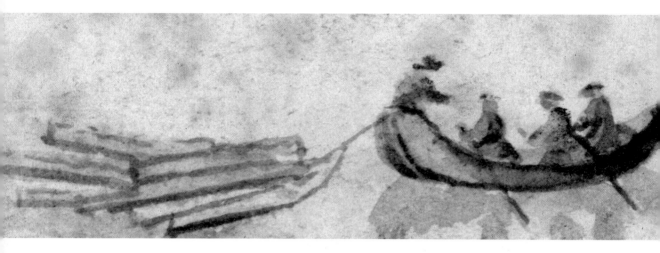

26. Boat towing logs on Loch Rannoch, 1758, from a plan by John Leslie (E 783/98, p. 26).

A vignette from a plan of a farm at Loch Rannoch illustrates timber transportation in the eighteenth century. This area was part of the estate of Robertson of Struan, which had been forfeited to the Crown after he supported the Jacobite side in the '45. The estate was being run by the Forfeited Estates Commissioners, many of whom were keen improvers. The commissioners were anxious to foster industry on the estates in their care and were developing the Black Wood of Rannoch commercially. According to James Small, the factor, Struan had exploited the wood with little care to its regeneration: 'The late Strouan took a very fatherless care of it and not only without judgement or mercy cast down young and old trees much more than he could dispose of, but likeways allowed his tenants and others to cutt and destroy vast quantities of it.'[12]

Before he became factor, Small had looked after the woods on the estate, and before that he had been an ensign in the army. He organised replanting, reduced the quantity of felling the previous factor had been carrying out and improved the existing sawmills. He also had parts of the wood enclosed to prevent damage to young trees by grazing animals.

The drawing shows logs being towed to a sawmill on the south shore of the loch. They were also floated down the rivers Tummel and Tay to Dundee. Timber from the Black Wood of Rannoch was used in projects to improve communications to this remote area: Wade's bridge at Aberfeldy and the West Highland Railway both used local wood.[13]

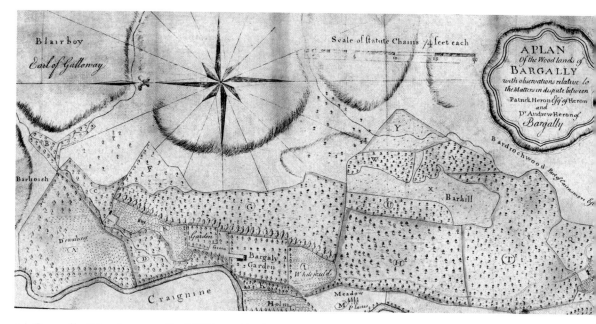

27. Bargally Woods, 1772, by William McCartney
(RHP 661).

A plan of woodlands in Kirkcudbrightshire shows the variety of trees favoured by improvers – fir, oak, birch, ash, willow, plane, lime, alder, gean, chestnut, beech, poplar and walnut. Much of this planting was done by Andrew Heron of Bargally (d. 1740), one of the most knowledgeable and enthusiastic tree-planters of the time. He started the garden and planting at Bargally in the 1690s, enclosed part of the estate and built the house. He planted all around the lower part of the valley which housed Bargally. An eighteenth-century history of the family describes his work: '[he] improved these grounds to good advantage having enclosed all his Low grounds, built a handsome little house, Large Gardens well stockt with variety of fine fruits both ston fruit and core, some parterres stockt with fine flowers, a green house stockt with oranges, lemons, pomegranats, passion trees, citron trees, oleanders, myrtils and many others'.[14]

Heron had one of the earliest collections of hothouse plants in Scotland and was one of the country's first plant specialists. When he was visiting a gardener near London, he displayed such expert knowledge of exotic plants that the man declared: 'Then sir, you must either be the devil, or Andrew Heron of Bargally.'[15] However, his enthusiasm for horticulture, planting and improvement caused him serious financial problems. In straitened circumstances he borrowed money from his nephew, Patrick Heron, using the woods of Bargally as security. Patrick took control of the estate after his uncle's death, and it took thirty years for Andrew's heir to recover possession.

7

Rural Housing

The miserable cottages, built of turf or sod, which are in some districts rapidly, and in others slowly disappearing, do not require any particular description. They are seldom well situated and their construction is despicable. Indeed nothing but ignorance of any thing better, or necessity, which must submit to every inconvenience, could have induced any human being to be satisfied with such wretched accommodation.[1]

MANY travellers commented on the primitive nature of Scottish rural housing during the eighteenth century. During a tour of Scotland in 1769, Thomas Pennant described Highland cottages as 'black mole hills'.[2] Improvements to cottages came later than other aspects of estate modernisation, and even in the early nineteenth century the state of rural housing was still a cause for concern. The disparaging description above appeared in 1814 in the *General Report of the Agricultural State and Political Circumstances of Scotland.*

Before the agricultural revolution, housing in the Scottish countryside was very basic. Most people working the land lived in timber-framed cottages where the roof rested on wooden arches known as crucks or couples. In cruck-framed houses the walls did not bear the weight of the roof, and so impermanent materials such as clay and turf were used. Rough stone was sometimes used for the lower courses of the walls. Visitors regularly commented on how low Scottish cottages were: five feet was the common height.[3] This lack of height was caused by the shortage of timber in seventeenth-century Scotland. As a result of this scarcity, crucks were the most valuable part of the house. In some parts of Scotland timber was provided by the landowner; in others, tenants provided their own building materials and took the timbers with them when they moved.

A variety of materials was used in roofing: heather, turf, straw, reeds, bracken and broom were all common. No building materials were wasted. When tenants needed a new roof, they recycled the old thatch, which had been enriched by soot from the peat fire, on the fields as compost. Most houses had wooden shutters rather than glass for windows, and earthen floors. Pre-improvement cottages in the Scottish countryside were by and large biodegradable.

Cottages were generally of the longhouse construction, with people and animals sharing one roof. The dwelling house was often separated from the byre by only a partition. This allowed the heat from the cattle to provide some warmth to the house. The size of houses varied according to the status of the tenant, but for those at the bottom of the social scale, one room was the norm. In poorer houses the family slept on the floor around the fire, which was usually in the centre of the room. Smoke escaped through a hole in the roof.

When an estate was modernised, fermtouns with their characteristic jumble of buildings disappeared from the landscape. New farms had substantial farmhouses, built of stone and lime, with two floors and slated roofs. They provided tenant farmers with a house of the standard a laird's house would have been earlier in the eighteenth century. Agricultural journals and numerous publications carried standard designs for farmhouses, offices and cottages. New steadings were often arranged round a courtyard, and the symmetrical new buildings reflected the geometric layout of the fields around them. From the late eighteenth century a trend started to separate the farmhouse and the farm workers' cottages from the steading, a situation which reflected the growing differentiation between the farmer and his workforce.

Building materials changed as the ready supply of turf from commonties was no longer available once these areas were divided. Slates and pantiles replaced turf or thatched roofs. The introduction of lime mortar (as opposed to the use of clay) meant that load-bearing walls could be built, and the need for crucks diminished. With longer leases, tenants were more inclined to build more permanent houses. Although these technological advances meant that houses of more than one storey could now be built, it was the nineteenth century before two-storey cottages for farm workers became common.

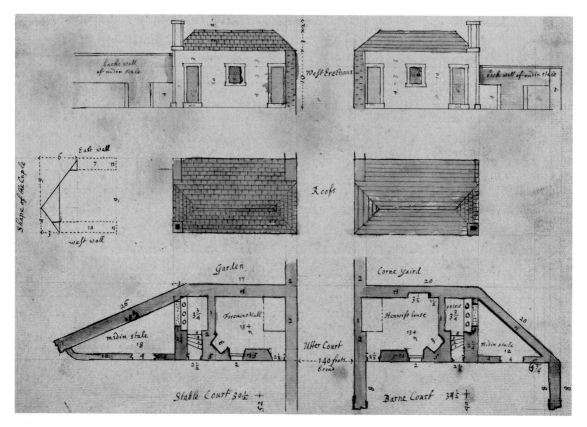

28. Cottages for the foreman and henwife at Panmure, 1701
(RHP 35157a: courtesy of the earl of Dalhousie).

Improvements on the earl of Panmure's estate near Carnoustie in Angus had been going on since the 1660s. By the beginning of the eighteenth century, better housing for farm workers was being provided. Each of these cottages has one room with a bed recess, allowing a degree of privacy, and a hearth. Next door is the privy for the farm workers.

The cottages measure thirteen feet by nine, which may seem very small, but even in 1814 a living room twelve feet square was felt to be sufficient to accommodate a family.[4] When proposing designs for new cottages, the improvers concentrated on ventilation, lighting and construction rather than increased living space. Slate roofs, fireplaces with chimneys, glazed windows, and stone and lime walls were usually advised.

29. Garrichrew cot houses, *c.*1804
(RHP 6769: courtesy of Viscountess Melville).

In 1783 Henry Dundas, later Viscount Melville, bought the Dunira estate at Comrie in Perthshire. He set about extensive improvements, rebuilding the house, laying out the grounds and creating a model farm. He wanted the estate put into perfect order, and the new farm buildings, along with enclosing, fencing and improved roads, were intended to add considerably 'to the Gentlemanlike look and appearance of the Place'.[5]

These cottages were for farm workers – the shepherd, henwife, gamekeeper and ploughman. Like most cot houses, even improved ones, they were built in a single-storey terrace. However, their steeply pitched roof would have contained an attic. The cottages measure twenty feet by fifteen and have one room with two bed recesses, a pantry, a fireplace with chimney and one window.[6]

Plan & Elevation for Farm house Holme.

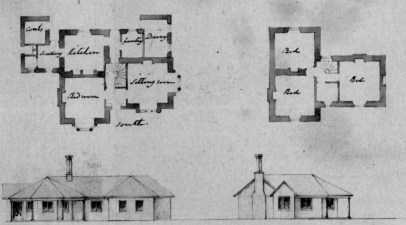

Plan & Elevation for Cottage - Wholestone Bank.

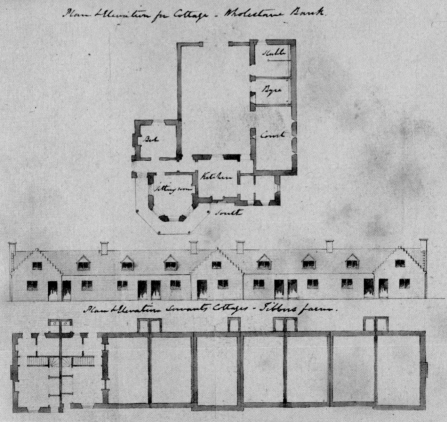

Plan & Elevation Servants Cottages - Tibbns farm.

30. (*Opposite*) **Farmhouse and cottages at Drumlanrig, 1830, by William Burn** (RHP 93718: courtesy of the duke of Buccleuch and Queensberry KT).

In the nineteenth century a second wave of improvements to farm housing took place. These buildings are a good example of the very substantial farmhouses and cottages that were built at this time. They were designed by William Burn, who built many mansion houses for the aristocracy, as well as public buildings. He was doing a lot of work for the duke at this time, including an addition at Bowhill.

      The buildings look remarkably modern. The farmhouse has a sitting room and four bedrooms as well as a large kitchen, a scullery, pantry and dairy at the back of the house. The detached cottage has a courtyard design with the stable and byre along one side. The terraced servants' cottages have two storeys. They are a world away from the Garrichrew cottages which were built only twenty-five years or so earlier. Burns described his thinking behind the designs to the duke:

> *I now send a rough sketch for the farm house Holme – for a cottage to be built on Wholestane Bank, & for servants cottages at Tibbers farm, which I have kept as plain as possible, & yet given as much feature to them as the situation & nature of the buildings appear to me to demand.*
>
>   *The cottage for Wholestane Bank I purposely kept low, from the precipitous nature of the ground, & the situation otherwise appearing most appropriate for that stile of building, and it occurs to me that it will both make a better & more convenient description of farm cottages to have one room above the other in place of extending so much accommodation on the ground floor.*[7]

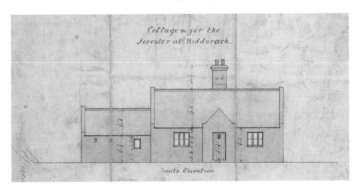

31. Forester's cottage, Rhidorroch, 1861 (RHP 45223).

This cottage is typical of Highland estate buildings of the mid-nineteenth century. It was on the earl of Cromartie's estate in Wester Ross. The cottage has two floors, with a room and kitchen downstairs and two bedrooms upstairs. The byre is attached to the side of the house. The cottage cost £200 and the elderly forester for whom it was built, Donald McLeay, was said to be very proud of his new home.[8]

8

The New Face of the Country

The present appearance of the parish is very different from its former state; the face of the country is naturally beautiful, and the natural beauty of the hills and vallies is increased by the windings of the Forth, by innumerable inclosures, by many young thriving plantations, by a variety of villages, and by several genteel houses, appearing in different parts of the parish.[1]

AS a Stirlingshire minister noted in the late eighteenth century, the country received a radical facelift from the dividing of commonties, enclosing of fields, draining of marshlands and planting of trees. Its new appearance was regular and ordered, embellished by new houses and farm buildings, trees and hedges. Large areas of moor and marshland were transformed into arable land and the acreage under cultivation increased considerably, e.g. by almost one third in Kincardineshire in the first half of the nineteenth century.[2]

Improving trends which started in the late seventeenth century accelerated dramatically in the second half of the eighteenth. As leases came to an end, smallholdings were amalgamated into self-contained, single-tenant farms. Like other improving trends, this process started in the fertile areas of the Lothians and gradually spread across the country. A recent study of poll-tax records of six Lowland counties has shown that, by the 1690s, there were twice as many single-tenancy farms as joint holdings.[3] By 1750 multiple-tenancy farms were in the minority in most parts of the Lowlands.

After improvement, new farms in the Lothians could be anything from 200 to 600 acres. Further north, smaller farms prevailed, and in the western Lowlands holdings of up to 150 acres were the norm.[4] The north-eastern counties of Aberdeen, Banff and Kincardine differed in having a large number of very small holdings, like the crofts of the Highlands. This was due to new areas of hill and moorland being brought under cultivation. In this area the smallholders cultivated their own few acres and also worked for neighbouring farmers.

With these developments the old fermtoun disappeared, its characteristic jumble of cottages and outbuildings replaced by trim new farmhouses and steadings. The new farms resembled touns in their size, as the farmhouse, workers' cottages and farm offices were all adjacent, but they had the improvers' stamp of regularity all over them. Gone too were the ridges and baulks of runrig cultivation. In their place were substantial flat geometric fields, enclosed by hedges, ditches, dykes or shelter belts of trees.

While early improvers such as Sir John Cockburn of Ormiston could bankrupt themselves with the expense of modernising their estates, by the end of the eighteenth century landowners could spend large sums on improvements in the knowledge that increased rentals would be assured. Rising grain prices during the Napoleonic Wars provided a particular impetus to improvements in the 1790s. Robert Barclay of Ury (1730–97), a noted Kincardineshire improver, managed to increase his estate's annual value from £200 to £1,650.[5] The minister of Campsie in Stirlingshire reckoned that the land rental of the parish more than doubled between 1763 and 1793.[6]

By the late seventeenth century, written leases were common, and from the early eighteenth, leases were lengthened to 19–21 years, giving tenants greater security of tenure. Previously tacks might only run for between three and nine years. This security, combined with freedom from the constraints of communal methods of farming, meant that tenants of the new farms could try out improved methods of agriculture unimpeded. Indeed most of the new leases stipulated that improvements such as tree planting, enclosure and new crop rotations had to be carried out.

The practice of converting rents from kind to money payments had begun towards the end of the seventeenth century, and over the next sixty years or so this practice became standard throughout Scotland. This development was one of the most important changes of the agricultural revolution as it brought tenants directly into contact with market forces for the first time. Farmers now had to sell their own produce direct to raise cash to pay the rent. Agriculture was no longer a subsistence affair, but a commercial enterprise.

Improvements brought new methods of working the land. Lime became very popular as a fertiliser. It had been used in Ayrshire since the late sixteenth century, and in the seventeenth its use spread throughout the Lowlands. Improved crop rotation was an essential part of the new agriculture. Legumes, such as peas and beans, were planted to fix nitrogen in the soil. Allowing the ground to recover by lying fallow for a season was a concept Scottish farmers needed a little persuasion to accept. Writing in 1729, William Mackintosh of Borlum, a noted improver in Inverness-shire, was loud in his praise of the practice: 'I am sorry to find some of our Gentlemen in that Error that Fallow can never be of Profit. Fallow is the Life of Improvement; for however better and more beautiful Inclosing and Planting will render our Country, 'tis Fallow will really make it fertile and rich, 'tis Fallow will make Wheat in Scotland as plentiful as now Bear [bere].'[7]

New rotations of crops included sown grass, such as clover and rye, and root crops, such as turnips, which allowed the ground to recover from a succession of cereal crops. Crop yields doubled and sometimes trebled with the new practices, while the introduction of turnips solved the perennial problem of providing winter feed for livestock. Turnips had been used for domestic consumption since the seventeenth century, but their use as field crops started in the south-east of Scotland in the 1740s. The old system of agriculture could provide little in the way of winter fodder, but turnips could feed stock for several months of the year.

Improvements in agricultural implements also made a great difference. The old Scots plough was a heavy instrument with a flat mould-board. These ploughs usually required eight, but sometimes up to ten or twelve, oxen or horses to pull them and two men to guide them. In the first half of the eighteenth century, improvers such as Grant of Monymusk tried new, lighter English ploughs, such as the Rotherham plough. In 1767 James Small, from Berwickshire, patented his swing or chain plough, in which he combined features from the old Scots plough with the Rotherham plough.[8] The new ploughs had curved mould-boards to turn the earth over, and needed only two horses and one man to work them. This represented another factor in the move away from the old communal methods of agriculture.

Scotland's growing towns and emerging manufactures opened up new markets and stimulated food production. They also provided employment opportunities, which were an essential safety net for those affected by the changes sweeping the countryside. These changes led to a transformation in rural society as well as in the landscape. Small tenants and cottars saw their patches of land absorbed into larger farms and lost their rights to pasture cattle as commonties disappeared. Previously almost all those involved in agriculture had had a piece of ground of their own to work, however small, but the new rural society consisted only of farmers and landless farm-workers. The cottar class disappeared.

Because the process of change in Lowland Scotland was gradual and because other work could be found, the alteration to rural society, though major, happened without the cataclysmic results which affected the Highlands. Those who lost their small patches of land often became paid labourers on the new farms. Arable farming still required a good labour supply at harvest time. The process of improvement itself required labourers for digging drains, planting hedges and trees, and building farmhouses. Craftsmen such as joiners found their skills in great demand for building and making farm equipment. Some cottars and small tenants moved into the many new villages being created and took work in developing rural industries, such as textiles, or jobs in constructing the growing transport system.

Others moved to urban areas for employment. The agricultural and industrial revolutions resulted in a huge shift away from rural living. In 1750 only one in ten Scots lived in a town of over 10,000 inhabitants. One hundred years later, one in three did so.[9] Some people, however, left Scotland altogether and sought new opportunities by emigrating abroad. For people who had lost their holdings, the attraction of cheap or sometimes free land in America or Canada was considerable.

Though there was only one sustained protest at the effect of the new farming practices, the Galloway Levellers' revolt, it has been suggested that the frequency of meal riots in the second half of the eighteenth century may be connected with the radical alteration in the traditional way of life caused by the move of so many people into towns.[10] Food shortages could cause major problems in a newly urbanised population which had been accustomed to living off the land. The reports in the Old Statistical Account, written by parish ministers in the 1790s, contain numerous references to the social upheavals the agricultural revolution brought in its wake. The minister of Currie in Midlothian remarked on the depopulation in the pastoral parts of the parish caused by the development of large farms:

> *The first and leading [cause of depopulation] here, as well as elsewhere, has been the*
> *extension of farms, by which several small ones have been swallowed up in one large*
> *one. This cause has operated very powerfully in thinning the inhabitants in the upper*
> *parts of the parish, where there is now much pasture ground. At present there are only*
> *three villages in the parish . . . but formerly there were a great many more . . . and*
> *many different places, where, in the beginning of this century, from 20 to 30 families*
> *resided, are now without an inhabitant.*[11]

32. (*Overleaf*) **The lands of Floors, 1736, by William Wyeth**
(RHP 9302: courtesy of the duke of Roxburghe).

This plan of the lands around Floors Castle shows a Borders estate after improvement. The castle, whose outline in red can be seen at A, was remodelled by William Adam in the 1720s and rebuilt by William Playfair in the nineteenth century. Adam was also responsible for laying out the grounds around the castle.

Here we see a formal landscape with intricate patterns of woodland avenues which looked out onto features of the Borders landscape, such as Smailholm Tower. The fields have been enclosed and lined with trees, and plantations surround the castle. The town of Kelso stretches out along the river Tweed on the right of the plan. The house stands on a natural terrace above the river and the sweeping view across the parkland to the river and town can still be seen today.

Defoe saw Floors in the 1720s as the improvements were under way and marvelled at the transformation taking place:

> *Floors is an ancient seat, but begins to wear a new face; and those who view'd it fifteen*
> *or sixteen years ago, will scarce know it again, if they should come a few years hence,*
> *when the present Duke may have finished the additions and embellishments, which*
> *he is now making, and has been a considerable time upon. Nor will the very face of*
> *the country appear the same, except it be that the river Tweed may, perhaps, run in*

the same channel: but the land before, lying open and wild, he will find enclos'd, culti-
vated and improv'd, rows and even woods of trees covering the champaign country, and
the house surrounded with large grown vistas and well planted avenues, such as were
never seen there before.[12]

33. (*Opposite*) **The lands of Houston, 1759, by Charles Ross** (RHP 10659).

This plan illustrates the partially modernised West Lothian landscape of the mid-
eighteenth century created by Thomas Shairp of Houston, a keen improver.

    Two large parks of fifty-seven acres each, Wester Park and Nettlehill Park, were
established, probably for cattle, with smaller sheep parks to the north of them. Leading
south from the house, parks are laid out in pairs on either side of an avenue of trees. At
the bottom of the parks, a new wood has been planted. Outwith the improved area, the
rest of the landscape consists mainly of moor and moss, sprinkled with fermtouns. The
appearance of Easter and Wester Drumshaggs indicates a fermtoun which had expanded
sufficiently to require division.

34. (*Overleaf*) **Leith Hall Mains, 1758**
(RHP 5198/1: courtesy of the National Trust for Scotland).

This plan of the mains farm at Leith Hall shows an Aberdeenshire laird's estate at an
intermediate stage of improvement. The house and gardens are surrounded by enclosed
parks, with two areas of plantations to the north. The house was extended to about this
time, and the new curved stable block can be seen above the house and gardens. At the
top of the plan a dyke is marked to be built to enclose a large acreage of improvable
pasture. The commonty is still in existence, on the bottom left, beside the river, with a
cluster of cottages beside it.

    The arable lands are coloured yellow and the pasture lands green. The infield
consists of the square fields near the house, between 4 and 8 acres in size, a total of 70
acres. The outfield is 57 acres and meadowlands account for 31 acres. A further 48 acres
have been planted with trees. The crofts beside the river are mostly 2 acres.

    The house and gardens, both of which have been altered since the eighteenth
century, are now in the care of the National Trust for Scotland.

North Mains

North Park

Washouse Park

Brox burn Paris's piece

Caningham's piece

Clos Park

Barn Park

Wester Sheep Park

Easter Sheep Park

Little Park

Garden

Miln Land

Carriers

Dechmont Lands

Land

Wester Park

Bigg

Park

Park Side

Stankards

Cox Park

Stonie Park

Hay Park

Knight

Canyland Tail

Bleugh

Burn

Wester Bleugh Burn Park

Easter Bleugh Burn Park

Ridge Land

Nettle hill Park

Bruclet Hall

Canyland

Moor

Mosside

Canyland Lands Park New hill Land

Lovats Park

Bruclet Hall Park

Mosse Side

Land

oun Moss

the New

Wood

Knight Ridge Moor

Easter

Wester

Drumshaggs

9-10.

PLAN
OF
LEITH HALL MAINS
WITH
MILL OF SIDE
CROFTS

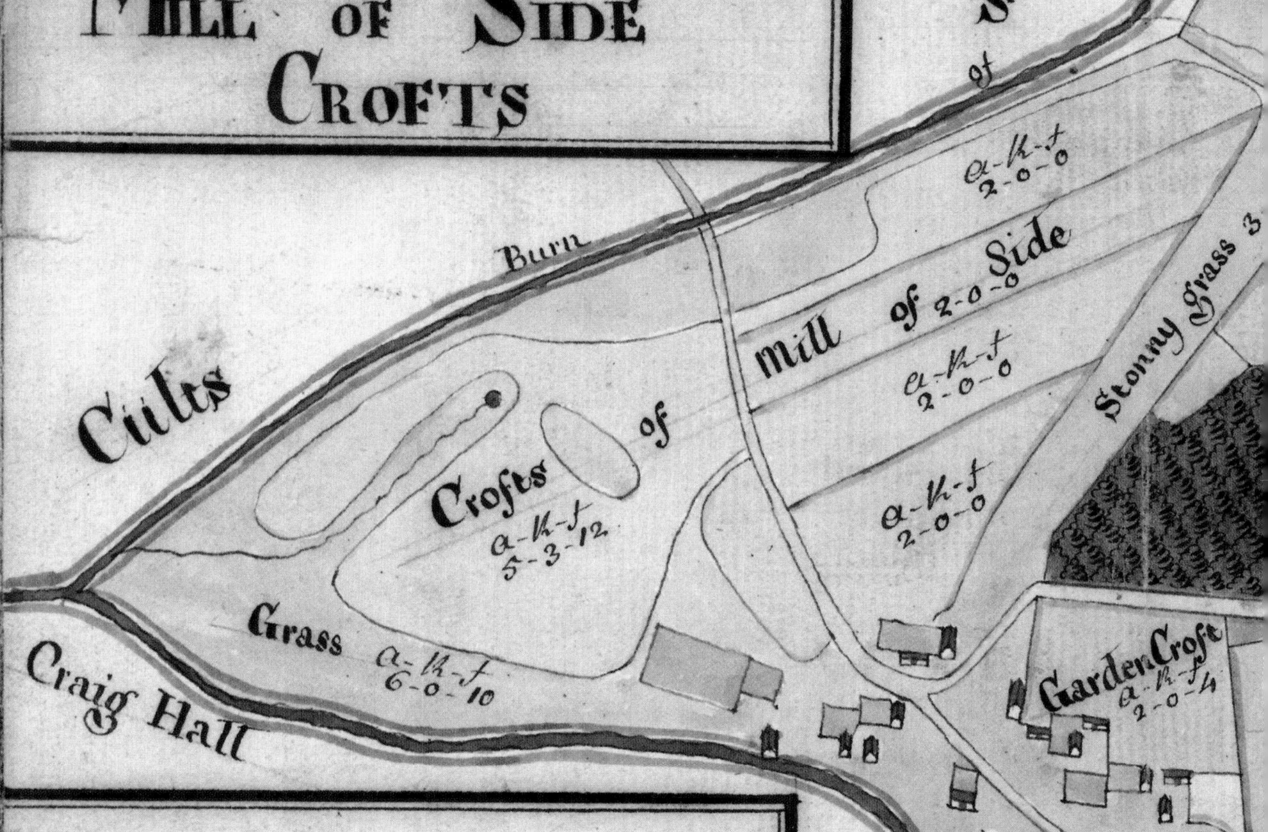

W · E
St
of

Burn

Ciils

Crofts of

Crofts
a-R-f
5-3-12

mill of 2-0-0 Side

a-R-f
2-0-0

a-R-f
2-0-0

a-R-f
2-0-0

Stonny Grass 3

Grass
a-R-f
6-0-10

Craig Hall

Garden Crofs
a-R-f
2-0-4

Commonty

2-3

This Sketch Exhibits the Situation and Extent
of The House Gardens Jnclosures, Planting And
Improvements on the Mains of Leith Hall
And the Crofts on Mill of Side
The Corn Lands are all of a Yellow Collour
Meadow & Grass a Green — Water Blue
The Jnclosures that are planted is markt with
Trees Representing planting
The Names and Extent of each Different
Jnclosure or Feild are markt on them
And all corrected in the Table of Contents

5198/1

Spring

A Dike along here

Improveable

Pasture
a-h-t
42-0-16

Foggie Leys
a-h-t
18-0-10

Matticks Leys

Floor Faulds
a-h-t
7-0-0

Hill of Side

Cummer Fauld
a-h-t
9-1-10

Brown hill
a-h-t
6-3-0

Over Bank
a-h-t
7-0-12

Broad Croft
a-h-t
6-2-0

Lang Croft
a-h-t
7-0-14

Side Park
a-h-t
8-3-0

East Park
a-h-t
6-2-0

Ley
h-t
-12

Little Park
2-0-7

Dovecoat Park
2-2-30

House Park
a-h-t
5-0-0

Meadow Park
a-h-t
5-2-0

Broom hill Park
a-h-t
4-0-0

Saughn Ward
h-t
2-1
5

Garden Meadow
a-h-t
5-1-12

East
a-h-t
4-2-0

Meadow
a-h-t
4-0-12

willow park
1-2-32

urn Meadow
h-t
5-2-0

Cuie

Keple crook
a-h-t
5-2-0

Burn

Moss of Earl

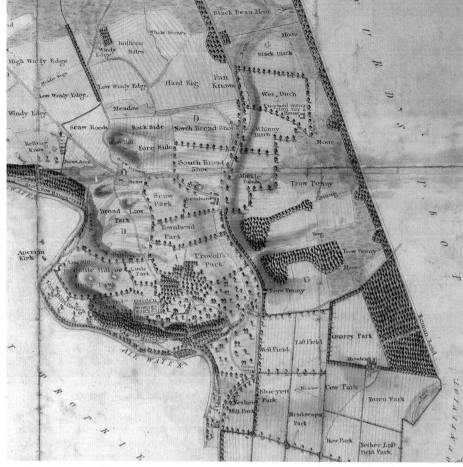

35. The estate of Ancrum, 1795, by John Ainslie (RHP 47938). See also p. xii.

By the late eighteenth century, much of this Roxburghshire estate had been improved. However, quite a quantity of moorland still exists, and above the centre right of the plan a site for a new house is proposed. The existing house has a formal garden, deer park and orchard, and much planting has been carried out on the estate. To the right of the house is an area of enclosed parks. A Roman road, Dere Street, runs down one side of the estate, while the Edinburgh–Jedburgh road runs through the centre of it.

Improvements started at Ancrum as early as the 1630s, when Sir Robert Kerr, later first earl of Ancram, gave detailed instructions to his son on altering the house and laying out the grounds. He planned draining, enclosing, planting and the establishment of 'a fayre orchard of the best fruits you can get in the Abbyes about you', indicating the continuing reputation of Borders monastery gardens for fruit trees. Like most improvers, Sir Robert had both aesthetic and practical considerations in mind: 'you must make all this of bewty and ornament and use, not only for your selff but other folk ... Wherever you fynd a spring cutt it a little channel to lett away the watter, that it turne not to a bogg and then both the bankes of it and all the ground about will be the better grass; for many a good peece of ground do wee loose in Scotland for not ordering our springs and not encloseing our grounds.'[13]

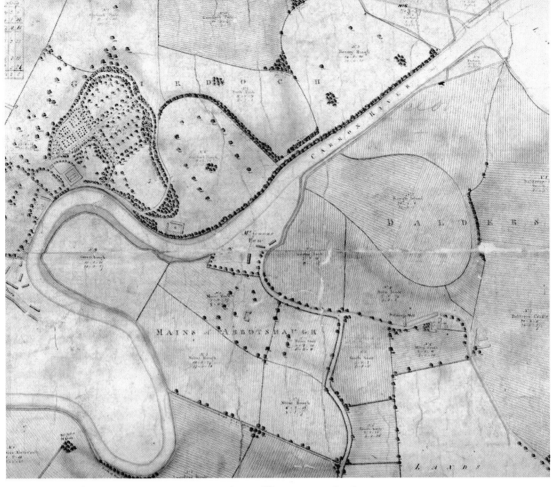

36. The estate of Abbotshaugh, 1819, by William Crawford
(RHP 1485: courtesy of Brodies WS).

By the early nineteenth century this estate near Falkirk had been fully improved. The house has gardens and plantations around it and all the fields on the estate are enclosed.

Abbotshaugh was at the centre of Scotland's developing heavy industry. In the 1760s it was bought by Charles Gascoigne, the manager of the Carron Company. He also ran a shipping company, and in the 1760s had two cuts made in the Carron to straighten out the loops in the river and allow larger ships to use it. The cuts also helped the estate by securing the river-banks against flooding. Gascoigne built Carron House, part of which was used as a warehouse for carronades, the guns produced by the company.

Gascoigne also laid out the parks and improved the farms. A rental of 1764 reported that 'the farmhouses are in exceeding good order, being all but one small one, rebuilt lately by the master with Stone & lime at a considerable charge'.[14] Gascoigne went bankrupt and the estate was sold in 1783 to John Ogilvie, who carried on with the improvements, removed the semi-industrial aspects around it and turned it into the private improved estate illustrated here.

37. Crop rotation at Murraythwaite, 1794 (RHP 6070).

The new fourfold rotation of crops introduced from Norfolk consisted of turnips, barley, clover and wheat. In Scotland oats often replaced wheat, and different areas had local variations, according to the type of soil and whether the farm was mainly arable or pastoral. East Lothian favoured a sixfold rotation, alternating grain with legumes: wheat, peas and beans, corn, sown grass (clover and rye), oats, fallow.[15] With improved practices and an increased demand from a population whose tastes now required wheaten rather than barley bread or oatcakes, there was an increase in the acreage of wheat cultivated. However, oats continued as the dominant crop for some time, particularly in the Highlands.

The crop rotation used at Murraythwaite in Dumfriesshire at the end of the eighteenth century included two crops of oats, followed by turnips or potatoes, then barley with clover, followed by two crops of hay, then pasture – see the field on the right called Woodfoot.

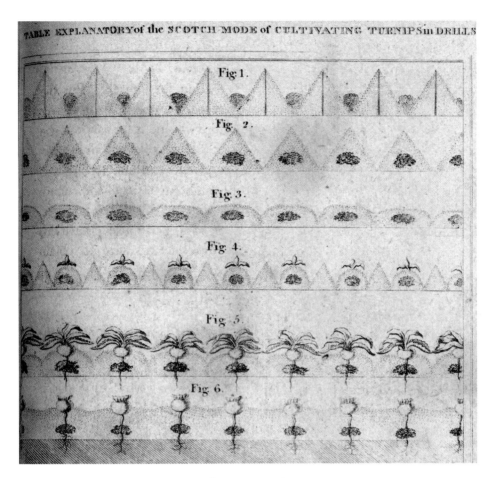

38. Turnip growing, 1814 (*General Report* I, 567).

Sir John Sinclair believed 'the benefits which are derived from turnip husbandry are manifold and of great magnitude'.[16] By planting grass and turnips, farmers could feed many more sheep and cattle over the winter. The availability of winter fodder permitted the building up of dairy herds, particularly in areas around cities and towns which provided a ready market for the produce. In other districts, such as Strathmore, cattle farming developed, and for the first time grain was not the main product.

Other benefits of turnip husbandry included the soil being cleaned: as turnips were planted in drills, weeding could be carried out between each row. The arrival of root crops also brought an improvement to the Scottish diet from the late eighteenth century. The over-wintering of larger numbers of sheep and cattle in good condition meant fresh meat was available during the lean months – a great advance on the salt variety that was previously the winter lot for much of the population.

**39. Limekiln and new plough, 1774, from plan of Bargany
by George Robertson** (RHP 1724: courtesy of Mr J. Dalrymple Hamilton).

Lime was invaluable in improving the quality of Scotland's acidic soils by raising its pH value. Its use as a fertiliser allowed plants to absorb nutrients better and led to greatly increased crop yields. Lime was made by burning limestone in kilns, and in the eighteenth century structures like this appeared on many estates. They were often built into sloping ground so that limestone and coal could be fed in at the top and the lime removed from the foot of the structure. The remains of limekilns can still be seen in many rural areas today.

The production of the fertiliser also took off on a commercial scale. In the 1760s the earl of Elgin created an enterprise on the shores of the Forth which employed 200 people. He established a new settlement at Charlestown, beside the village of Limekilns, to house the workforce.

Improvements in farm implements were an essential part of the agricultural revolution. The plough illustrated beside the limekiln in this vignette is a representation of the improved Scots plough, along with a five-barred harrow. The change from wooden to iron teeth on such harrows meant more effective tilling could take place. The illustration is taken from a plan of improvements to Bargany in Ayrshire.

9

Mining

This improved cultivation is in no small degree to be attributed to the advantages arising from the extensive distribution, easy conveyance and moderate price of coal; for wherever fuel is most abundant, there the population is greatest, and manufactures, commerce and agriculture mutually aid and stimulate each other.[1]

THIS writer was aware of the interrelations between the agricultural and industrial revolutions. The development of Scotland's agriculture and industry went hand in hand, and both brought changes to the landscape. During the eighteenth and nineteenth centuries, industry, both heavy and light, added its mark to the face of the country. Mining and quarrying left very obvious scars.

Coal and lead had been mined in Scotland since medieval times, though early mining technology permitted only basic methods of extraction. The first mines were simply opencast, with miners digging coal from a surface outcrop. When they exhausted the readily available coal, they would dig mines or roads (known as *ingaun e'es* – ingoing eyes) along the seam. The other early method of mining was used where coal was known to be at a shallow depth below the surface. A bell-shaped pit was dug, and miners extracted coal from an area around the foot of a shaft accessed by ladders. Work proceeded until the pit was deep enough to require draining or propping up, when the owner would close it and open another.

At the end of the sixteenth century the first machinery for draining mines appeared in the form of water-powered wheels with wooden buckets attached. These 'gins' were sometimes powered by windmills or by horses. Such improvements in drainage led to deeper mines, like the workings under the Forth at Culross. During the seventeenth century, large numbers of pits opened in the Lothians, in Fife, in Ayrshire and around Glasgow to supply coal needed for the production of salt, lime, glass and pottery.

The eighteenth century brought further technological advances which led to the expansion of all Scotland's industries. The arrival of the Newcomen atmospheric steam engine allowed better pumps for drainage and provided a mechanical method of bringing coal to the surface. The first in Scotland was installed in 1719; collieries in Saltcoats and Airth both claim the honour. James Watt's more advanced steam engine, which appeared in the 1760s, allowed further improvements in drainage, which in turn permitted deeper pits. Along with better ventilation and easier methods of moving the coal, a huge expansion in mining took place to meet an ever-increasing demand.

Many landowners were as much involved in industry on their estates as they were in agriculture. Fostering the growth of mines, salt pans or textile production was just as much part of improvement as enclosure or new crop rotations. All these activities made their estates more productive and more profitable. The increased use of lime required large quantities of coal for lime burning: the earl of Elgin's limekilns at Charlestown used about 12,000 tons of coal annually.[2] As more of the population moved off the land and into towns and cities, fewer people had access to peat. In the nineteenth century coal took over as the most common source of fuel in the Lowlands. Other industries such as salt production and ironworks also required increasing amounts of fuel. In the 1790s the Carron Iron Works at Falkirk consumed 800 tons of coal a week.[3]

The change from water to steam power increased demand further. During the eighteenth century coal production in Scotland increased dramatically, possibly as much as eight- to tenfold.[4] In 1814 one writer estimated that consumption had reached 2,500,000 tons.[5] The transport revolution also played its part. The first railways were waggon-ways attached to mines, and Scotland's developing road and canal systems made transporting coal to markets much easier.

As technology advanced, mining became a much more expensive operation and landowners who had worked their own collieries found it more profitable to lease them to mining companies. By the mid-nineteenth century, there were 368 collieries in Scotland, with a workforce of almost 33,000 people.[6] Mining on this scale inevitably left blots on the landscape: abandoned mine shafts, waste heaps and ruined engine houses are often all that remain of one of Scotland's major industries.

The extraction of Scotland's other natural resources has also left its legacy in the countryside. The remains of lead-mining operations can be seen in Argyll and the south-west of Scotland. Aberdeenshire is littered with granite quarries, while the West Lothian landscape shows its industrial past in the form of shale bings, the slag heaps from the paraffin oil industry which flourished in the area from the 1850s. Argyll was the centre of the Scottish slate industry, the main quarries being at Easdale and Ballachulish. The operation at Ballachulish lasted from 1693 to the 1950s and, though the resulting scars in the immediate vicinity of the village are healing, the results of large-scale extraction can still be seen in the hinterland. Several parts of the Highlands housed iron-smelting enterprises and the charcoal-burning operations which accompanied them. Though it is difficult to imagine today, Loch Maree in Wester Ross was the location of a thriving iron industry during the seventeenth century. The ironworks at Bonawe in Argyll, now in the care of Historic Scotland, give an indication of how these pockets of industry affected Highland areas.

40a (*Above*) **& b.** (*Overleaf*) **The village and mines of Strontian, 1733, by Alexander Bruce** (GD 241/164/1: courtesy of Garden Haig solicitors).

In the 1720s Sir Alexander Murray of Stanhope, an enthusiastic mineral prospector, discovered lead near Strontian in Argyll. He leased the mineral rights in 1724 to a partnership of adventurers which included General Wade and Sir Archibald Grant of Monymusk. They in turn leased the operation to the York Buildings Company, which had bought several Jacobite estates forfeited after the 1715 rising and attempted various enterprises in the Highlands, with little commercial success.

The company had to put in the infrastructure necessary to support a mining operation in the west Highlands and bring in a skilled workforce from England and the Lowlands. It built roads to transport the ore and put up the buildings in Strontian illustrated here: furnaces, a smelting mill, stores, a quay, and houses for the manager and workers. It also paved the streets of the village, 'whereby it is become wholesome and pleasant'.

Despite the company's substantial investment, working conditions at Strontian were never easy. The miners were not popular with the local people, who refused to sell them food. As many of the miners' supplies had to be imported, they suffered from a lack of fresh produce, and scurvy was not uncommon. Because of the company's financial difficulties, the miners did not always receive their wages. Despite the hardships and dangers of a lead-miner's life, one man who worked at both Strontian and Leadhills allegedly lived to the age of 132 – the normal lifespan for a lead-miner was thirty-five to forty.[7]

The vein of lead at Strontian is shown on the plan to the north of the village:

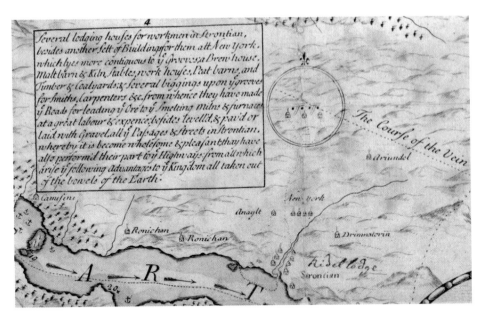

it was over a mile long and two and a half feet thick. Although prices rose because of increasing demand for lead as a building material and in the production of glass and pottery, the mines were not profitable and the company pulled out in 1742. Lead-mining at Strontian continued intermittently until 1904. In 1790 the element strontium, named after the village, was discovered at the mines. The mines were reworked for a time in the 1980s to supply barite for the North Sea oil drilling industry. The results of two centuries of operations in the form of ruined buildings and spoil heaps can be seen still in the countryside near the village.

41. Spoil heaps near Strontian, 2004 (R.M. Gibson).

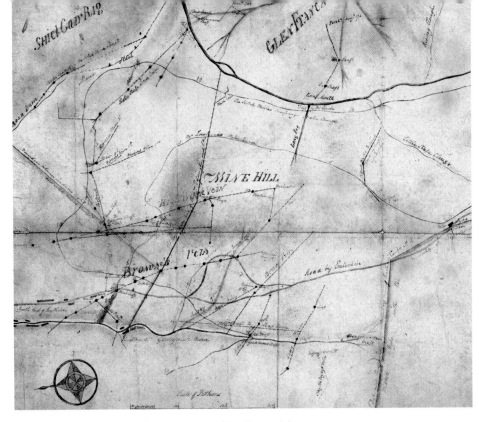

42. Leadhills mining district, 1764 (RHP 405/1).

Lead had been mined in upland Lanarkshire at least since the thirteenth century and perhaps as early as Roman times. In 1638 the mines came into the possession of the Hope family, who made their fortune from the profits. They became earls of Hopetoun and at the end of the seventeenth century commissioned Sir William Bruce to build the magnificent mansion-house of Hopetoun.

This plan was drawn at a time of expansion at Leadhills. As technological improvements provided engines for drainage, new veins were discovered. The veins of lead are marked: in places they were up to 21 feet wide. At this time most of the mines were leased to the Scotch Mining Company. It and the earl of Hopetoun ran them on paternalistic lines. In the 1790s about 200 miners worked these mines. They were encouraged to build their own houses and cultivate smallholdings. The village of Leadhills, on the left of the plan, had the first subscription library in the country.

The remote and inhospitable upland nature of the area is clear from the plan. The nearby lead-mining village of Wanlockhead, at an altitude of 1,500 feet, is the highest village in Scotland. One visitor described the area as 'dreary beyond description, uncommonly subject to Stormy Weather in all Seasons'.[8] The effects of this particular industrial enterprise are still obvious today. The restored former miners' cottages contrast markedly with the industrial scars on the area. Lead-mining ceased here in the 1950s, but a visit to the Museum of Lead Mining at Wanlockhead will give a good idea of living and working conditions for lead-miners through the centuries.

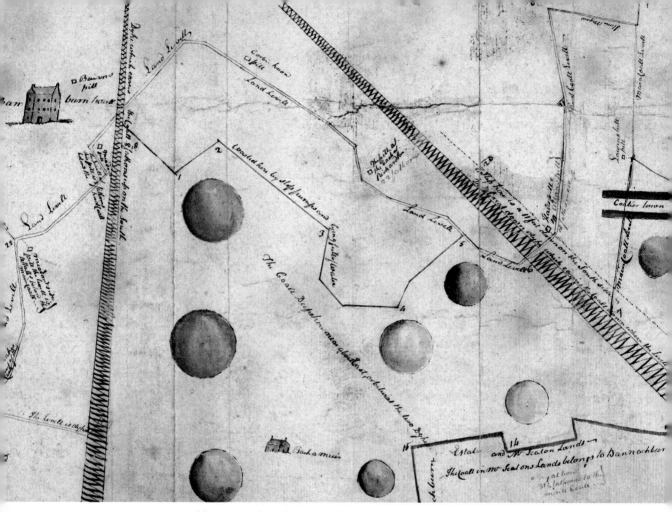

43. Bannockburn coalworks, 1783, by William Thomson
(RHP 1489: courtesy of Brodies WS).

This mining plan shows the outcrop of coal seams and the location of pits in part of the Stirlingshire coalfield. Bannockburn was one of several collieries opened up in the area after the Restoration to serve local needs. Along with the nearby mines of Plean and Auchenbowie, these collieries supplied about 600 tons of coal a week to the surrounding country.

The circles on the plan represent coal seams as yet unworked. Bannockburn House, where Bonnie Prince Charlie stayed during the 1745 Jacobite rising, appears in the upper left of the plan. The 'collier town' is depicted by two black oblongs on the right of the plan. The zigzag lines indicate dykes or vertical fissures of hard rock cutting across the strata of coal.

Bannockburn was a profitable pit producing high-quality coal. In 1825 Robert Bald, the mining engineer, described the operation as 'uniformly prosperous, the coals of the best quality, and commanding a very high price in the market'.[9] The mine continued in operation until 1964.

44a & b. Colliers from a plan of Gilmerton coal, 1786, by John Ainslie
(RHP 93582: courtesy of the duke of Buccleuch and Queensberry KT).

These details show colliers' working conditions in the 1780s. At this time serfdom in Scottish mines was coming to an end. In 1606, with demand for coal expanding rapidly, the Scottish parliament had passed an act binding colliers to the owners of the pit in which they worked, in an effort to retain enough labour for a dangerous and unpopular job. It was not until the late eighteenth century that acts of 1775 and 1799 put an end to the system of servitude.

Colliers' families also worked in the pits. Men cut the coal and their wives and children generally took it to the surface. Children as young as six could work in the pits. When machinery to wind coal to the surface came into use, women and children were still used to move coal to the bottom of the shaft. The illustrations show a hewer cutting coal with a pick, and two men sending it up to the surface. A young boy with a candle provides illumination for the work. This vignette also illustrates the 'stoop and room' method of mining: the stoops are columns of rock left in place to prop up the roof and the rooms are the excavated areas where the miners cut the coal.

In the lower vignette, women bearers carry coal in creels on their backs and light their way with candles. These loads could weigh up to four and a half hundred-weight[10] and often needed two men to lift them onto the bearer's back. Female bearers carried these creels up ladders through the different levels of the mine. It was not until a royal commission reported on conditions in mines in 1842 that the employment underground of women, and children under ten, was forbidden.

Rural Industries

The works at Deanston seem to possess every facility and recommendation: they have changed the aspect of the country – beautiful and romantic as it is – by introducing into it habits of industry, order and the highest mechanical genius and dexterity; they cause a circulation of money to the extent of about £20,000 per annum; they furnish employment for people of all ages; they have called forth the spirit and activity of the agriculturalists to meet the ever-recurring demands of the place.[1]

A description of the cotton mill at Deanston in Perthshire in 1844 illustrates the effect lighter industries such as textile production had on the economy of rural areas. Scotland had produced woollen cloth and linen since medieval times, and in the eighteenth century started to manufacture cotton goods as well. The textile industry at this stage was still carried out on a domestic scale. The raw materials of wool and flax were produced locally; every family had a spinning wheel and every fermtoun had its weaver. Most wool and linen cloth was produced at home by people who also worked the land. As one minister remarked, 'Every family is a small factory for both linen and woollen cloth.'[2]

Although textiles were one of Scotland's staple exports, until the mid-eighteenth century the quality of cloth produced was poor. From the 1720s the government made great efforts to develop the industry. In 1727 it set up the Board of Trustees for Fisheries, Manufactures and Improvements in Scotland to improve the production processes. In 1746 the British Linen Company was founded to produce and market linen. Under the attentions of these two bodies, the textile industry could hardly fail to expand. The Board of Trustees brought experts from Europe to train Scottish workers in better practices. It also gave subsidies for growing flax, set up bleachfields and spinning schools, and established a quality-control system for cloth. In the thirty years after the founding of the board, linen production trebled. At this stage the industry was still a dispersed rural one, operating in a series of small establishments and most homes throughout the country.

As the eighteenth century progressed, textile manufacturing developed from a cottage industry into a commercial, factory-based enterprise. The industrial revolution brought mechanisation to all Scotland's rural industries. Water power had long been used in milling grain and in fulling woollen cloth, and every estate had its small meal mill and waulk mill. From the late 1720s water power came to be applied to other processes in textile manufacture and in other industries also. This resulted in the spread of mills of all types along river valleys: these included paper mills, sawmills and iron mills, as well as mills processing yarn.

The first significant development came in 1728 with the application of water power to the scutching of flax or lint, the process which separated the fibres of the flax before it was heckled (combed) in preparation for being spun. Small lint mills driven by waterwheels soon made their appearance in all parts of Scotland. Water power was subsequently used in the intermediate processes in yarn production, such as heckling. However, it was the mechanisation of spinning which changed the scale of the textile industry and took it out of the home and into the factory. The first water-powered mill for spinning cotton opened in Penicuik in 1778, and the first mill for spinning linen yarn was set up in Brigton in Angus in 1787. The final part of the production process, weaving, continued to be done by hand until the 1830s.

Just as linen had taken over from wool as Scotland's main textile in the late seventeenth century, so in the later eighteenth century cotton overtook linen in popularity. The cotton industry's rapid development, with machines such as the spinning jenny, water-frame and mule, resulted in the building of large mill-complexes in many parts of the country. These brought huge changes to the areas where they were established. Not only were the cotton spinning mills on a scale hitherto unseen in Scotland, but they brought with them housing for mill workers. Since these mills needed a good water supply, they were sited in rural areas beside fast-flowing rivers. Mill sites were inevitably some distance from population centres, so accommodation had to be provided for the factory workforce, either in planned villages, such as New Lanark on the Clyde or Stanley on the Tay, or in the expansion of existing villages, as in Penicuik, Midlothian. By 1812 there were 120 spinning mills in Scotland and over 150,000 people working in the cotton industry alone.[3]

The large premises and expensive machinery that cotton production involved needed substantial infusions of capital. Developments of this scale were beyond the resources of most estate owners. Some simply leased out land for mills, while others developed partnerships with mercantile interests. As the mechanised parts of the production process now required full-time workers, mills provided employment for former agricultural workers put off the land by the new, less labour-intensive methods of farming, and for migrants from the Highlands. Mill villages also provided ready markets for local farmers.

The application of steam power to textile production from the 1790s led to the gradual transfer of the industry from the countryside to the town. While water power required mills to be beside rivers, steam engines' need for coal led to the building of factories near coalfields. From the 1820s textile production became centralised in urban areas with easy access to fuel supplies, markets and raw materials coming in by sea. At the start of the nineteenth century there were eleven cotton mills in and around Glasgow: by 1839 there were ninety-eight.[4] By the time of the 1851 census, some 257,000 people, 20 per cent of Scotland's workforce, were employed in the textile industry.[5]

Scotland's brewing and distilling industries also operated on a domestic scale for much of the eighteenth century before taking off as commercial concerns. Distilling for private use was originally permitted on a limited scale, so, like textile manufacture, whisky production was carried out on most estates. However, in 1779 the government drastically reduced the quantity allowed and in 1781 banned private distilling altogether. Although an illicit trade in whisky continued to flourish, licensed distillers' business expanded rapidly. So too did the number of distilleries. They formed another strand in the web linking Scotland's agricultural and industrial development. Distilleries provided a convenient market for barley from surrounding farms, and their by-products were recycled as foodstuffs for cattle.

In 1786, during a period of intense debate on the industry, Lowland landowners expressed support for licensed stills of a considerably smaller size than the 400 gallons then permitted, as this would allow farms to start distilling. Thus 'agriculture and distillery will be united to their mutual advantage whereby the wastelands will be cultivated'.[6] Their lobbying was successful, and from July that year licensed stills as small as fifty gallons were allowed.[7] By the end of the eighteenth century many rural areas of the Lowlands housed distilleries, and several had large-scale operations. Further north, illicit stills remained a popular method of production: one legitimate distiller reckoned that in Glenlivet alone there were 200 illicit stills.[8] However, by the second half of the nineteenth century the traditional architecture of the commercial distillery was a common sight in the Highland landscape.

45. (*Opposite*) **Saltoun bleachfield, East Lothian 1762, by Lewis Gordon** (RHP 6695: courtesy of Mr W.G. Drummond Moray).

As part of the drive to encourage Scotland's linen industry, commercial bleachfields were established to improve the quality of bleaching. Bleachfields were expensive to set up as they needed a considerable amount of equipment, a good water supply and a large area of flat land. This level of capital investment was beyond the reach of many estate owners, but the Board of Trustees could provide grants. The British Linen Company started the bleachfield at Saltoun in 1746 to finish linen to a high quality and to train apprentice bleachers. It represented a large investment of capital, costing the company over £2,000 to establish.

The plan shows the bleaching field, where pieces of cloth from thirty to forty

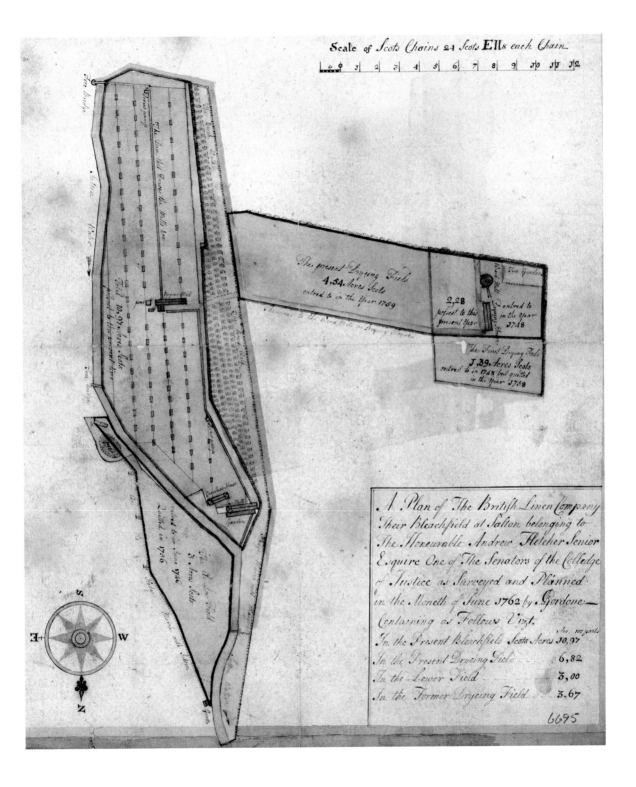

Scale of Scots Chains 24 Scots Ells each Chain

The present Dryeing Field
4,54 Acres Scots
entred to in the Year 1759

2,28 perfeit to this present Year

entred to in the Year 1748

The First Dryeing Field
1,39 Acres Scots
entred to in 1748 but quitted in the Year 1759

A Plan of The British Linen Company
Their Bleachfield at Salton belonging to
The Honourable Andrew Fletcher Senior
Esquire One of The Senators of the Colledge
of Justice as Surveyed and Planned
in the Moneth of June 1762 by G. Gordone
Containing as Follows Vizt.

Acr. 100 yards

In the Present Bleachfield Scots Acres 10,97
In the Present Dryeing Field ___ 6,82
In the Lower Field ___ 3,00
In the Former Dryeing Field ___ 3,67

6695

yards long were pegged out to whiten from their original greyish-green colour. There is a pond and a dam to draw water from the Saltoun Water. The squares on the bleaching field are the canals from which water was taken to dampen the cloth as it bleached. The drying field, drying house and windmill which pumped the water are on the right of the plan. The whole bleaching process took from five to eight weeks. During the season from April to October, up to sixty workers would be taken on, some of them from the Highlands. In 1772, as a result of falling profits, the company sold the

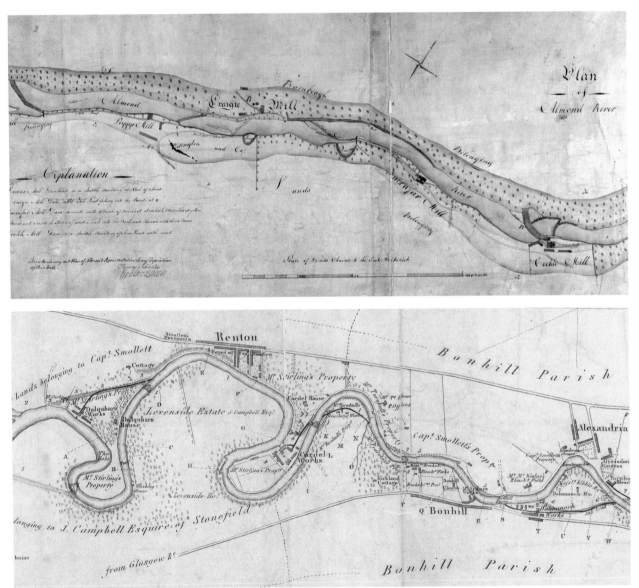

bleachfield to Andrew Fletcher of Saltoun, who turned it into a pleasure ground.

By the 1770s there were about ninety bleachfields in Scotland. One or two have survived in the form of village greens, e.g. in Gifford in East Lothian and Eaglesham in Renfrewshire.

46. (*Opposite top*) **The river Almond, 1786, by Thomas Johnston** (RHP 2).

The history of these mills at Cramond, near Edinburgh, illustrates the uses of water power. These buildings were used for a variety of purposes during their lifetime, from humble grain mills to iron production as part of the mighty Carron Company enterprise. Downie's Mill, Peggy's Mill and Craigie Mill were originally grain mills. Fairafar Mill was both a grain mill and a waulk mill. Cockle Mill, on the right, also started life as a grain mill: there had been a mill on this site since the twelfth century.

In the 1750s the Carron Company bought the mills, and Cockle Mill became an iron splitting mill. In the 1770s the mills became the property of the Cadell family when they left the Carron Company, but their role in the iron industry continued. The mills produced rod iron for nails, spades, files and hoops for barrels. By the 1870s all iron production in the area had ceased. Peggy's Mill subsequently became a paper mill, then a gelatine works and in the twentieth century a furniture-making business.

47. (*Opposite bottom*) **The river Leven, 1824, by Hugh Baird** (RHP 967/4).

This plan shows how an area became associated with one particular industry, in this case the textile industry. The soft waters from Loch Lomond were particularly suited to bleaching linen and in 1728 a bleachfield was established at Dalquhurn, which continued in production for 100 years. Others followed, and textile production ensured the prosperity of the Vale of Leven.

By the time this map was drawn there were eight mills on the Leven, six printfields and two bleachfields, including Mr McKinlay's bleachfield at Alexandria in the middle of the plan. Dalquhurn works, on the left, was owned by the firm of William Stirling & Sons, who were also the main shareholders in the Monkland Canal.

The textile industry was the major employer in this area and the scale of production was substantial. When the new cylinder method of printing cloth was established, up to 360 handkerchiefs could be printed in an hour. In the 1790s three printfields in Bonhill parish alone employed almost 1,000 people. Pressure on housing was so great that in 1782 Mrs Smollett of Bonhill founded the village of Renton to accommodate the labour force. In the nineteenth century the area turned to turkey-red dyeing, and by 1879 there were 6,000 people working in the industry in the Vale of Leven.[9]

48. Mill from a plan of Renfrewshire, 1796, by John Ainslie
(RHP 9439: courtesy of the duke of Buccleuch and Queensberry KT).

The impact of technology on the manufacture of cotton was enormous. The move to a factory-based industry started in 1764 when James Hargreaves invented the spinning jenny, which could spin eight threads at once. Richard Arkwright's water-frame and Samuel Compton's mule (a combination of the spinning jenny and the water-frame) followed soon after, and by the 1790s one mule could spin as much yarn as 150 hand spinners.

These machines required substantial buildings to house them, and in the last two decades of the eighteenth century large mills like these began to appear in Scotland. The size of these mills, with their workers' housing alongside, was impressive. One commentator described them as 'stately edifices of four, five or six stories, and their spacious floors are laden with machinery of the most ingenious and beautiful construction'.[10]

The waterwheels alone dwarfed anything seen before: the wheels at the Catrine mills in Ayrshire were fifty feet in diameter, whereas meal mills usually had twelve- to fourteen-foot wheels. The best-known mill village is New Lanark, founded in 1785, which housed 2,000 people. It had four mills which were seven storeys high, 160 feet long and 40 feet wide.[11] The complex has been restored and a visit to New Lanark gives a vivid impression of working conditions in buildings such as these.

49. New Lanark village, 2004 (New Lanark Conservation Trust).

50. (*Overleaf*) **Craigend distillery, 1798, by William Drummond** (RHP 80866).

This colourful plan of a Stirlingshire distillery illustrates whisky production in the late eighteenth century, when small distilleries were numerous, before the major concerns attained near monopoly of the industry. In the 1790s there were six in this parish alone, employing up to 100 people.[12] Many distilleries were, like this one, attached to farms. They grew their own barley and kept herds of cattle. The cattle were fed with the draff from the distilling process, and their manure fertilised the crops.

The whole property of Craigend distillery consisted of thirty acres of land, including twenty fields of crops. On the left of the plan is the barn for malting the barley and on the right, next to the dunghill, is the distilling house with the engine shed beside it. Opposite are the house, with the garden behind, and the byre for the cattle. The vignette shows a field being ploughed, a cart bearing barrels and the still itself. By this time the still at Craigend was being discharged 44 times in 24 hours, compared to a large distillery like Canonmills in Edinburgh, whose rate was 96 times in 24 hours. [13]

Craigend was owned by James and William Miller, who were also spirit dealers in Glasgow. They sold their whisky to vintners, spirit dealers and individuals, mostly in the Stirling area, but also in Edinburgh, Glasgow and Biggar. They went bankrupt in 1825.

MR JAFFRAY'S
GROUND

Road

from

THIS FIGUR

shaded bloc

is the property of

MR JAFFRAY

Barn

Malt

Kiln

Miln

Caig-

ler

by

THE

BARR

C

Craigend

washing
green

PLANN
OF
CRAIGEND
Measured Aprile
1790

MR

jaffray

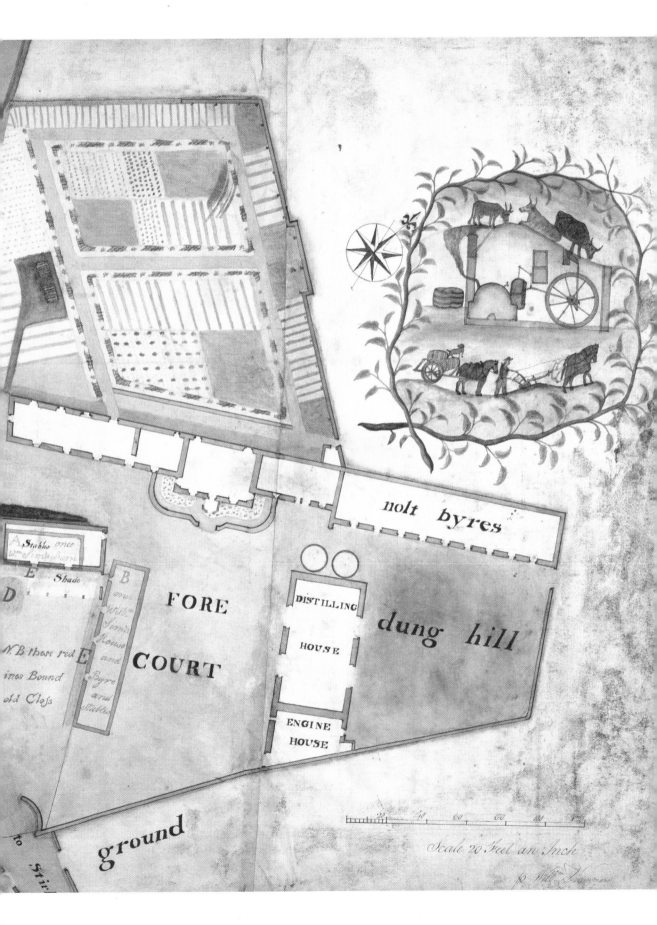

nolt byres

DISTILLING
HOUSE

dung hill

FORE

COURT

ENGINE
HOUSE

A Stable once
w.m Sim's Barn

E   Shade

D

N.B these red
ines Bound
old Closs

B
one
w.th
Sim's
House
and
byre
and
stable

ground

to
Stirl

Scale 20 Feet an Inch

The Highland Landscape

[T]he rage for sheep farms which has for some years obtained among Highland Proprietors: the high advancement of Rent they have obtained and the many great Tracts of country which have been dispeopled in consequence. On this very account, the Society have been obliged to remove many of their Schools from Stations once full of Inhabitants, but now occupied only by a Shepherd.[1]

IN 1791 the Scottish Society for the Propagation of Christian Knowledge expressed its concern about the depopulation of the Highlands caused by the introduction of sheep farms. This was the form which the commercialisation of many Highland estates took, with devastating consequences for the indigenous people. Changes to the Highland landscape came later than in the Lowlands and, because of the different nature of the land, took a different form. Some aspects of estate modernisation were common, e.g. the disappearance of the jointly held farm, but in the Highlands the lack of alternative economic prospects led to a painful period of change. In the north and west of Scotland, landowners' efforts to improve their estates caused huge upheavals in Highland society.

The traditional role of clan chiefs began to alter in the late seventeenth century. As they became more integrated into southern society, they became caught up in the consumerism affecting other Scottish elites. They came to view their estates less as a power base and source of fighting men, and more as a means of income. In consequence their need for cash increased, as did their absences from their estates. In common with the Lowlands, the first sign of change was the conversion of rents paid in kind to money rents. The failure of the '45 Jacobite rising brought the chiefs' military power over their clansmen to an abrupt end and hastened this move away from traditional values.

The first group to feel the effects of this change of attitude were the Highland middle class, the tacksmen. They acted as middlemen by getting tacks of large areas of land from the chiefs and subletting it at a profit to smaller tenants. Before the '45 the tacksmen had also been responsible for raising the clan's fighting force. With this military requirement gone, estate owners, looking for ways of increasing their income, decided it was more profitable to rent direct to tenants, and so started to phase out the tacksmen. This was mostly a feature of the second half of the eighteenth century, although on the duke of Argyll's estate the process started as early as 1710. Many tacksmen emigrated to America and Canada, taking other tenants with them.

Government initiatives to 'civilise' the Highlands after the '45 also played their part in bringing change to the area. Jacobite estates were forfeited after the rising. Some were annexed to the Crown and run until 1784 by the Forfeited Estates Commissioners. This forty-year absence on the part of indigenous owners hastened the process of change in the Highlands. The commissioners tried to develop the area's economy by modernising the estates in their care, encouraging industries such as textiles and fishing, and improving communications. The work of the British Fisheries Society and the Highland Roads and Bridges Commission was also directed towards improving the region's economic prospects.

As in the Lowlands, the traditional jointly held farming system was broken up by the process of improvement. The Highland *baile*, or clachan, went the way of the fermtoun. Auchindrain Museum in Argyll preserves the last example of the *bailtean* to survive. In more fertile areas of Perthshire and Argyll, single-tenant farms were created from these holdings. However, in the west Highlands and islands the landscape of moorland and hill ground presented particular difficulties for improving landowners. Here the proportion of arable land to pasture was pitifully small. Only about 10 per cent of land in this part of Scotland was capable of growing crops. The other 90 per cent was either too high, too acidic or too rocky to be cultivated. Short growing seasons and high rainfall added to the difficulties of the Highland farmer. As much of the area was more suited to livestock than cultivation, estate owners came to see large-scale sheep farming as the best method of increasing rent rolls. All Highland landowners and tenants kept sheep, but on a domestic scale. It was the arrival of non-native sheep in huge numbers which caused major changes in the area.

51. (*Previous page*) **Auchindrain Museum, 2004** (R.M. Gibson).

Commercial sheep farming came to Argyll in the 1750s and Perthshire in the 1760s, and in the following decade reached Easter Ross. Landowners found it profitable to let out large areas of land to sheep farmers. They cleared their tenants from inland valleys and settled them on small plots of ground, often near the coast. It was this process which broke up the *bailtean* and created the crofting landscape, the Highland equivalent of the new farms of the Lowland improvers. The newly created crofts were single-tenant holdings with common grazings. These holdings could be up to twelve acres, but many crofters had only three or four acres. Crofts were made deliberately small so that tenants were obliged to find other work. Sir John Sinclair estimated that a crofter would need an additional 200 days' work a year to survive.[2]

When the population of the Highlands expanded by over 50 per cent between 1750 and 1830,[3] subdivision of these crofts into even smaller units was necessary. In the more crowded areas of the Western Isles, by the mid-nineteenth century some families were trying to survive on holdings of as little as an acre or two. It was the introduction of the potato in the 1740s which allowed crofters to live on such small plots. Potatoes could be grown on very poor ground. They tolerated wet conditions better than grain crops and provided a much higher yield than oats or barley. By the late eighteenth century, potatoes had replaced grain as the main source of food in some parts of the country. This dependence on one crop later had tragic consequences, but in the late eighteenth and first half of the nineteenth century, the potato provided crofters with a basic level of food supply. Provided they had other work, they could use their income to buy further provisions.

Many got seasonal work in herring fishing or migrated south annually to work on Lowland farms. Other employment opportunities were provided in constructing roads, canals and railways. Highland girls regularly went into domestic service in Lowland homes and some took work in the textile industries. Until the 1820s the kelp industry was the other mainstay of the Highland economy. Kelp, or potash, was used in industries such as soap and glassmaking, and in bleaching linen. For many years it provided a good income for cash-strapped Highland landowners. Kelp was obtained by burning seaweed. As twenty tons of seaweed had to be gathered to produce one ton of kelp, the industry required a substantial labour force. At first, therefore, landowners were happy to have large numbers of crofting tenants to support kelp production. As many as 30,000 people may have been employed in the Highland kelp industry.[4]

However, after the Napoleonic Wars, the price of kelp halved when a cheaper alternative, barilla, became available from Spain. In addition, the two other staple industries of the Highlands suffered in the post-war slump of the 1820s. The fishing industry went into the doldrums, and cattle prices fell by 50 per cent between 1815 and 1830. While landowners had encouraged large crofting populations as long as kelp was profitable, when the bottom dropped out of the market a wholesale change took place in their attitude towards the small tenant – they regarded them as redundant.

When crofters could no longer sell their cattle or find employment in fishing or kelping, they were unable to pay their rents, and arrears climbed steeply. Sheep, however, remained profitable, and most Highland landowners and their factors believed they provided the only means of making their estates viable. Sheep farms, however, required large areas of land free of people, and so the crofting population had to go. Removing tenants was easier in the Highlands than in the Lowlands as few crofters had leases. Instead they held land on an annual basis, while the cottar class held no land officially. It was therefore a relatively straightforward process for factors to remove small tenants by giving them notice to remove at the next term day.

Clearances had started in the central Highlands in the 1770s. The most infamous took place in Sutherland between 1811 and 1821, when between 6,000 and 10,000 tenants were cleared to coastal areas. The first phase of clearance, from the 1760s to the 1820s, generally aimed to resettle tenants on coastal or marginal land. However, from the 1820s the process of clearing people to make way for sheep increased as the failure of several previously profitable traditional markets brought many Highland estates to bankruptcy. This phase of clearance was concentrated in the Western Isles, though some removals also took place in the central and eastern Highlands. Clearances from the 1820s to the 1860s were intended to remove crofting tenants altogether, preferably by emigration.

Any remaining links with traditional Highland society were severed when huge areas were sold to incomers. Most owners of Highland estates preferred to spend their time in the south, but the effort of trying to maintain their position in British society proved too much for their estates to support. The collapse of the kelp industry affected estates in the Western Isles particularly badly. Profits from their kelp shores had been the only thing standing between several estate owners and bankruptcy, and when this source of income failed they were obliged to sell. By the mid-nineteenth century, all the estates in the Outer Hebrides and many on the west coast and in Inverness-shire had been sold by their debt-ridden owners. Joseph Mitchell, who had travelled the Highlands for decades in the nineteenth century as engineer to the Highland Roads and Bridges Commission and the Scottish Fishery Board, reckoned that in his time almost two-thirds of the estates in the Highlands had changed hands.[5] The new owners were generally industrialists, merchants, bankers or lawyers from England or the Lowlands.

When the potato famine started in Scotland in 1846 the impossibility of supporting large numbers of people on pitifully small holdings of land became tragically clear. The famine was the final straw for an area whose fragile economy had been devastated since the end of the Napoleonic Wars. The potato blight of the 1840s and 1850s was accompanied by another fall in cattle prices and an industrial recession in the

Lowlands, which again reduced the availability of seasonal employment. The loss of the staple crop, which accounted for four-fifths of their food supply, along with a fall in their alternative income, meant disaster for the crofters. They had to put what little cash they had towards buying meal and had no reserves to pay rent. Arrears rocketed again and estate owners, old and new, were faced with supporting a large and starving tenantry, when their own income was severely reduced. Sir James Riddell's Ardnamurchan estate saw rent arrears climb from £269 at the start of the famine to £3,219 in 1852.[6]

Despite the government's efforts, no viable industries such as textiles had established themselves on any scale in the Highlands, and so there was no other permanent employment for the tenants. A fund for the relief of Highland destitution provided meal to starving crofters in return for work on projects such as the 'destitution roads', but such measures did not provide a long-term solution. Landowners continued to regard large-scale sheep farming as the remedy for the Highlands' economic ills, and encouraged their tenants to leave by offering assistance to emigrate to Canada and Australia. The Highland and Islands Emigration Society was set up in 1852 to deal with the crisis caused by the potato famine. For as little as £1 per head, estate owners could secure passage to Australia for their destitute tenants. Some crofters also found their way to Lowland towns and cities. Almost 17,000 people were helped to emigrate from crofting areas during the famine years.[7]

The post-clearance landscape of empty valleys scattered with ruined cottages, and coastal areas cluttered with crofts, was the result of a century of such traumatic changes in the social and economic structure of the Highlands. Writing in 1879, Joseph Mitchell eloquently described the results of 'improvement' in the area. Speaking of a strath he had visited on Skye in 1825, he commented:

> A year or two before, it had been cleared of the tenantry, to the number of 1500 souls. They had emigrated, and the whole valley was converted into two great sheep farms. The ruined cottages and green spots of the once cultivated crofts were to be seen scattered on the hill sides, indicating the sites of the abodes of the expatriated families. But all was then a solitude, and nothing was heard by the passing traveller but the bleating of sheep.[8]

52. (*Opposite*) **Little Gruinard, 1756, by Peter May** (RHP 3401).

This area of Wester Ross illustrates the barren nature of much of the Highland landscape. This area was part of the Cromartie estates, which had been forfeited after the '45 and were being run by the Forfeited Estates Commissioners. This plan forms part of their original survey of the estates.

Like many Highland farms, Little Gruinard had very little arable land and a

Lochuacareild

BARREN   HILLY   GROUND

ROCKS

Lands

A Hill

Head

called

FULL   OF   ROCKS

Meaulnagory

A small
Shielling
called
Achabatroan

ROCKS

AND   COVERED   WITH   HEATH

of

March Line

Moss

Little Gruyard

Mungostown

A Smooth bottom of Beech   here

great
Steep
Rocks
called
Craigimore

Mackenzie of Dundonnate

large quantity of hill pasture. Its few arable strips cling to the coast. Small cultivated areas, known as *feannagan* or lazy-beds, were created in such inhospitable landscapes. Working land like this was labour-intensive, requiring much manuring with seaweed, shell sand, peat and old roofing material impregnated with peat smoke. Behind these small strips is an expanse of 'barren hilly ground full of rocks and covered with heath'. In the middle of this area is a shieling, an upland area where the cattle were pastured in summer. The surveyor noted the poor nature of the ground and the dependence on fishing: 'This farm of Little Gruinard is but a very middling one, and would make a poor subsistance being little else but hill and Rocks with very bad pasture either at the farm, or at the shieling, were it not that the fishing is annexed to it, upon which the bulk of the living depends.'

The Highland climate was also a problem. While surveying the estate, May was forced to ask the commissioners to provide him with a tent, since he had difficulty in finding accommodation in such a remote area. He had been obliged to sleep in the open fields, 'which is dangerous in a Climate where so much rain falls'.[9]

53. (*Opposite*) **Easter Carwhin, 1769, by John Farquarson** (RHP 973/1, p. 8).

The landscape of the Perthshire Highlands looks a little more hospitable. Carwhin was one of several townships on the earl of Breadalbane's estate on the north side of Loch Tay. Great improvements had already taken place at the house and grounds of Taymouth earlier in the century, and this earl had continued the modernising of the estate with the building of Kenmore village. In 1769 he commissioned a survey of the farms on both sides of the Tay with a view to improving them also. Two surveyors were employed for ten months each, one on the north side and one on the south side of the loch.

The township of Carwhin is a cluster of buildings at the bottom right of the plan, with a mill a little to the north. The areas marked A–H are infield land. Like most Highland townships, this arable land is scattered in irregularly shaped lots. The outfield land belonging to the township was situated further up the slopes which lead to Ben Lawers. The road along the north side of the loch runs just north of the township of Cary. To the left is Blairmore, with a smithy. The surveyor noted that, apart from the large field by the loch (G) and land at Croftvellich, the infield was of poor quality. However, the outfield above Blairmore was good. Below the road the grass was poor because of the rocky nature of the ground. There were trees at the lochside 'but the high part of this and several adjoining farms looks very bleak'. On the bottom right of the plan is the head dyke, which separated the arable from the pasture land.

The number of buildings shown on the plan gives a good indication of the high population in the area. In his tour of Scotland taken at the same time as this survey, Thomas Pennant described how the houses of the Highlanders in the area appeared

'not singly, but in small groups, as if they loved society or clanship'. He also estimated that the population on the north side of Loch Tay was 1,786 people.[10] The year after the survey was carried out, the tenants of Crannich and Carwhin petitioned against a rent rise, saying they had difficulty paying the existing rent because of the number of people trying to subsist on the farms: 'There are no fewer than fifty nine families in the said officiary, exclusive of cottagers, and at the most moderate computation there are in every family six souls besides servants. How difficult it is to maintain such a vast number of souls upon so small possessions as the memorialists have may very easily be conceived.'[11] From these figures, it seems there were well over 350 people trying to support themselves from the land around these townships.

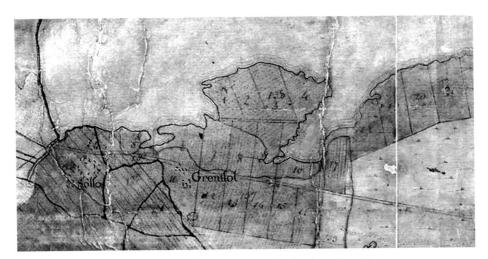

54. Sollas and Grenitote, North Uist, 1799, by Robert Reid
(RHP 1306: courtesy of Brodies WS).

This plan shows the origins of the crofting landscape in North Uist. In 1799 Lord Macdonald had his estates surveyed with a view to increasing his rent roll. The surveyor, John Blackadder, recommended that the jointly held runrig farms on North Uist, each occupied by about thirty tenants, be done away with. He recommended replacing them with individual crofts, whose tenants would continue to work in kelp manufacture. At this time, Lord Macdonald's income from the kelp shores was twice the island's land rent. 'As the making of Kelp is the Staple of this Country, the encouraging of a number of inhabitants to settle or remain in it is the sure means of Keeping up the advantages and Revenue to be derived from the Manufacture of that Article. But the improvement of the Land cannot be effected or brought about while the present system of Run-rig possession exists.'[12]

The tenants were not keen on the proposals and, because the estate was afraid of losing valuable kelp workers through emigration, it took some time for the North Uist farms to be reorganised. In 1813 Blackadder was employed again to divide the lands into crofts: the gridlines on the plan were added at this time. The straight lines of the crofts are the Highland equivalent of the geometric fields of the Lowland single-tenant farms. Sollas was divided into twenty-three crofts of seven acres each. Holdings of this size ensured that their tenants would have to work on the kelp shores to survive.

The surveyor described the ground: 'The soil in general is good except no.17 & 18, which are wet, but capable of improvement by drainage. The Machair produces fine grass, either as pasture or hay.'[13] The neighbouring township of Grenitote was turned into twenty-five crofts, mostly of eleven acres.

55. (*Overleaf*) **Evidence on Sollas clearances, 1849**
(AD 14/49/249, p. 37. Crown copyright).

The next stage in the development of the Sollas area came in 1849. By this time the boom years of the Napoleonic Wars were long over and, with the end of the kelp industry, the high population which the estate had previously encouraged had become an embarrassment. The population of North Uist had risen by 141 per cent since 1755,[14] and even before this dramatic increase one visitor had remarked on the lack of arable land in relation to the island's population: 'The Quantity of cultivated land in North Uist is extremely small compared to the number of the Inhabitants.'[15]

Despite over 1,300 tenants being assisted to emigrate from the island, by the late 1840s the crofts in Sollas and the neighbouring townships housed 600 people. When the potato famine began, rent arrears climbed steeply, and as a result Lord Macdonald's debts reached over £200,000. He tried to sell the island, but no buyers could be found in the middle of the crisis. The estate was put into the hands of trustees, who tried to improve the balance sheet by clearing off the crofters to create sheep farms. The Sollas tenants vigorously resisted the first attempts to evict them and a force of thirty policemen had to be sent to the island.

Police Constable Ewan Macdonald related what happened when they put the crofters out of their cottages:

> We went first to Malaglete and put the furniture out of the house of Norman MacPherson there, during which time I observed a crowd gathering in the neighbourhood and coming towards us. We then proceeded to the house of Alexander MacPherson which is within a few yards of Norman's to remove the furniture from it, and immediately on our commencing to do so, a volley of Stones was thrown at us from the mob which had collected near the door and might then have amounted to about a hundred and fifty.

Several crofters were arrested and charged with mobbing and rioting. There was a great deal of public anger at the evictions, and even though the defendants were found guilty the jury recommended clemency. Many of the evicted tenants emigrated to Canada or Australia. The estate's efforts to avoid financial disaster were not successful, and in 1856 Lord Macdonald sold North Uist. The subsequent history of the area will be found in Chapter 17, on land settlement.

8 Ewen Macdonald Constable residing
at Knockline in the Parish of
North Uist and County aforesaid

Declares in the Gaelic language
On Saturday the 14th day of July
last I was employed by Roderick
Mac Donald Sheriff officer to accompany
him to the District of Sollas to execute
Warrants of Ejectment against the
Tenants there. I accordingly accompanied
him and several other assistants,
Consisting of Eight in number
being those named in Roderick
Macdonald's Declaration. We went
first to Malaglete and put the
furniture out of the house of
Norman Macpherson there, during
which time, I observed a Crowd
gathering in the neighbourhood
and coming towards us. We then
proceeded to the house of Alexander
Macpherson which is within a
few yards of Norman's to remove
the furniture from it, and immediately on our commencing to do
so, a volley of stones was thrown
at us from the Mob which had
collected near the door and might
then have amounted to about
a hundred and fifty but none

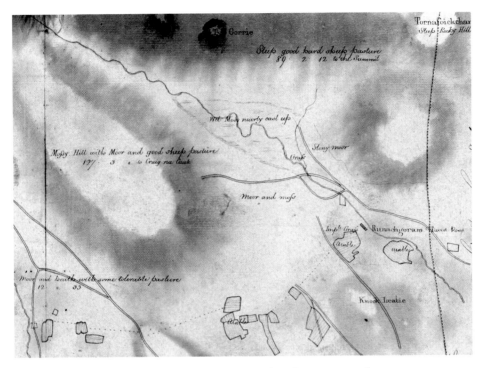

56. Hill of Struie, 1808, by George Brown (RHP 13299, p. 30).

This farm is in Easter Ross, the first area in this part of the Highlands to start sheep farming. Sir John Lockhart Ross of Balnagown introduced blackface sheep here in the 1770s after he had seen how profitable they could be in Perthshire, and by 1781 he was running a flock of 3,000 sheep.[16] Sir John was reckoned to be the best sheep-farmer in the country and the most enterprising Highland landowner of the time. He enclosed, drained and planted his estate, and regarded the promotion of sheep as the best method of improving the Highlands.

The plan illustrates why he and many other Highland landowners were keen to introduce sheep. It shows a bare upland farm with a few small patches of arable land surrounded by large expanses of moorland. Several places are noted as good or tolerable sheep pasture. The introduction of sheep to Easter Ross led to opposition by the local people, who were concerned at the loss of their grazings. In 1792, *Bliadhna na Caoraich* (the year of the sheep), they rounded up 10,000 sheep from farms in the area and drove them towards Inverness, hoping others would join them. However, soldiers were sent in and the protesters dispersed. Their action did little to stop the inexorable spread of the white tide: sheep numbers in Ross-shire increased from 51,000 in 1811 to 251,000 in 1854.[17]

12

Planned Villages

*A country so thinly inhabited, and its towns so inconsiderably peopled, can never be
in a state of much prosperity. A people scattered over the face of the territory they are
possessed of may be happy, but unless large bodies are collected in towns they are not
likely to be rich or powerful, not being able to combine their efforts for any object,
however necessary or important.*[1]

SIR John Sinclair, like many of those involved in improvements in the Highlands, saw
the creation of new villages as the salvation of the area. New settlements would
promote a spirit of trade and industry among the Highlanders, develop the economy
and 'civilise' the inhabitants.

Lowland improvers also favoured the establishment of model villages. Indeed
planned villages were felt to be a vital part of agricultural improvement. They absorbed
the population put off the land by the consolidation of farms, and served as markets for
the produce of the new, more efficient farms. They were centres of employment and
manufacture for rural industries such as textiles. On the coasts new fishing villages
would encourage the industry and provide a living for those cleared off inland glens.
They also had the advantage of increasing the landowner's rent roll. New settlements
were usually sited on previously uneconomic land such as moorland, and rent from
plots in the villages was a welcome addition to the income of many landowners. The
founder of Cuminestown in Aberdeenshire was delighted to see the rent from part of
his estate increase from £11 to £150 through the establishment of the village.[2]

Landowners were keen on planned villages for aesthetic as well as economic
reasons. To the improvers, the trim appearance and grid layout of a new village was
more fitting to the new landscapes they were creating than the haphazard look of the
fermtoun. In some cases estate owners moved a village from close proximity to their
improved mansion house and resited it further away to preserve their privacy and the
amenity of their policies. The dukes of Argyll and Gordon removed settlements from
the gates of their castles and established the handsome new villages of Inveraray (1743)
and Fochabers (*c.* 1778) at a respectable distance away.

One writer has estimated that over 450 villages were created in the period 1720
to 1850.[3] Like other aspects of improvement, the height of village founding was in the

sixty years between 1760 and 1820. Most areas of Scotland saw the start of new settlements, though the greatest concentration was in the counties of Moray, Banff and Aberdeen. While many villages were established by landowners improving their estates, public bodies also played their part. The Forfeited Estates Commissioners were enthusiastic village founders. As well as trying to foster villages as centres for textile manufacturing in the Highlands, they also established settlements for soldiers and sailors coming back from the Seven Years War, e.g. Strelitz in Perthshire, established in 1763.

The British Fisheries Society set up several communities in the Highlands to encourage the fishing industry. The establishment of fishing villages was an important component of government policy to develop the economy of the area. The society was established in 1786 and wasted no time in founding new settlements. In 1788 it started Ullapool, and bought land for Tobermory on Mull. In the mid-1790s the society established Lochbay near Dunvegan on Skye, and in 1803 set up Pulteneytown at Wick. Of these, only Ullapool and Wick flourished as fishing settlements as intended. Although Tobermory did not develop as a fishing centre because of its distance from the fishing grounds, it soon became a thriving port. Lochbay was not a great commercial success, but it did become a focus for a crofting community. The Highland and Agricultural Society also encouraged the creation of villages in the Highlands by offering premiums to landowners who established new settlements.

Planned villages were usually laid out on the geometric lines so beloved of improvers. Generally they had a central tree-lined square, where the most prestigious public buildings such as the church, courthouse, school and inn were sited. Residential streets were arranged on a grid pattern spreading out from the square. Some villages like Tomintoul were built on a linear plan, with only one street built along an existing road, generally a highway, as good road links were essential for the success of a new development. Building regulations were used to ensure a proper appearance to the new settlements. Houses were built hard up against the pavement, both to save land and to prevent dunghills being placed in the street. With new and strictly regulated housing, the inhabitants of the new communities enjoyed a higher standard of accommodation than many other rural dwellers in the eighteenth century. Houses in planned villages were built of stone and had slate or tile roofs. They had at least three, and often five, rooms, and many were two-storey buildings.

Most houses had large plots of ground to the rear for growing fruit and vegetables and to house the workshops of tradesmen. Villagers generally also had a couple of acres in lotted lands around the settlement, where they grew oats and hay. These lands also provided grazing for the inhabitants' few cows, sheep and horses, and peat mosses for fuel. Villagers worked the land part-time on a small scale while making their main living from trades such as shoemaking or weaving. Some people also had employment on the larger farms around the settlement, often on a seasonal basis.

The naming of planned villages was generally unimaginative. One common practice was to name the new settlement after the founder or one of his relatives. Cuminestown was founded around 1740 by Joseph Cumine of Auchry, and Grantown-on-Spey was established in 1766 by Sir James Grant. The other method was to add the prefix '*New*' to the name of an existing settlement, as in New Scone (1805). Some landowners founded more than one village: in addition to moving Fochabers, the duke of Gordon set up Huntly around 1765 and Tomintoul in 1779. Tomintoul was intended to gather together the scattered communities in that remote area and to act as a centre for linen manufacture.

New villages were founded in most regions of Scotland, though not in Orkney or Shetland. Helmsdale, on the Sutherland coast, was set up in 1814 to house crofters cleared from Strathnaver, so that they could support themselves by fishing. Athelstaneford in East Lothian was an agricultural village. Deanston (*c.* 1790) in Perthshire and Catrine (1787) in Ayrshire were factory villages for the textile industry, as were Keith (1750) and Huntly in the north-east and Newcastleton (1793) in the Borders. In the south-west, Glencapel (1746) and Port William (1770) were centres for fishing and shipping. On Speyside, Grantown was founded with a distillery and sawmills as a centre for local industry. Transport developments also provided an impetus to village founding. Grangemouth was established in 1777 as a port at the eastern end of the Forth and Clyde Canal, and Newtyle developed at one end of the Dundee to Newtyle railway.

Even when the original hopes of the founder to attract industry to the area failed to materialise, as happened in Tomintoul, the new villages were, at the very least, successful in mopping up some of the surplus agricultural population and in providing service centres for the surrounding area. Although many of the original buildings in these settlements have been replaced, the distinctive layout of planned villages makes them easily recognisable today.

57. (*Overleaf*) **Gordon Castle policies and the village of Fochabers, 1764, by William Anderson** (RHP 2312/3. Crown copyright).

The present village of Fochabers was the result of the enthusiasm of the dukes of Gordon for improving their estates. The original village, which can be seen clustered on the edge of the castle grounds, was described by Pennant as 'a wretched town, close to the castle gates'.[4] The third duke decided to resite the village, but his death in 1752 caused the scheme to be shelved. In the 1760s and 1770s his son Alexander, who had been on the grand tour of Europe, carried out major improvements to the castle and policies and revived his father's plan to move the settlement. He decided on a new site a suitable distance away: it is marked on the map as 'New Town of Fochabers'.

In 1776, being 'desirous to remove the present town or village of Fochabers upon account of its inconvenient nearness to Gordon Castle',[5] the duke commissioned his factor to buy up feus in the existing village. It was, however, a thriving community with a courthouse, school and several inns, and not everyone was willing to move. The factor complained about the difficulty of getting people to leave their homes:

> The Duke is anxious to have the present Town of Fochabers removed and with that view has marked out a Situation for a new Town. I have bargained with a few of the present Tenementers and some houses are going on in the New Town. The fact however is, that many of the present possessors are unwilling to part with their old Habitations, but as the Duke is determined, and intent upon it, Every method must be taken to force their removal.[6]

The duke was obliged to pay inducements to his tenants to move to the new site, on average about £20. Even with this encouragement, it took until 1802 for the last of the old village to disappear.

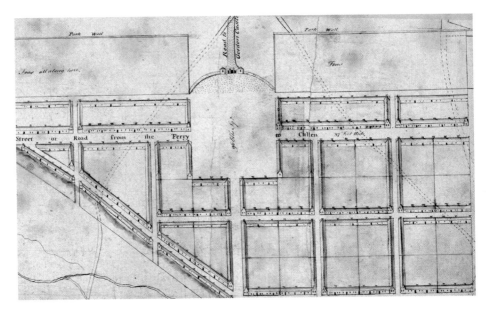

58. Fochabers street plan [1770s] (RHP 2358. Crown copyright).

Fochabers was laid out by John Baxter, who also carried out extensive alterations to Gordon Castle for the duke. The duke himself took a close interest in the planning of the village. This plan shows his original intention of having the drive to the castle leading off from the square. In the end, the castle drive entered the village a little to the east. As in most other planned villages, the main road ran through the middle of the square.

The plan shows terraced single-storey cottages, but the duke stipulated that the buildings around the square had to be two storeys tall. The grid pattern of Fochabers contrasts greatly with the picturesque disorder of unplanned older settlements like Garmouth (see Fig. 7), a few miles away.

59. (*Opposite*) **Callander, 1774, by John Leslie** (E 777/313, p. 290. Crown copyright).

The duke of Perth began planning the village of Callander in the 1730s. When he lost his estates after the '45, the Forfeited Estates Commissioners continued the development of the settlement. Their factor believed the advantages of the settlement's location would make a successful manufacturing village:

> *Callendar is a Small Village pleasantly Situated on the North Side of the water of Teith 14 miles distant from Stirling . . . It lyes in the very entry of the North and West highlands; a publick Road from Stirling to Fort William . . . lyes thro the Said Village; whereby its a proper place for erecting and carrying on Several Branches of*

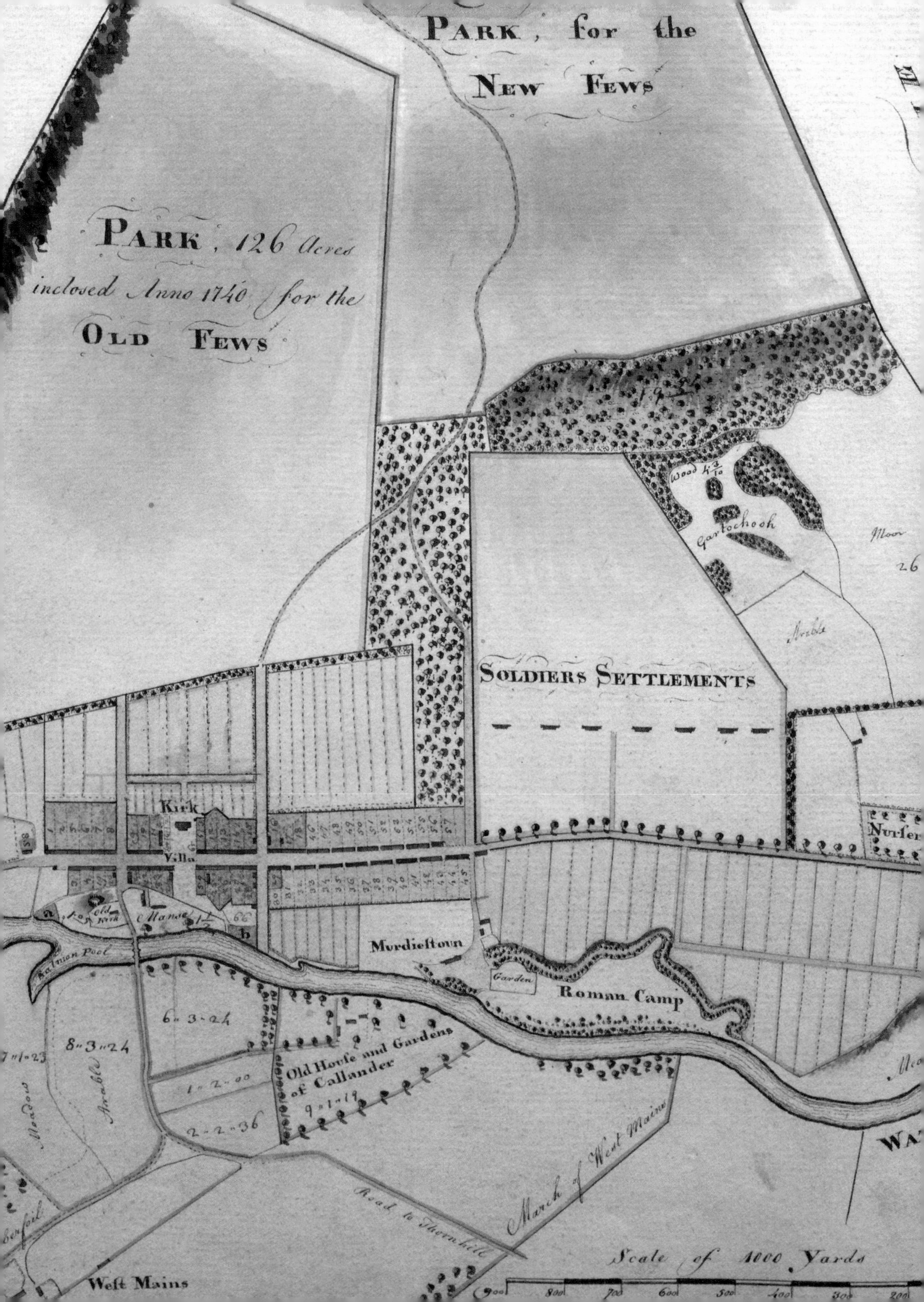

PARK, for the
New Fews

PARK, *126 Acres*
inclosed Anno 1740 for the
OLD FEWS

Wood 4 3/10

Gartochook

Moor
2.6

Arable

SOLDIERS SETTLEMENTS

- - - - - - - - - - - - - - - - - - -

Nurser

Kirk

Villa

Old with

Manse

68

b

Murdieftoun

Garden

Roman Camp

Salmon Pool

6 3 24

7 1 23

8 3 24

Meadow

Arable

1 2 40

Old House and Gardens
of Callander

9 1 19

Ma

2 2 36

Wa

March of West Mains

Road to Thornhill

West Mains

Scale of 1000 Yards

900   800   700   600   500   400   300   200

Manufacture which would tend to bring Industry in Practice in the highlands and civilising the Inhabitants therin.[7]

The plan shows the new bridge to which the commissioners contributed, a soldiers' settlement, the new feus (shaded green) and the original feus (in yellow), and the nursery which raised substantial numbers of trees for planting in the surrounding areas. The new church can be seen in the centre of the square and the houses, shown in red, leading off from it. The houses were on quarter-acre plots and the frontage of each building was sixty feet. In addition the settlers had an acre of arable ground and a quarter-acre of meadow in the acre-dales around the village and on the hill behind.

The soldiers' settlement here did better than the others attempted by the commissioners, because it was attached to an existing village and because the soldiers placed there were local men. Although it became a thriving little town, the early days of Callander were not without their problems. In 1765 the factor made some heartfelt remarks about the quarrelsome nature of the villagers: 'I had more trouble in examining into pretended grievances in this village than one half of the estate of Perth. The inhabitants are eternally at law with one another, which makes their feus be often in the market . . . Altho' they are at variance with one another, yet they all join in distressing any stranger settled amongst them by the Board.'[8]

The Commissioners believed that education, both mainstream and technical, was vital to their plans for developing the Highlands. They were keen that Callander should be a centre for education. As well as an ordinary school, the village had schools to teach sewing, knitting, stocking-making and cooking.

60. (*Opposite*) **Archiestown, 1865, by Peter McBey** (RHP 46730).

In 1760 Sir Archibald Grant of Monymusk started the village of Archiestown in Morayshire as part of his extensive improvements to his estates. He planned to improve the barren moor of Ballintomb by establishing a manufacturing village and attracting 'Honest and Sober tradesman & Honest Sober Industrious Labourers to Settle.' An advert seeking settlers for the new village described its situation as 'well accommodated with very near unexhaustable Moss and good Water and Stone for Building, and very convenient and healthy pleasant Situation'.[9]

In 1763 Thomas Anderson, a linen manufacturer who had settled there, petitioned the Forfeited Estates Commissioners for financial support. He described the development of the community in the three years since its foundation. The village by then housed nine weavers, as well as a variety of other tradesmen: 'Bellintomb, before your Petitioner went there was nothing else than a Barren muir, no house nor person near it, but since building the houses abovementioned 2 Weavers, 2 Taylors, 1

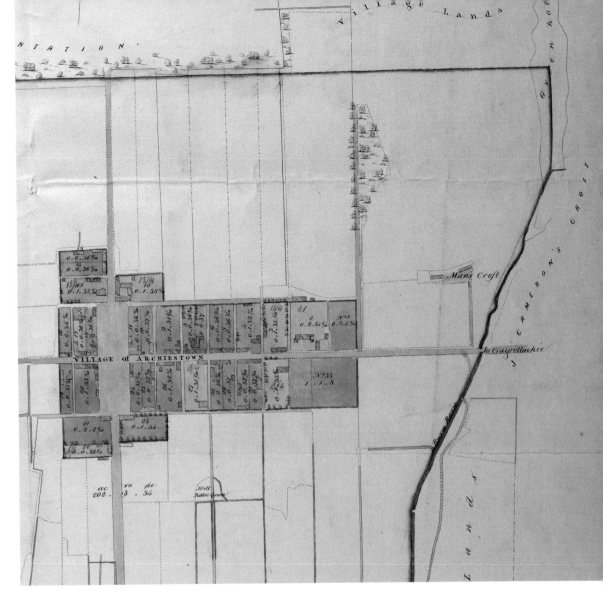

Shoemaker, 3 Masons, 2 Wrights and a Merchant have also built houses & Settled there, besides 7 Weavers and a Heckler in the Service of your Petitioner.'[10]

  Archiestown was based on the village of New Keith, founded by the earl of Findlater in 1750. This plan shows the village about 100 years after its founding, at another stage of its development, when more lands were being feud out. The original village is shaded pink and green: at this time it had twenty-three plots. Like other planned villages, it was laid out on a grid pattern with the main street running through the square. The village lands can be seen at the top of the plan. Possibly because of its distance from markets and its altitude – 747 feet – Archiestown never flourished as some of the other settlements did. Consequently it remains today a good example of an eighteenth-century planned village, although most of the original buildings were replaced after a fire in the 1780s.

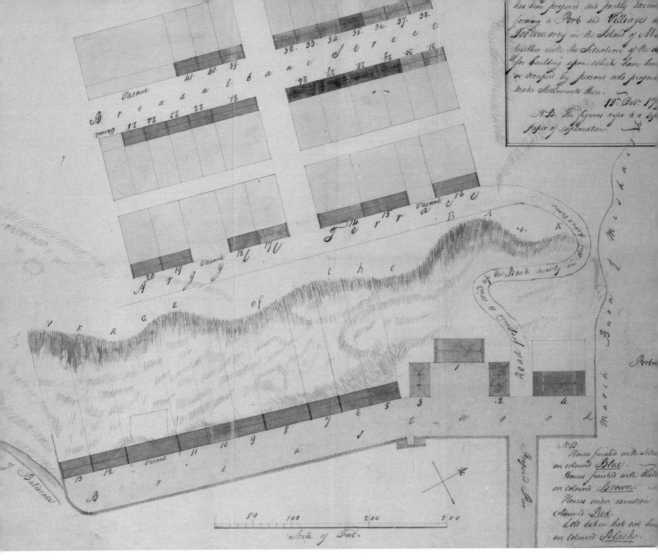

61. Plan of Tobermory, 1790 (GD 9/4/313).

The British Fisheries Society chose this site for a village because of its good sheltered harbour, and the distinctive layout of the settlement was dictated by the topography of the area. Round the sweep of the bay were the public buildings such as the customs house, storehouse and the inn, as well as houses and tradesmen's premises. Above the harbour, two residential streets were laid out, Argyll Terrace and Breadalbane Street. Unlike most planned villages, Tobermory had some thatched houses.

    The first settlers in the village included three merchants, a shoemaker and a mason. All these took sites along the harbour. Those who took houses in Argyll Terrace included a landowner from across the Sound of Mull, Sir James Riddell of Ardnamurchan, as well as an excise officer, a wheelwright and a quarrier. Tobermory's population grew rapidly, from 100 in 1791 to 900 thirty years later. It was clear in its first year that the village would flourish:

The face of the place already assumes an air of industry highly pleasing. By the returns of the Custom House, from May 21st, the time it was established, to August 15th, it appears that there has been seven Hundred & eighty eight Bushels of Salt already sold & delivered to Fish Curers from that Port. Their stock at the latter date was exhausted . . . so great was the demand. A considerable quantity of corn is also sold here.

A Woolen Manufactory is soon to be established and Mr Stevenson of Oban . . . proposes trying a manufactory of soap. This spirit of enterprise promises to be of great utility to the place . . . The number of Boats fitted out this season from this Port for the Fishing amounted about the middle of August to twenty four.[11]

Many of the boats which used Tobermory were involved in carrying kelp and wool to Lowland and English markets rather than in fishing. The opening of the Crinan Canal in 1801 encouraged the village's commercial success.

62. Sketch of Tobermory, c.1790 (GD 9/4/117).

The customs house, storehouse and inn are situated at the head of the pier. These and the breastwork around the bay were built first to allow the commercial life of the settlement to start. The buildings along the front had to be at least two storeys high, with slate roofs. Above the slope are the single-storey houses of Argyll Terrace. This was the more expensive of the two upper streets as it had better views.

13

Roads and Bridges

It is impossible that any Country and the Inhabitants thereof can be brought to a civilized state, good Manners & encreasing Improvements . . . except it be Accessible for Men & Carriages.[1]

MANY writers calling for improvements in the Highlands after the '45 believed, like this commentator, that a proper road system was essential to the area. His remarks could have applied equally to the whole of Scotland. The lack of decent roads in Scotland was a frequent lament in travellers' tales. In the first decades of the eighteenth century there were very few areas of the country accessible to carriages. Paved roads generally existed only in towns: most routes were simply beaten tracks worn by centuries of use rather than constructed. Most routes were impassable to wheeled vehicles: bad weather turned the tracks into quagmires and many were closed for the winter months. People travelled on horseback, or walked, and goods were transported by packhorse. A network of drove roads existed to drive cattle from the Highlands and islands to markets in the Lowlands and England, but as they tended to avoid population centres and kept to high ground where it was easier to move large numbers of beasts, these routes were not always suitable for domestic traffic.

The minister at Rannoch reckoned the normal travelling speed to be one mile per hour. He provided a colourful account of travel in the Highlands at the beginning of the nineteenth century, remarking that in large parts of the west Highlands 'there is hardly anything that deserves to be called a road':

A person is astonished to see the natives scrambling with beasts of burden (there are no carts) over precipices that would frighten a stranger . . . From Inverness to the Point of Kintail, what a road! If it can be so called, for it is hardly agreed upon by travellers which is the line, every one making one for himself . . . The paths, such as they are, take such oblique and whimsical directions, not even excepting General Wade's roads across the Grampians, that they seem hardly to have been drawn by rational beings.[2]

A marked lack of bridges was another impediment to travel. A journey of any length involved numerous fords and ferry crossings, which were at the very least time-consuming and at worst dangerous in bad weather. Sites of former ferries are indicated by place names such as Boat of Garten in Strathspey. Although thousands of bridges were built in the eighteenth and nineteenth centuries, the replacement of ferries with bridges was still going on in the late twentieth century. Until 1975 the Glasgow to Fort William road involved a ferry crossing at Ballachulish or a long detour by Kinlochleven, and it was only in 1984 that the Kylesku Bridge replaced a ferry on the main highway in the west of Sutherland.

The eighteenth and nineteenth centuries saw a transformation of Scotland's transport infrastructure, which went hand in hand with the agricultural and industrial revolutions. In his *Wealth of Nations* (1776) Adam Smith described good roads, canals and navigable rivers as 'the greatest of all improvements'. Better communications were developed not only to facilitate travel, but also to take farm produce to market and transport coal and materials to supply burgeoning industries.

Ironically the first area of Scotland to benefit from better roads was the least populated and least industrial – the Highlands. This area saw a road-building programme in the 1720s, for reasons of law and order, however, rather than economic development. After the 1715 and 1719 Jacobite risings, the government decided proper roads were essential to policing the area. They needed to be able to move troops swiftly around the network of forts and barracks they were building or repairing at places such as Fort George and Fort Augustus. In the 1720s and 1730s General Wade constructed 250 miles of military roads across the Highlands, giving rise to the couplet 'Had you seen these roads before they were made, you would throw up your hands and bless General Wade.' Wade was responsible for the roads linking Fort William to Inverness, Dalwhinnie to Fort Augustus by the Corrieyairick Pass, Dunkeld to Inverness (now the A9) and Crieff to Dalnacardoch, south of the Drumochter Pass, which provided a connection all the way from Stirling to Inverness.

The road-building programme in the Highlands continued under Wade's successor, Major Caulfeild. Old military roads are often referred to generically as 'Wade roads', but Caulfeild was responsible for about 800 miles of them, including the road between Stirling and Fort William and the link between Dumbarton and Inveraray. The 1745 Jacobite rising reinforced the need for good communications and Caulfeild remained in charge of the military roads in Scotland until his death in 1767. A welcome by-product of military roads was the provision of kingshouses or inns to serve the needs of travellers. These generally developed out of camps which housed the soldiers working on the roads. Some still carry out their original function today, e.g. the Kingshouse Hotel in Glencoe. The building of roads and the provision of inns were encouraged by the Forfeited Estates Commissioners, who were aware how crucial a transport system was in opening up the Highlands to influences from the south and in promoting industry.

Government initiatives on roads in the Highlands continued into the nineteenth century. In 1801 they asked Thomas Telford, then engineer to the British

Fisheries Society, to report on communications in the Highlands, identify sites for fishing stations and consider linking the east of the Highlands to the west by canal. In his report Telford described the dangers of travel before the military roads existed, but also pointed out the drawbacks of these roads, which had not been planned with commercial or civilian traffic in mind, either in their locations or in their gradients:

> *Previous to the Year 1742, the Roads were merely the Tracks of Black Cattle and horses, intersected by numerous rapid Streams, which being frequently swoln into Torrents by heavy Rains, rendered them dangerous or impassable. The Military Roads, which were formed about this Time, having been laid out with other Views than promoting Commerce and Industry, are generally in such Directions, and so inconviniently steep, as to be nearly unfit for the Purposes of Civil Life.*[3]

As a result of Telford's recommendations, the government set up the Commission for Highland Roads and Bridges, and appointed him engineer. One of the concerns behind the commission was the draining away of the population of the Highlands through emigration. It was hoped that better roads and the canal would improve the area's economy and encourage people to remain, as well as providing immediate employment in construction. The commission was also given responsibility for the upkeep of the existing military roads. In twenty-five years Telford and his successors built over 1,100 bridges and about 900 miles of roads across the Highlands. Road making also took place as a relief measure during the potato famine of the 1840s, as a result of which some areas have highways known as 'destitution' roads: for example, the road at Loch Maree was built during the famine years.[4]

Roads in the Lowlands were almost as much of a problem as in the Highlands. Road and bridge building was originally the responsibility of the Justices of the Peace and Commissioners of Supply, who operated the statute labour system introduced in 1669. Landowners had to pay assessments towards the building and maintenance of roads and bridges, and local people were obliged to provide six days' labour on the roads every summer. Statute labour was unpopular, partly because tenants were required to work at the very time when they were busy on their farms. Sir John Sinclair succinctly summed up the disadvantages of the system: 'experience sufficiently proved that statute-labour, or work done without pay, cannot be depended upon. The roads in general being imperfectly made, soon became useless.'[5]

During the eighteenth century the practice of commuting labour obligations to money payments became common. It was more effective to build roads with a skilled workforce than with reluctant amateurs. Even with this improvement, however, the system was rarely effective in providing a network of good roads. As a result, road building in the Lowlands remained a piecemeal affair until the mid-eighteenth century. Many bridges and roads were built at the personal expense of estate owners to improve access to their properties and to facilitate taking produce to market. In the second half of the eighteenth century the earl of Breadalbane built the road along the north side of Loch Tay, a project which involved the construction of thirty-two bridges.[6] In some cases bridges were built by subscription: for example, the bridge over the Forth at Drip near Stirling was partly funded by local farmers. Churches sometimes held collections to fund local projects, often to ease their congregations' route to church.

63. Carr Bridge *c.*2004 (R.M. Gibson).

The well-known bridge at Carrbridge, the oldest stone bridge in the Highlands, was commissioned in 1717 by the local laird, Sir Alexander Grant of Grant, partly to facilitate burials in Duthil churchyard (hence its by-name of 'the coffin bridge'); it was financed from the unused stipends of the parish.

From the 1750s the pace of road and bridge building increased as developments in agriculture and industry demanded a proper transport network. This was due largely to the development of turnpike trusts, which put road building on a much firmer footing. Turnpike trustees, who were usually local landowners, raised money for new roads and employed professionals to build them. They recouped their investment by charging tolls. The first turnpike trust was set up in 1713 in Midlothian, but it was the middle of the century before turnpikes were extensive enough to bring a marked improvement to the roads of central Scotland. However, by the end of the eighteenth century over 3,000 miles of turnpike roads had been constructed. These roads have

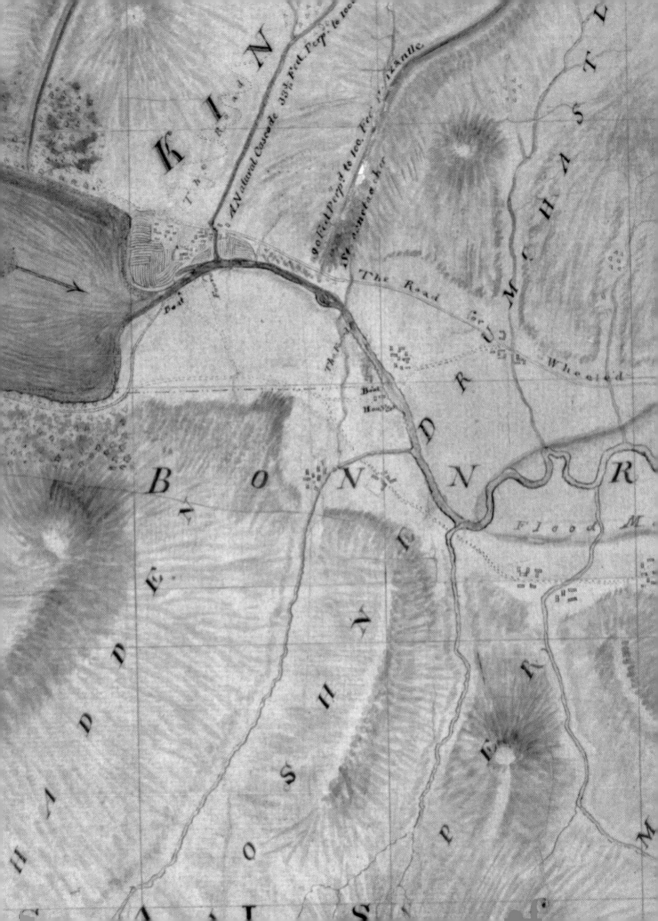

M A C H U I N

Aultree na Stochtan

Craig low

Craiggiproild

Feopatestill

L

GARBULEINE

Loinemore

MUILUIN MADDIDH

R

U

Achtarshan

Barinteem

M

N COULNASAUCH

Carriages

Mount Alexander

S COULNASAUCH

Mill

A

M

N

O

C

A

K

W O O D

of

The Nw to S Road from Rannoch

D U K E of

often been overlaid with the roads we use today, but signs of them can still be seen in the surviving toll houses. These are usually cottages at the roadside with a large bow window at the front so that the toll-keeper could see the traffic in both directions. Milestones are another legacy of turnpikes. One turnpike trustee in Ayrshire in the 1780s was John Loudon McAdam, who invented the modern road surface: before his surface came into common use, road builders had been using technology little changed since Roman times.

The work of turnpike trustees and the Highland Roads and Bridges Commissioners led to a revolution in Scotland's transport. By the 1820s coaches were running as far north as Wick, at a speed of ten to twelve miles per hour. Telford has left a 'before and after' description of travel in Caithness:

> In surveying for the future Roads, it was with difficulty and not without danger that I could scramble along a rugged, broken, sandy shore or by narrow tracks on the edge of precipices, frequently interrupted by rude and inconvenient ferries . . . Now, in the year 1828, a mail coach passes daily from Tain, by Bonar Bridge, the Fleet Mound, Dunrobin, Helmsdale, and the Ord of Caithness, to the extremity of the island at Wick and Thurso, without being interrupted by a single ferry.[7]

64. (*Previous pages*) **Roads in Rannoch, 1756, by John Leslie** (RHP 3480. Crown copyright).

This area, part of the forfeited estate of Struan, was until the mid-eighteenth century a lawless place. Its unenviable reputation was due to its inaccessibility. The lack of roads into Rannoch made the region a convenient refuge for cattle rustlers and other undesirables. According to the estate factor, James Small, 'scarce a single man in it but either stole or connived at theft', and no part of the Highlands needed a road more, 'both for the introduction of trade and marching of troops for civilizeing the country'. He believed that the estate's previous owner, Alexander Robertson of Struan, a notorious Jacobite, had been happy to keep the area inaccessible since it prevented his enemies reaching him:

> there could be no country worse of access or with fewer conveniences for communication than Ranoch, as there was no road to it but was extreamly bad and even dangerous for riders. It was a saying of the late Strouan's that be the roads never so bad, his friends would see him and he wanted no visits from his enemys, and very likely he had thieving in his view in this, as well as his circumstances.[8]

Colonel David Watson, who supervised the military survey of Scotland in the 1750s, wanted to build a road right across the centre of Scotland, passing through Rannoch. By this stage, roads were under construction between Kinloch Rannoch and Alyth in

Angus, from where existing highways led to east-coast ports. James Small calculated that the project required expenditure of only £150 to cover the remaining nine miles between the western end of Rannoch and the king's high road to Fort William at Glenorchy. However, this last stretch was never built and the factor's vision of Kinloch Rannoch as a busy commercial centre never came to fruition.

However, the Forfeited Estates Commissioners did invest considerably in roads in Rannoch to open the area up to lawful influences. The plan shows the road which soldiers and local people constructed from Tummel Bridge to the east end of Loch Rannoch. It runs above the river and is described as the 'Road for Wheeled Carriages'. The road was essential for the villages that the commissioners were setting up for former soldiers at Kinloch Rannoch and at Black Park. The commissioners funded the road east towards Alyth and in 1764 built the bridge at Kinloch Rannoch at a cost of £531: it is still in use today. On the bottom right of the plan is the road to Perth via Cushieville, completed in 1756.

It took another stage of the transport revolution, the railway, to provide the final link from Rannoch through to the west (see Fig. 83). Although it has long since ceased to be a nest of cattle thieves, Rannoch still retains the distinctive atmosphere of an area lacking a through road.

65. Bridge intended to be built at Dumbarton, 1684 (RHP 3493).

This bridge was originally proposed in 1680 when the town petitioned the Privy Council to allow contributions to be made from all over Scotland towards its building. The magistrates were conscious of the need for a bridge to foster the area's economy. A safe river-crossing at Dumbarton was particularly important for the cattle trade between the Highlands and the Lowlands. When weather conditions were too severe to cross the Leven at Dumbarton, men and beasts had to make a twenty-four mile detour to the bridge over the Forth at Stirling or risk drowning:

> *No effectuall meanes can be used for preserveing of any commerce except by the building of a stone bridge upon the river of Leven, lying in the mouth of the Highlands and being the passe and inlett of all trade betwixt them and the Lowlands. The want of a bridge in that place does very much prejudge the trade of cowes, which is one of the most considerable commodities of the nation, and which cowes are either stopt when the storme is great and so starved, or in swimming over are extreamlie weakned and oft times drowned. Nor is there any safety for his Majesties subjects themselves in these great stormes, they being very often stopped and too frequently drowned, so that they are forced to goe about by the bridge of Striveling, which is twenty four myles of unsecure and rough gate, where there is neither meat nor safety for the passingers nor cowes.[9]*

In the event, work on the bridge did not begin until 1754 after the town councillors were alarmed to discover plans to bridge the Leven at Bonhill. They feared this would lead to Dumbarton being 'drained of its inhabitants'. The bridge was not completed until 1765, eighty years after the first plan was drawn up.

66. (*Opposite*) **Bridges built by Highland Roads and Bridges, 1803–21** (RHP 2006/1).

In his report on communications in the Highlands, Telford had commented on 'the want of Bridges'. Consequently one of the objectives of the Commission for Highland Roads was to bridge the main river crossings in the area. This illustration shows part of an engraved plate in the Commissioners' 9th Report (1821), depicting some of the 1,117 bridges they built or improved. Many of them were designed by Telford, whose poet friend Robert Southey nicknamed him 'Pontifex Maximus' and 'Colossus of Roads'. Telford's bridges include the magnificent seven-arched bridge at Dunkeld (1809) and the elegant Bonar Bridge (1813), described by one grateful inhabitant as 'like a spider's web in the air . . . the finest thing that ever was made by God or man'.[10]

These bridges and the parliamentary roads, as they were known, laid the basis of the road system in the Highlands today. Through his roads, bridges, harbours and canals, Telford did more for opening up the Highlands than any other individual. Among the highways constructed by the commission were the road to Loch Hourn, the Road to the Isles from Invergarry to Kyle of Lochalsh, and the highway up the east side of the Highlands, from Dingwall to Thurso and Wick.

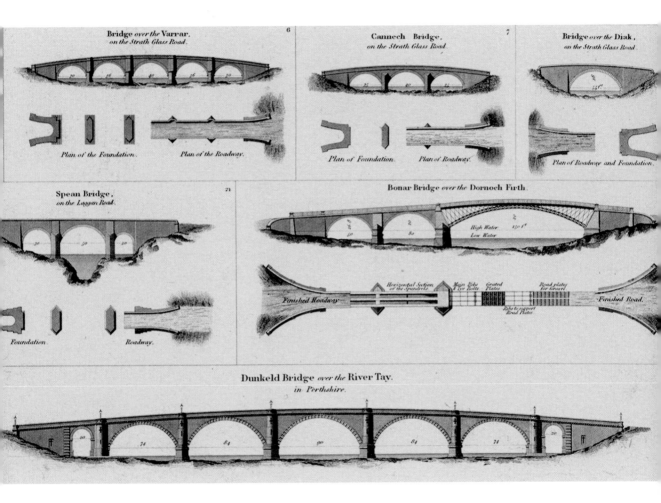

Bridge *over the Varrar,*
on the Strath Glass Road.

6

Plan of the Foundation.

Plan of the Roadway.

Cannech Bridge,
on the Strath Glass Road.

7

Plan of Foundation.

Plan of Roadway.

Bridge *over the Diak,*
on the Strath Glass Road.

Plan of Roadway and Foundation.

Spean Bridge,
on the Laggan Road.

21

Foundation.

Roadway.

Bonar Bridge *over the* **Dornoch Firth.**

High Water

Low Water

Horizontal Section
of the Spandrels.

Main Ribe
Eye Bolts

Grated
Plates

Road plates
for Gravel

Finished Roadway.

Rebe to support
Road Plates.

Finished Road.

Dunkeld Bridge *over the* **River Tay,**
in Perthshire.

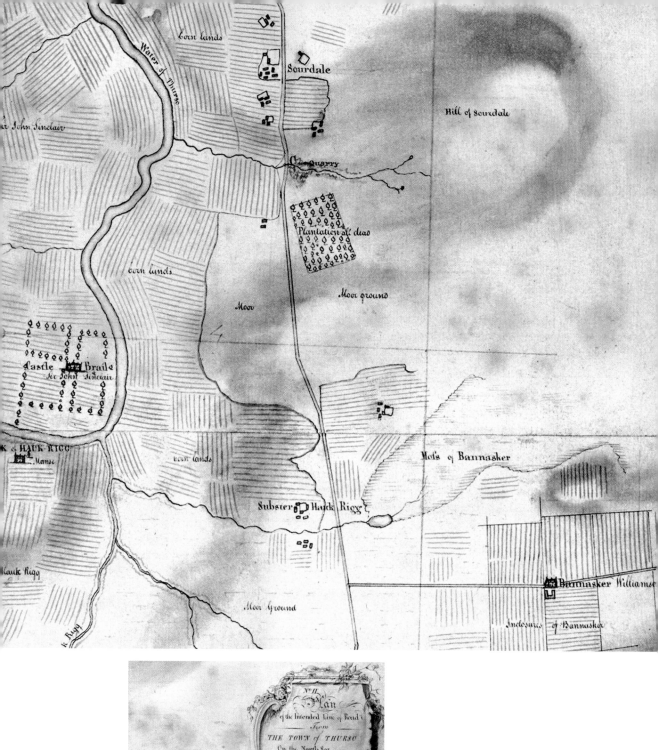

Corn lands

Water of Thurso

Sourdale

Sir John Sinclair

Hill of Sourdale

Quarry

Plantation all dead

corn lands

Moor

Moor ground

Castle Braile
Sir John Sinclair

K of HAUK RIGG
Manse

corn lands

Moss of Bannasker

Subster Hauk Rigg

Hauk Rigg

Moor Ground

Bannasker Williamse

Inclosures of Bannasker

Nº II
Plan
of the Intended Line of Road
from
THE TOWN of THURSO
On the North Sea
Across the County of Caithness
to
DUNBEATH
On the Murray Firth
or
East Sea
Surveyed Summer 1797
By Geo Brown

67a & b. (*Opposite*) **Thurso to Dunbeath road, 1797, by George Brown** (RHP 11610/1).

In 1779 the landowners of Caithness complained that the area was 'miserably retarded in the almost total want of roads'.[11] The episcopal bishop of Ross and Caithness has left a vivid picture of what this meant for travellers. In 1762 Bishop Forbes made an expedition to Thurso, having taken the precaution of leaving his wife at Inverness, then the northern extremity of travel by coach. He needed a guide to take him across the notorious Causeway Mire, between Latheron and Spittal, where horses were not allowed to stop, lest they sank. According to the bishop the mire was 'one continued piece of mossy ground for about two miles at least, full of sloughs and quagmires, directly across the road to Thurso, but why it is called by such a name I could not conceive, as the smallest vestige of a causeway we could not discover in the whole. However at Thurso they told me that a causeway had been there of old, but it had sunk down out of sight by the ruins of time.'[12]

Sir John Sinclair of Ulbster, who owned Braal Castle, on the left of the map, was as keen on road making as on other forms of improvement. In 1780 he used the statute labour system to its utmost to try to improve the road. He assembled almost 1,200 men, and in one day they completed a six-mile stretch to allow vehicles to travel over a hilly section at Benachielt, north of Latheron. Aware that a more permanent solution was needed, Sinclair obtained a private act of parliament for a proper road system in Caithness. Plans, including this one, were drawn up and assistance sought from the Highland Roads and Bridges Commission. The commission provided half the costs and the county had to find the other half. In the early nineteenth century several highways were completed in Caithness, bringing huge benefits to the county's economy. James Mitchell described the great north road to Wick and Thurso as 'a fertilising stream': 'The Parliamentary road through this county in 1817 seemed to have acted like a fertilizing stream. On each side farms sprang up, houses and steadings were built, and in a few years the necessity and advantage of roads throughout the county became strikingly apparent.'[13]

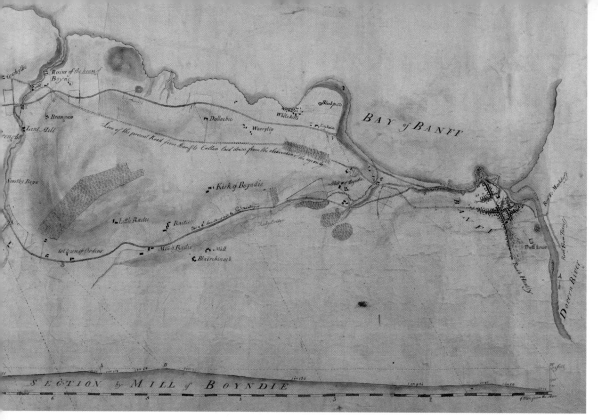

68. Banff to Fochabers road, 1802, by Thomas Shier (RHP 46014).

At the beginning of the nineteenth century, the roads in Banffshire were 'in bad repair, narrow, incomodious, and dangerous to travellers'.[14] This road was one of several proposed by the turnpike trustees for the area. The duke of Gordon promised £3,000 towards the cost of the programme, and Thomas Shier, a road surveyor at Aberdeen, was commissioned to make a survey. His estimate for twenty-three miles of road and nine bridges was £6,863. A turnpike act was obtained and by 1807 the road had been completed from Banff to Cullen. Toll-bars were put up and the old roads closed to stop people evading payment.

The plan shows two lines of road, one near the coast and one inland. Shier explained the advantages of the inland route, which would serve the hinterland better than a coastal route:

> I have also surveyed and laid down another line from Banff to near Portsoy, by Mill of Boyndie and Mill of Raitie etc, which, except one short pull near the sea side where it departs from the other line at letter W is as level, and no more expensive in execution, and would give more accommodation to the Country, as it goes more into the interior part thereof; and will also save near five miles of Road making to Keith and Huntly if the Roads to these Towns from Banff should be made.[15]

A further Turnpike Act in 1825 set tolls on the road at 8d for a cart, 1s 4d for a coach, 6d per score for a drove of sheep and 4d for a horse.[16]

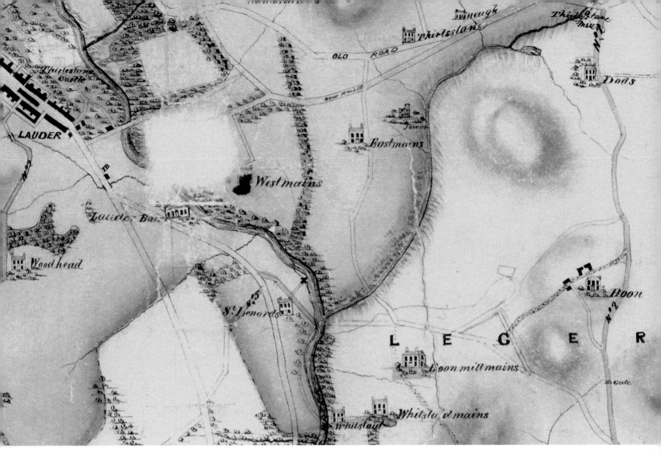

69. Lauder district roads, 1842, by Thomas Mitchell (RHP 30041).

This part of the Borders had had the advantage of a good road system since the mid-eighteenth century. The London to Edinburgh road ran through Lauder, and a regular coach service had been operating on the route since 1753. In the 1790s the minister of Greenlaw described how better communications improved access to markets around Edinburgh for local farmers:

> When a spirit of improvement in agriculture first appeared in this part of the country, the roads were in bad repair. The only way of transporting grain or meal to the Lothian markets was on horses backs . . . besides being expensive, it was attended with another, and even greater inconvenience: in winter the roads, or rather tracts, were often impassable. But since that branch of the great road from London to Edinburgh was made (which is nearly 30 years ago) there has been constant access with carts to the Dalkeith market. A cart with 2 horses, carrying 5 load of meal, can perform 2 journeys in the week, and returns home laden with coal or lime.[17]

By the time of this plan there were turnpikes from Lauder to Coldstream and to Jedburgh, on which coaches travelled between Edinburgh and Newcastle, as well as many miles of parish roads. The town of Lauder had four public coaches passing through daily.

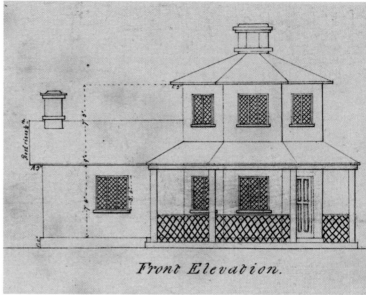

70. (*Left*) **The Aviemore Inn, 1807**
(RHP 9039: courtesy of the earl of Seafield).

Visitors to Scotland regularly complained of poor tourist accommodation, and both the government and landowners tried to improve matters. Aviemore had boasted an inn since the 1720s, provided by the local laird. In 1766 James Grant of Grant built a new hostelry, shown here some forty years later. As well as two parlours and bedrooms for guests, it had stabling for their horses and its own brewhouse and farm to provide food and drink for customers. The building survived until 1969. During its long history the inn was variously described as 'this comfortable inn' and 'that horrible house'.[18]

71. (*Right*) **Tollhouse at Conon Bridge, 1828**
(RHP 12645: courtesy of Drummond Miller WS).

This elevation illustrates the octagonal shape common to many tollhouses. The Conon Bridge tollhouse was designed by Joseph Mitchell, who was general inspector to the Highland Roads and Bridges Commission for forty years. It survives today as a private house.

14

Harbours and Lighthouses

Safe and Commodious Harbours are of the greatest importance to the Nation in general, and are much wanted on the East Coast of Scotland in particular.[1]

HARBOURS were also an essential part of the communications infrastructure. Communication by sea was of great importance in a country whose terrain did not lend itself to easy inland transport. Until the eighteenth century, most of Scotland's towns were either on the coast or near the mouth of a river. They were served by small coastal vessels which berthed simply by drawing up on beaches or mud flats or tying up in creeks. If there was a natural shelter, larger ships could drop anchor and unload their cargoes using small boats. Most early harbour works were simple quays or occasionally breakwaters. Until 1725 Arbroath was served by a wooden pier which had been erected by the townspeople and the abbey in 1194.[2]

From the late sixteenth century, towns began to build more protection, often utilising rocks bordering a bay to create an enclosed shelter. In cases where there were no natural structures to use as a basis, two piers might be built out to form a harbour. By the end of the seventeenth century, the east coast of Scotland had a number of harbours. In Fife and the south-east, harbours were developed to facilitate the east-coast burghs' trade with Europe. The south-west of Scotland was also reasonably well served with harbours by this time. However, from Argyll northwards there were no shelters for ships and on the east coast there were few refuges north of the Moray Firth.

The eighteenth century brought a marked increase in Scottish trade, particularly with the British colonies. From the 1780s, as her industries developed, Scotland's coastal shipping also increased and so too did the size of vessels. In 1760 Scottish trading ships were normally about 54 tons burden: by 1840 they had more than doubled to 123 tons.[3] Despite the growing road system, water-borne transport still remained the most efficient method of moving bulk goods over long distances. Along with the expansion of the fishing industry, these developments brought demand for safer harbours around the coasts to provide better shelter for the rapidly expanding number of ships using Scottish ports.

From the early eighteenth century much building and improvement of harbours took place. Towns and cities set up harbour trusts and port authorities to take forward river and harbour improvements. By the mid-eighteenth century, Glasgow's development was being hampered by the shallow Clyde, which prevented vessels larger than thirty tons coming upriver to the city. In 1768 inexpensive improvement works started with the building of jetties, which narrowed the river channel and had the effect of scouring and deepening the river bed. By the 1780s, ships of 100 tons could reach Glasgow. Later dredging works allowed ships of 400 tons upriver by the 1830s and enabled Glasgow to achieve its position as the second city of the empire. Major harbour developments also took place in Edinburgh, Perth, Dundee and Aberdeen.

In villages a landowner might pay for harbour works. The Earl Marischal built the first harbour at Peterhead in the late sixteenth century, the earl of Cromartie established the harbour of Portmahomack in the 1690s and in the same decade Sir Patrick Ogilvie of Boyne had Portsoy harbour constructed to export Portsoy marble. Before publicly funded works started in the eighteenth century, towns issued appeals for contributions towards harbour building, sometimes through churches, but more often through the Convention of Royal Burghs. The government provided finance for new harbours first through the Forfeited Estates Commissioners and then by the British Fisheries Society, whose work included the establishment of harbours at its fishing stations. In 1809 the Scottish Fishery Board was set up to develop the industry, partly in the hope of providing employment in the Highlands. The board originally paid bounties for catches, but in 1828 switched its funding to building harbours. Joseph Mitchell, who had been appointed by Telford as superintendent of Highland roads and bridges, was given the additional job of engineer to the Fishery Board. The board funded over 100 harbours around the coast of Scotland. As with the Highland Roads Commission, the Fishery Board provided part of the cost, and local people, whether landowners, town councils or local fishermen, provided the rest.

Several of the harbours built in the eighteenth and early nineteenth centuries were designed by three of the great engineers of the day, John Smeaton, Thomas Telford and John Rennie, while many of those built slightly later by the Fishery Board were designed by Joseph Mitchell. Much of the harbour-building activity was concentrated on the east coast, where there were fewer natural shelters and more fishing boats. Better harbours provided safety for ships once they had reached port, but help was needed further out to sea as well.

As shipping increased, losses of ships grew and demand rose for lighthouses to make the coasts safer. Until the late eighteenth century very few existed. Tradition tells of a beacon maintained by the monks of the Isle of May in the Forth as early as the tenth century, and beacons in the Minch and on the Moray Firth in the fifteenth century. Early lights on record are fire beacons on the Isle of May from 1636 and at the entrance to the Tay in 1687. Southerness on the Solway had a light from 1748 and Little Cumbrae in the Clyde acquired a coal beacon in 1757. Until the late eighteenth century, these and a few other lights were all that stood between Scotland's shipping and her dangerous coasts. Surveys of the coastline after particularly bad storms in 1782 emphasised the need for lights. In 1786 the Northern Lighthouse Board was founded to improve 'the security of navigation and the fisheries'. Since that date 200 lighthouses have been built around the coasts of Scotland, many of them by the Stevenson family of engineers.

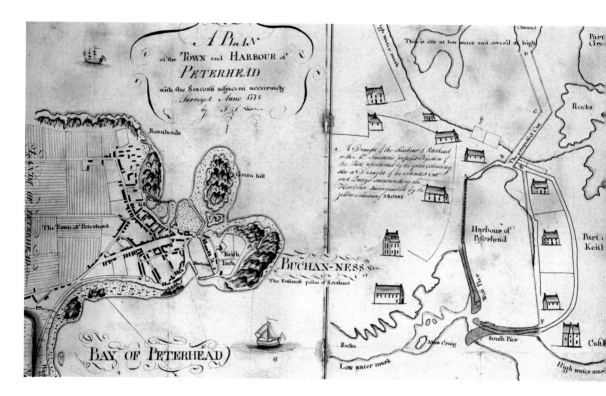

72. The town and harbour of Peterhead, 1775, by John Smeaton
(RHP 37949).

Peterhead harbour had been in existence since the 1590s. In the first half of the eighteenth century repairs were carried out with funding from the Convention of Royal Burghs. By the 1770s the port was expanding and major improvements were needed. John Smeaton designed the new south harbour. He had built the Eddystone lighthouse in the 1750s and played a considerable part in improvements to Scotland's communications, including engineering the Forth and Clyde Canal. Smeaton's other harbour works in Scotland include Eyemouth, Aberdeen and Cromarty.

This plan of Peterhead harbour and town, with its pictorial representations of buildings, formed part of the town's petition to the Forfeited Estates Commissioners for funds. Fishing was the town's lifeblood and the councillors were aware of the drawbacks of the existing harbour. They highlighted the port's value as a national harbour of refuge for both international and coastal shipping:

> Its Port, or rather two Ports, upon the German Ocean [North Sea], looking South & North . . . are divided by a shallow Chanel & Sand Bridge . . . The Coasting Ships from South & North, with Westerly Winds, are taken Short, & must Stop at this Critical Point, and Ships to & from the Baltick & Eastern Coast, North America, the West Indies, Greenland & Hudsons Bay, As well as Ships drove from the Coast of England & many Ports of Scotland, can fetch the Harbour of Peterhead when they Can no other port in great Britain.[4]

Smeaton's intention was to realign the south pier to direct the sea away from the harbour mouth and to alter the west pier to provide an entrance eighty feet wide. The cost of the improvements was estimated at £6,891, of which the town raised £2,000, including a contribution from the other royal burghs. Work was completed in 1781. In 1818 Thomas Telford designed the north harbour and later a canal was cut to join both harbours. By the mid-nineteenth century Peterhead was one of the busiest harbours in Scotland.

73. (*Opposite*) **Pulteneytown and harbour, 1807, by Thomas Telford** (RHP 42242/1).

Unlike the west coast, the north-east coast had no good harbour to allow boats to take advantage of the productive fishing grounds in the area. In 1789 Sir John Sinclair of Ulbster emphasised the drawbacks this posed for the development of the fishing industry when he asked the British Fisheries Society to build a harbour at Wick:

> From Helmsdale to the Neighbourhood of Wick in the County of Caithness there are a variety of small Ports where Fishings are carried on to some extent, and which are capable of very material Improvements, but in the situation of Wick the Neighbourhood possesses Advantages very superior in nature, that it seems to be peculiarly intitled to the attention of the Society . . . All these natural advantages are rendered useless by one unfortunate circumstance, namely the want of a Harbour along that valuable and extensive Coast . . . The Society has it in its power by establishing a Fishing Station in this Neighbourhood, and forming a Harbour there . . . to do more for the Fisheries of the North of Scotland than can be accomplished by any other means.[5]

The following year Telford also recommended Wick as a fishing station. The society bought land on the south of the river and obtained grants of £7,500 from the Forfeited Estates funds and £1,000 from the Commissioners for Highland Roads and Bridges to

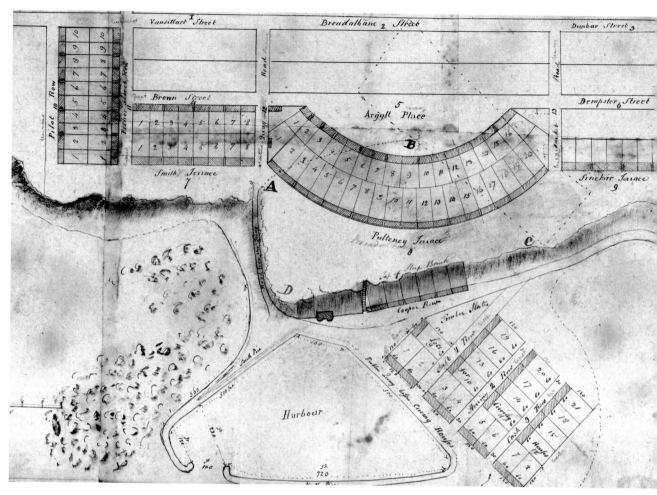

build a new bridge. The harbour was finished in 1810 at a cost of £1,400. Telford designed the harbour and the town, which was named after Sir William Pulteney, former governor of the society. The town thrived, partly because it was beside an existing settlement, and Pulteneytown became the society's most successful project.

The population grew from 300 in 1813 to almost 1,000 in 1819, when settlers included an architect, a surgeon, 16 fish curers, 41 fishermen, 63 coopers, 7 merchants, 2 bakers and a bookbinder.[6] During the fishing season numbers generally trebled as seasonal workers poured in. The major factor in Pulteneytown's growth, however, was the plentiful supply of herring: twenty years after the harbour was built, over 200,000 barrels were being caught annually.[7] In 1819 a customs house was set up and foreign trade followed, mainly with the Baltic and America. Pulteneytown also attracted industry in the form of shipbuilding, brewing and distilling. Such was the scale of growth of the port that in 1823 Telford had to design a larger harbour.

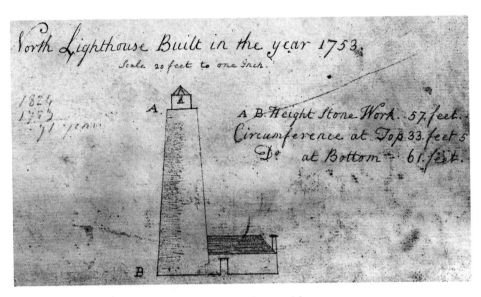

North Lighthouse Built in the year 1753.
Scale 20 feet to one Inch.

A

A B. Height Stone Work. 57. feet.
Circumference at Top 33. feet 5
Do. at Bottom = 61. feet.

B

74. Buddon Ness lighthouse, 1767, by John Holden
(RHP 1158: courtesy of Brodies WS).

Buddon Ness is on the north side of the Firth of Tay, where treacherous sandbanks were a great danger to shipping approaching Dundee. In 1687 local fishermen asked the earl of Panmure if they could set up fire-beacons on his land to make the area safer. They described the firth as:

> ane narrow entry betwixt two dangerous banks so that it cannot be entered under night by the best experienced seamen without imminent hazard, there being no assistance of lights or beacons, so that strangers ordinarily in stress are forced to run ashore and lose all, and even the natives keep off to the outward bay with great danger, to the great prejudice and discouragement of trade and ruin and loss of men's lives.[8]

The earl readily gave permission for a project which would encourage trade in the area, and two beacons were set up. The system was known as 'leading lights': safe entry to the firth was ensured by lining up the two lights. This drawing comes from a plan of Lord Panmure's farms in Barry parish. It shows the north lighthouse, which was built in 1753. It was a stone tower fifty-seven feet tall with a lantern on top, and had a house attached.

15

Canals

Navigable Canals afford great facilities for the conveyance of commodities and both from lessening the expence of land carriage and from conveying safely many articles liable to be injured by the motion of carts, wagons etc, they are a valuable improvement on the means of communication.[1]

CANALS formed a major part of the transport revolution of the eighteenth and nineteenth centuries. They gave safe passage for ships across the country rather than long and dangerous journeys by sea around the coasts. They allowed efficient transportation of materials used in expanding industries – coal, timber, lime and iron – as well as general trade goods. Before steam-powered vessels were common, one horse-drawn barge could carry the equivalent of forty cartloads of goods. At a time when the country's road system was just developing, canals became a popular method of travel for passengers as well as freight.

Scotland's rugged topography ensured that her rivers were rarely navigable more than a few miles from their estuaries, so a comprehensive canal network like England's was not feasible. Nonetheless seven major canals and several small ones were built, most to provide links between rivers or lochs, or coast-to-coast connections. The promoters of all of Scotland's canals had specific commercial benefits in view.

In the seventeenth century Charles II believed a canal linking the east and west of Scotland would be of great benefit to his navy, but it took a long time for the Forth and Clyde Canal to get under way. A survey was carried out in 1726 and the subject was raised several times thereafter, but it was not until the Board of Manufactures employed John Smeaton to carry out a detailed survey in 1763 that things began to move. The board believed the canal would be 'an Improvement of great Consequence to the Trade and manufactures of Britain and Ireland'.[2] It was intended to open a route across Scotland for seagoing ships to save the journey around the north coast. Glasgow merchants were particularly keen to have a canal as it would provide a direct link to Baltic and European markets for their imports of tobacco and other goods from America.

The canal ran for thirty-five miles from Grangemouth on the Forth to Bowling on the Clyde, with a branch into Glasgow. Although construction work began in 1768, the canal had reached only Hamiltonhill in 1777 when funds ran out. However, freight and passengers were able to use the route as far as it existed, and in 1785 the government gave a loan from the Forfeited Estates funds to complete the project. The canal finally opened along its full length in 1790. The waterway was successful in fostering industrial development in the towns it passed through, such as Falkirk and Kirkintilloch, and it established Grangemouth as a major port. In its heyday the Forth and Clyde Canal carried 3,000 vessels a year. However, the opening of the Glasgow–Edinburgh railway in 1842 affected passenger traffic badly. Commercial traffic continued healthy until the First World War when the closure of the Firth of Forth to civilian shipping had a drastic effect on the waterway. Thereafter traffic on the canal declined rapidly, and it closed in 1963.

The Monkland Canal was built to reduce the price of coal in Glasgow by providing a more economic method of transport from the Lanarkshire coalfields than overland carriage. Work started in 1770, but funds ran out four years later and the work was not completed until 1792. The canal ran from Calderbank, east of Coatbridge, to join the Forth and Clyde Canal at Port Dundas in Glasgow. Although it was only twelve miles long, the canal proved a profitable enterprise. It was popular with passengers and became Scotland's busiest canal for freight, carrying 1 million tonnes of coal and iron annually. The railway between Glasgow and Coatbridge proved its downfall, however. Commercial traffic ceased in 1935 and the canal closed in 1950. Part of the route is now covered by the M8 motorway.

The object of the Crinan Canal was to shorten the distance between the west coast and the Clyde by cutting across the Kintyre peninsula. The nine-mile shortcut from Ardrishaig on Loch Fyne to Crinan on the Sound of Jura saved ships a journey of almost 100 miles around the Mull of Kintyre. The magistrates of Glasgow, who proposed the canal to the Forfeited Estates Commissioners in 1771, believed the opening of the route would have great benefits for the herring fishery and trade in general:

> one half of the Herring Busses could pass and repass that way, without going round the dangerous Mull of Cantire, and it would open an easy and short communication between Clyde and the West Coast as far North as Cape Wrath, and with all the Western Isles, so that Timber, Bark, Kelp, grain, Fish or whatever these Countrys could spare, might be brought to market cheaper and with less danger than by doubling the Mull.[3]

This canal was also intended to discourage emigration. It was hoped it would decrease the isolation of the Highlands by bringing people closer to areas of commerce and industry. Part of the route opened in 1801, but it was 1809 before it was completed. Workmanship was poor and major repairs were needed. Although a popular route for all types of vessel, the canal was always in financial difficulties and the company had to be bailed out by public funds. Management of the canal was eventually given to the

Caledonian Canal Commissioners. Passenger traffic ceased in 1929, but fishing and commercial vessels continued to use the route. The Crinan Canal has always been popular with leisure traffic and is now used by 2,000–3,000 pleasure craft annually.

The Aberdeenshire Canal, which opened in 1805, ran for eighteen miles through the valley of the Don from Aberdeen Harbour to Port Elphinstone, near Inverurie. It was built to bring grain, timber and granite to the city, and to take coal and lime to the hinterland. It was reasonably successful on a small scale and fostered the growth of Inverurie, but its life was short. It was bought by the Great North of Scotland Railway Company in 1845 and closed in the 1850s, when part of the route was converted to a railway line.

The Glasgow, Paisley and Johnstone Canal was part of a project to link Glasgow with Ardrossan, the Ayrshire town developed by the twelfth earl of Eglinton. It was planned before the deepening of the Clyde and was intended to give Glasgow easy access to a port on the Atlantic coast. It opened in 1811, but lack of funds meant only eleven miles of the canal were built, from Glasgow to Johnstone. However, this route ran a very successful passenger service, carrying almost 400,000 people annually at its peak in the 1830s. The canal also transported raw materials to Paisley's textile industries. Like other waterways it found it difficult to compete with railways. In 1869 the Glasgow and South Western Railway Company bought the canal and it closed in 1881, being replaced with a railway from Glasgow to Paisley.

The Caledonian Canal has the distinction of having been prophesied some 200 years before it was built. In the early seventeenth century the Brahan Seer predicted that ships would sail behind Tomnahourich, a hill in Inverness. Although the canal was the subject of more concrete proposals in the 1720s, no action was taken for another fifty years. In 1773 James Watt surveyed the route for the Forfeited Estates Commissioners, who were considering ways of improving the fishing industry. However, it was not until Telford recommended the canal in his report on communications in the Highlands in 1802 that things started to move. The government hoped the project would stem the tide of emigration both by providing employment for Highlanders during the construction and by fostering commerce. According to Telford,

> The Improvement of . . . all the Highlands may be expected to follow from forming the Inland Navigation . . . Besides facilitating the Intercourse when completed, Habits of Industry would be introduced during the Execution of the Works. The industrious Part of the Inhabitants would thereby obtain sure Capital which would enable them to embark on other Employments, at present totally out of their Power.[4]

The canal linked the Atlantic to the North Sea by joining the lochs of the Great Glen to allow passage from Fort William to Inverness. By providing a safe route from the west coast to the north-east, it allowed fishing boats and other vessels to avoid the long route around the treacherous Pentland Firth. As it was planned during the Napoleonic Wars, the canal was also intended to have the strategic advantages of allowing ships to escape the attentions of French privateers and of providing speedy passage to warships. This was the only canal to be fully funded by the government. Work began in 1804 but ran into difficulties, and the canal required huge injections of government cash to complete it. It did not open along its full length until 1822. The opening of this route and the Crinan Canal allowed steamboats to run between Glasgow, Fort William and Inverness, a service which was well used by travellers. The Caledonian Canal also proved popular with fishermen and commercial traffic. In the 1960s the waterway was improved to allow large vessels to reach the pulp mill at Corpach. The canal has remained in use and is now an important leisure resource for the Highlands.

The Edinburgh and Glasgow Union Canal was built to provide a link with the Forth and Clyde Canal, and allow east-coast merchants to share Glasgow's trade with America and Canada. A more local aim was to break the monopoly of Midlothian pit-owners by bringing cheap coal to Edinburgh from the Lanarkshire and West Lothian coalfields. As this waterway was a contour canal, i.e. it was on one level, construction took only four years. It opened in 1822. Together these two canals provided a good service to passengers travelling between Glasgow and Edinburgh. However, the start of the Edinburgh to Glasgow railway in 1842 affected the canal considerably. Commercial traffic stopped in 1933 and the canal closed in 1965.

The construction of these canals involved massive and very expensive engineering works, and played a major part in changing Scotland's landscape. Gangs of navvies (shortened from 'navigators') dug channels and built basins, locks and aqueducts. The precise route of a canal was often hotly debated. Engineers such as Thomas Telford, James Watt, John Smeaton and John Rennie tried to keep to the natural contours of the land to facilitate building, while interested parties sought to wring maximum benefit from the passage of the canal. Landowners had to be persuaded to part with areas of their property, and though some did so readily as major investors, others were concerned at the loss of privacy a canal would bring. One landowner on the route of the Union Canal sold his entire estate to the canal company rather than endure this major public work on his doorstep. With the exception of the Caledonian Canal, Scotland's canals started off as privately funded ventures. They all ran into financial difficulties, usually caused by over-optimistic estimates of construction costs, and several required government loans to complete them. Delays in building were also caused by shortages of skilled labour, particularly in sparsely populated areas such as the Highlands.

Canals saw their maximum use between 1820 and 1840. Thereafter the coming of the railways provided strong competition and most canals were bought over by railway companies. They continued to carry commercial traffic into the twentieth century, though on a much reduced scale. All the waterways were nationalised in 1948 and thereafter came under pressure of closure. The road-building programme of the 1960s spelled the end for some, and the Forth and Clyde and Union canals closed during that decade. Only a few years later, however, the value of these inland waterways as a leisure resource was being realised. In 1971 the Scottish Inland Waterways Association was formed to keep the canals going and this was followed by the establishment of several local canal societies.

During the 1970s volunteers campaigned to keep the canals from being filled in, and carried out clean-up operations on the waterways. Four of Scotland's canals are still in use today, run by the British Waterways Board. The Caledonian and Crinan canals have continued in operation since they were built, apart from spells of closure for repair works. In the 1980s efforts started to restore some of the remaining parts of the Monkland Canal. Leisure traffic was restarted during the 1970s on sections of the Forth and Clyde and Union canals. In 1994 the British Waterways Board set up the imaginative and ambitious Millennium Link project to restore them fully and re-establish the coast-to-coast route across Scotland. In 2001 the canals reopened to navigation, and the following year the link between them was re-established by the opening of a rotating boat lift. The Falkirk Wheel is a magnificent feat of modern engineering, adding to the achievements of earlier canal engineers and navvies.

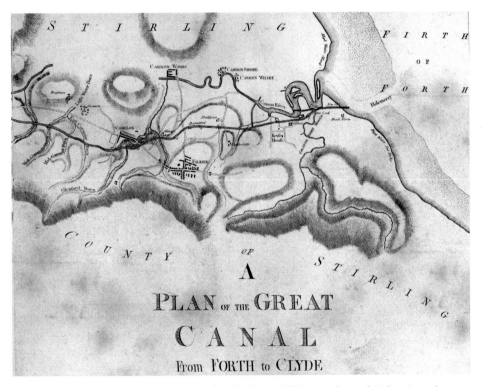

75. Forth and Clyde Canal, 1785, by Robert Whitworth and John Laurie (RHP 44612).

The route of the Forth and Clyde Canal, Scotland's first and longest waterway, was debated for many years. John Smeaton suggested two routes: a northerly route by Stirling and Loch Lomond, and the more direct route shown here, from the mouth of the river Carron in the east, through the valley of the Kelvin, to Bowling on the Clyde. The former was never a serious contender, and the main rival was a smaller barge canal, proposed by Glasgow merchants, which would terminate in the city at the Broomielaw. However, the smaller canal was dismissed as 'a mere puddle', and supporters of what became known as the 'Great Canal' won the debate.

A public subscription was opened in 1767 and raised £106,000 in a month. Subscribers included six dukes, two marquesses and sixteen earls, most investing £1,000–£2,000.[5] The canal's investors expected great things of the project. The earl of Kinnoul enthused: 'I look upon the great Communication betwixt Clyde & Forth to be the most noble & useful work that ever was undertaken in this Country, & that the memory of those who have been the principal Promoters of it will be held in Respect & Esteem by Posterity.'[6] Many landowners were affected by the new waterway. One of the main promoters of the canal was Sir Lawrence Dundas of Kerse, who received considerable financial benefit from the development of Grangemouth, which was part of his estate. Less enthusiastic, however, was Colonel William Forbes of Callendar, who regarded the canal as an intrusion onto his property at Falkirk.

Smeaton resigned as engineer in 1773, Robert Whitworth was appointed in 1785 to complete the project, and the canal was fully open in 1790. Despite taking twenty-two years to build, the canal was a great success for many years. Revenue increased tenfold between 1773 and 1810. By 1815 some 85,000 passengers were being carried each year on the route, encouraged by comfortable boats boasting a library and on-board entertainment by a fiddler.[7]

76. (*Opposite*) **Caledonian Canal, 1821, by A. Arrowsmith** (RHP 10651/1).

At its opening the Caledonian Canal was described as 'one of the most stupendous undertakings which Europe had seen'.[8] Telford was principal engineer, and all his engineering skills were required to construct a waterway through such difficult country. The route of the canal is sixty miles long, of which twenty-two miles were constructed, and includes twenty-nine locks. The eight locks known as Neptune's Staircase, at Banavie near Fort William, are still an object of admiration today.

Construction work was carried out at the east and west ends simultaneously so that the newly built stretches could be used to transport materials to the workers in the middle. Rising costs and labour difficulties, however, led to fears that the project would have to be abandoned. As intended, many of the navvies were Highlanders, but they were apt to leave for the herring fishing or to go home to tend their crofts. However,

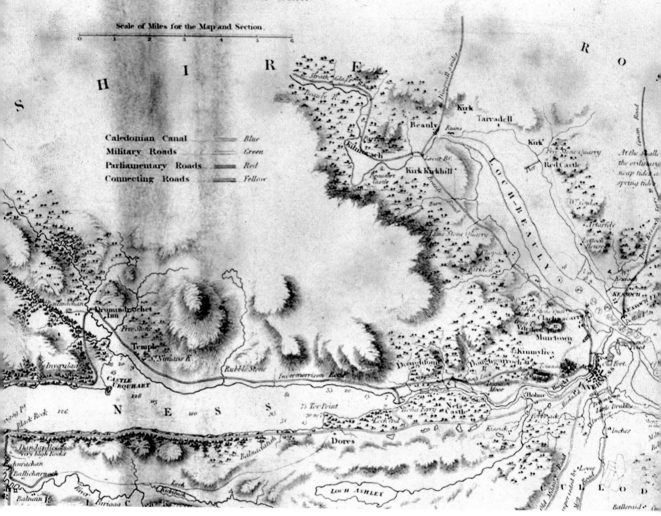

ALEDONIAN CANAL or INLAND NAVIGATION.

From the EASTERN to the WESTERN SEA.

Scale of Miles for the Map and Section.

Caledonian Canal —— *Blue*
Military Roads —— *Green*
Parliamentary Roads ══ *Red*
Connecting Roads ══ *Yellow*

since the project was successful in providing large-scale employment in the area – at one stage 1,200 men were working on it – the government continued to make grants. Telford's original estimate was that the canal would take seven years to build and cost £350,000. In the event, construction took sixteen years and the final cost was £912,373 – a colossal sum of money for the time.

    One landowner added to the delays with numerous objections and claims for compensation. The canal ran past the house of Alasdair Macdonell of Glengarry, on the shores of Loch Oich. Glengarry was the last of the traditional Highland chiefs, and on

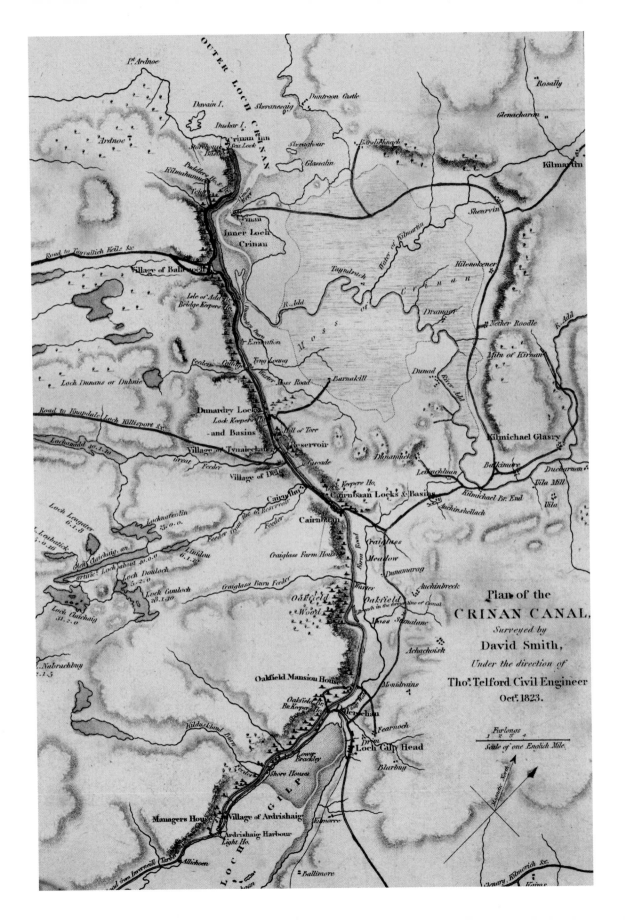

Plan of the
CRINAN CANAL,
Surveyed by
David Smith,
Under the direction of
Tho. Telford Civil Engineer
Oct. 1823.

Furlongs
1 2 3 4
Scale of one English Mile.

one occasion he and thirty armed retainers seized one of the company's boats and drove the workmen off. His claim for damages illustrates the profound effects the canal had on the environment and on the people round about. Glengarry wanted £14,000 compensation for the loss of part of the loch and land on the shore, for destruction of fishings, for the flooding of grounds, for damage to quarries and gravel pits, and for injury to 'the privacy, amenity, comfort and security of Glengarry's paternal mansion grounds and Gardens by the uncontrolled resort of strangers and in the continual passage and neighbourhood of Steam Boats and vessels of all descriptions'.[9] The case was not settled until 1851, long after Glengarry's death, when his son accepted £11,729 in compensation.[10]

The opening of the canal in 1822 was quite an occasion. The official party included the canal commissioners, the magistrates of Inverness and the Inverness militia band. They sailed from Inverness to Fort William over two days, to the accompaniment of gun salutes along the route. Over forty toasts were drunk at the official dinner, and 'a plentiful supply of whisky' was provided to assist the celebrations in the streets outside.[11]

77. (*Opposite*) **Crinan Canal, 1823, by David Smith, under the direction of Thomas Telford** (RHP 5489).

Although James Watt carried out a survey for the canal in the 1770s, the project did not take off until after the British Fisheries Society added their support in 1789. A few years later a subscription was opened. Work started in 1794, with John Rennie as engineer, but was held up by lack of labour and funds. The canal eventually opened in 1801, but it was not fully operational until 1809. It had been poorly built and in 1811 had to be temporarily closed when part of it collapsed. Telford reported that the canal was 'in a very imperfect condition'[12] and major repairs were undertaken, which took until 1817 to complete.

The local gentry were very heavily involved in the Crinan Canal. One of the main promoters was the earl of Breadalbane, who wanted to use the waterway to transport slate from his quarries at Easdale. Freight traffic also included herring, cattle, sheep, pigs, coal and general goods. Passenger traffic on the canal was provided by Henry Bell's steamship *Comet*, which ran between Glasgow and Fort William. When the Caledonian Canal opened in 1822, a service ran from Glasgow to Inverness, taking three days, and by 1827 over 13,000 passengers a year were travelling on the canal. Queen Victoria sailed on the Crinan Canal in 1847; though she thought the views of the hills 'very fine indeed', she found the passage through the locks tedious. However, her visit had the effect of increasing tourist numbers on the route.

16

Railways

From Edinburgh to Inverness the whole people are mad about railways. The country is an asylum of railway lunatics . . . The misfortune is that railways have come too late, they should have put in their claim before the country was made up.[1]

LORD Cockburn's pithy comments on the railway mania which swept the country in the mid-1840s reflect his concern for the natural heritage which they affected. In this case he was alarmed by the suggestion that Perth's beautiful South Inch might be turned into four railway stations. He lamented the city fathers' failure to appreciate 'how turf or trees could be of any use to a town'.

The country had indeed been 'made up' by the time railways came along, but the final and most important strand of the transport revolution brought further radical changes to the landscape. The first lines were colliery waggon-ways which had wooden rails and horse-drawn trucks. Scotland's first waggon-way, which opened in 1722, carried coal from Tranent to nearby harbours on the Forth, and by 1824 there were thirty-one such routes in the country. They were built to exploit the country's natural resources by reducing costs in transporting coal or iron to the nearest waterway, whether harbour or canal. The first real railway in Scotland was the Kilmarnock and Troon line, which opened in 1812. It too was constructed to transport coal, but it was not long before its promoters realised that considerable economic benefits were to be gained by carrying passengers as well.

The public were quick to appreciate the advantages of the new form of transport for trade, travel and food supply: 'While the merchant and manufacturer save in the carriage of their goods, the householder gets cheap coals, the professional man and tourist a cheap and speedy means of conveyance and the landholder finds an extensive market for his mineral and agricultural produce.'[2]

With railways providing a cheaper and faster means of carrying freight and people than either roads or canals, the opening of new lines proceeded apace, and by the 1820s Scotland boasted around ninety miles of railway track. Most of the lines were built to bring cheaper coal to towns and cities. Many of the early lines in the west were linked to the Monklands coalfields, e.g. the Monkland–Kirkintilloch line which opened in 1826. After the Garnkirk and Glasgow Railway opened in 1831, the price of carrying coal to Glasgow dropped by almost two-thirds.[3] The first railway in the east of the country, the Edinburgh–Dalkeith line (1831), was also built to transport coal.

By the 1840s a new stage in Scotland's railway development had been reached with the construction of lines linking towns and cities. The first was the Glasgow, Paisley and Ayr route in 1840, and in 1842 a line joining Glasgow to Edinburgh was opened. By the middle of the century most of the central belt was linked by rail, and the focus of the railway system had shifted from exploiting Scotland's mineral wealth to transporting passengers and general freight between population centres. Scotland now had about 200 miles of track. A major step was taken in the 1840s when Glasgow and Edinburgh acquired rail connections to London: this slashed the travelling time south from forty-three hours to seventeen. By 1850 the network extended as far north as Dundee and Aberdeen, and in 1863 Inverness acquired a direct line south.

Early railways used horses to pull the carriages, but from the 1830s steam locomotives became the favoured method of propulsion. As they allowed travel at the previously unheard-of rate of twenty miles an hour, compared to about five miles an hour by horse-drawn canal boat, the public took to the new method of travel with gusto. In the early days of trains, helpful advice was necessary to alert passengers to unaccustomed hazards. In 1849 the *Kelso Mail* issued this timeless rule for safe railway travel: 'When near tunnels or buildings, do not put your head at the windows. A fatal blow may be got by this indiscretion.'[4]

Enthusiasm for railways reached its peak in Britain in the mid-1840s. The public turned out to be just as keen to risk their savings in railway speculation as they were to risk their persons on the new means of travel. In the 1844/5 session of parliament 104 railway acts were passed for a total of 2,746 miles of line, and the staggering sum of almost £32 million was subscribed.[5] Side effects of railway mania included a lack of money for borrowing as so much capital was being devoted to 'the railway disease',[6] and a shortage of sheep shearers caused by Irish seasonal labourers' desertion to better paid work in railway construction.[7]

Scotland's railways had a profound effect on the country. By bringing people and places closer together, they played a vital part in unifying her economy during the nineteenth century. Perishable goods such as milk and fish could now be carried long distances and food supply was no longer dependent on what could be produced locally. With all sorts of goods becoming much more readily available, a national economy, rather than a collection of local ones, developed. By providing the first speedy and reliable transport links with England, railways did much to integrate Scotland's economy with the rest of Britain. The cross-border links allowed the sale of a variety of Scottish goods to English markets. By the 1880s fish landed at Aberdeen could be sold at Billingsgate twenty-four hours later. Railways were also ultimately responsible for the end of water-borne transport, though the demise of the canals was a long-drawn-out affair.

Railway companies put a great deal of effort into passenger services, and a new travelling public emerged. With train travel allowing people to commute a distance to work for the first time, the workforce became considerably more mobile. People used trains not only for work, but also for leisure purposes. Now all classes of society could travel long distances, and this provided a huge boost to Scotland's developing tourist trade. The upper and middle classes used railways to go on holiday, while working-class people were able to take advantage of day excursions. Hotels were built near railway lines, with their own halts to attract guests, such as the Loch Awe Hotel on the Oban line.

Railways had a huge effect on the landscape. They created new communities and developed existing settlements. Cities expanded rapidly as another phase of railway construction in the 1890s focused on commuter traffic and encouraged the middle classes to move out of city centres to semi-rural suburbs and beyond. New villages grew up along railway lines to serve both commuters and the tourist trade. Railway companies offered 'villa tickets' to commuters who built houses near the railway, and settlements of handsome stone houses appeared in the hinterland of Scottish cities as a result. Lenzie was one such development, while Strathpeffer in Easter Ross grew up as a spa resort after the opening of the Highland line.

Like canals, the building of a railway affected thousands of people who lived along the route. Landowners and tenants alike were usually delighted to hear that a railway was coming to their area: the former as it would increase the value of their property and allow them to negotiate a good price for any land the railway company needed; the latter as the line would bring greater opportunities for both work and leisure. Some estate owners had halts built near their property, e.g. Carbisdale Station, beside Carbisdale Castle. In cities, however, the building of a new line or major station was not always as welcome, as it could involve the displacement of thousands of people.

By the end of the nineteenth century the rivalry of Scotland's 200 railway companies ensured that the face of the country was lined with routes. Gangs of navvies spread railway lines, embankments, tunnels, bridges and viaducts across Scotland. These men worked in difficult conditions, constructing miracles of engineering, sometimes in remote and scenic areas. Though Lord Cockburn was not alone in his concern for what railways would do to the countryside, some of the structures built by Victorian railway engineers quickly became much loved features of the landscape. Doubts were expressed about building a railway in the stunning surroundings of Loch Shiel, but the Glenfinnan viaduct was soon seen as an asset to the environment: 'Many authorities on matters of taste declared when this viaduct was first proposed, that it would prove a monstrosity, sufficient in ugliness to take away all the charm and beauty of the scene. Few would endorse this opinion now. Viewing the work as you sail up Loch Shiel, it gives the idea of a light and fragile thing, as if a gigantic spider had stretched his web across the glen.'[8]

78. Glenfinnan viaduct, 2004 (National Railway Museum, York).

79. (*Overleaf top*) **Kilmarnock and Troon Railway, 1807, by John Wilson, copied by Peter Potter** (RHP 34790).

Although this railway can claim to be Scotland's first in that it was the first to get an act of parliament, it started as a horse-drawn waggon-way. The duke of Portland had it built to carry coal from his mines near Kilmarnock to his new harbour at Troon for markets in Ireland and the west Highlands and islands. The line opened in 1812, and carried timber and lime as well as coal.

This was the first railway to carry passengers, who could travel from Kilmarnock to Troon for a shilling. The coaches did five return-trips daily and soon established Troon as a seaside resort. In 1816 or 1817 the line saw the first experiment with steam, when one of George Stephenson's locomotives was tried out. This caused alarm among spectators, one of whom was the artist John Kelso Hunter:

> the first locomotive engine that ever appeared in Scotland . . . was set down on the
> Duke of Portland's tram road about 400 yards below Kilmarnock House. As the
> steam got up the people stood further back. The liability to burst at the start had been
> much speculated on, and a strong desire that it should was fearlessly expressed . . . the
> engineer opened the safety valve, with a grand burst, which struck the air and the ears
> of the crowd at the same moment. It seemed to me as if the whole mass had been
> blown to fragments . . . I was petrified . . . quite uncertain whether the people were
> killed, or if I were still alive.[9]

Though there were no casualties, steam did not immediately catch on, as the loco-motive was too heavy for the track; trains on this line remained horse-drawn until 1841.

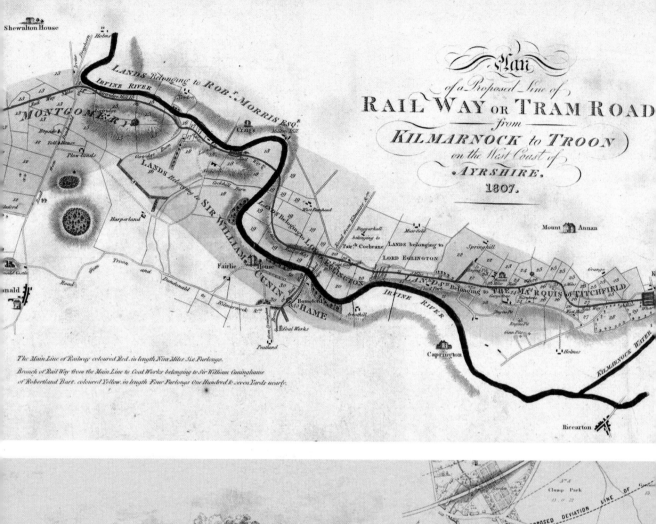

Plan

of a Proposed Line of
RAIL WAY or TRAM ROAD
from
KILMARNOCK to TROON
on the West Coast of
AYRSHIRE.
1807.

The Main Line of Railway coloured Red, in length Nine Miles Six Furlongs.

Branch of Rail Way from the Main Line to Coal Works belonging to Sir William Cuninghame
of Robertland Bart. coloured Yellow, in length Four Furlongs One Hundred & seven Yards nearly.

80. (*Opposite bottom*) **Westburn House, Cambuslang, and railway, 1845** (RHP 92273).

The Clydesdale Junction Railway was built to bring coal from Lanarkshire to Glasgow and to link the city with the Caledonian Railway at Motherwell. The promoters' prospectus, which outlined their intentions to prospective investors, also illustrates the number of other railways in the area. The route was to provide:

> *a direct and uninterrupted communication between the City of Glasgow and the inexhaustible fields of coal and other minerals, lying in the lower valley of the Clyde, as well as those traversed by the Wishaw & Coltness Railway, the Wilsontown Railway and other communicating lines; a union between the Caledonian Railway and the City of Glasgow, possessing the terminus at that city.*[10]

The plan shows the line cutting through the garden of Westburn House, with the railway embankment towering beside the property. Not surprisingly the owner of the estate, John Graham of Craigallion, objected and proposed another line further away from the house, shown on the plan as 'proposed line of deviation of railway'. The railway company was not happy with his suggested route as it would affect the gardens of thirty householders in Cambuslang and cost £7,000 more to build. In the end the line did avoid Westburn House and the privacy of the family was preserved.

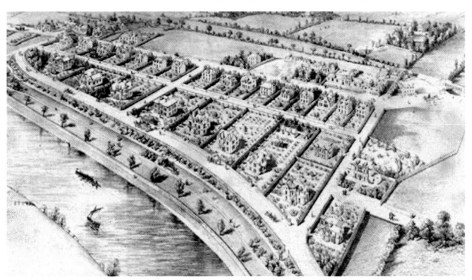

81. (*Above*) **Feuing plan of Ruthrieston, Aberdeen, 1875, James Forbes Beattie & Son** (RHP 6912).

Ruthrieston was on the Deeside line, which ran from Aberdeen to Ballater. The promoters of the route wanted to open up the agricultural area along the Dee and provide travellers with the opportunity to see some of the finest scenery in Scotland. The *Aberdeen Herald* predicted that the railway would 'cause the whole of Deeside to be studded with villas and cottages as thickly as the Banks of Clyde'.[11] Though the development was not quite on the scale envisaged, the line did lead to the rapid growth of settlements along its route.

The Deeside Railway opened as far as Banchory in 1853 and Aboyne in 1859. Plans to build a cross-country link through to Strathspey and on to Fort William were shelved when Queen Victoria expressed concern over the likely invasion of her privacy at Balmoral and the railway was taken only as far as Ballater. As well as carrying royal trains, the Deeside line provided excursions for substantial numbers of tourists and day trippers, enticed by railway guides and adverts describing the delights of the route: 'The scenery's grand, the air, oh it's charming, / Deeside being famed for excellent farming; / The mountains stupendous, and sweet heathery plains – / The travelling's pleasant, there's well arranged trains.'[12]

The railway was also popular with commercial users, carrying timber and agricultural produce from fertile Deeside down to Aberdeen and serving the paper mill at Culter. The route was also a boon to commuters into Aberdeen. In the few years after the line opened, several intermediate stations were added, including Ruthrieston in 1856.

The village was two miles from the centre of Aberdeen and was originally a hamlet at the Bridge of Dee, seen on the left of the plan. In 1875 James Forbes Beattie proposed this riverside development of broad streets and handsome villas: some of the houses cost around £5,000 to build.[13] The railway can be seen behind the development. It provided a regular service for commuters and helped in the expansion of Aberdeen's suburbs. The travelling time from Ruthrieston to the city centre was only five minutes. Several more suburban stations were opened, and by 1904 nineteen trains a day, known as 'subbies', ran on the line. Because of competition from buses, the suburban service ceased in 1937, and the line closed in 1966 as part of the Beeching cuts.

82. (*Opposite*) **The Forth Bridge** (BR/FOR 4/3. British Railways copyright).

The Forth Bridge brought a very dramatic change to the appearance of the Forth estuary. This magnificent monument to Victorian railway engineering still dominates the landscape at Queensferry. Before the bridge was built, the east-coast railway route came to an abrupt halt at South Queensferry, where passengers had to take the ferry across the Forth to Fife. The alternative was the long way round by Stirling and Dunfermline. In the 1770s John Smeaton had considered bridging the Forth but decided it was not feasible. In the first half of the nineteenth century other schemes

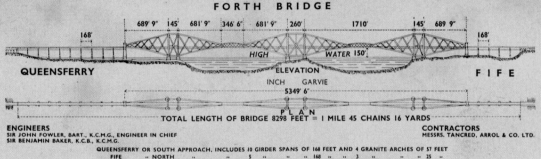

FORTH BRIDGE

689' 9" 145' 681' 9" 346' 6" 681' 9" 260' 1710' 145' 689' 9"

168' 168'

HIGH   WATER 150'

QUEENSFERRY   **ELEVATION**   F I F E

INCH   GARVIE

5349' 6"

P L A N

TOTAL LENGTH OF BRIDGE 8298 FEET = 1 MILE 45 CHAINS 16 YARDS

ENGINEERS
SIR JOHN FOWLER, BART., K.C.M.G., ENGINEER IN CHIEF
SIR BENJAMIN BAKER, K.C.B., K.C.M.G.

CONTRACTORS
MESSRS. TANCRED, ARROL & CO. LTD.

QUEENSFERRY OR SOUTH APPROACH, INCLUDES 10 GIRDER SPANS OF 168 FEET AND 4 GRANITE ARCHES OF 57 FEET
FIFE   „ NORTH   „   „ 5 „   „ „ 168 „ „ 3 „   „ „ 25 „

were proposed, including a tunnel, but they came to nothing. In 1878 Thomas Bouch started a suspension bridge, but the following year the collapse of the Tay Bridge, which he had also designed, put paid to his Forth Bridge project.

However, a crossing was urgently needed to provide the last link in the chain of railways up the east coast of Scotland, and within eighteen months Benjamin Baker and John Fowler produced a new design using cantilevers. The Forth Bridge was the first cantilever bridge in Britain, and the first in Europe to be built of steel. The contractor was William Arrol, who was also building the new Tay Bridge. Work started in 1883, and even while it was under construction the bridge attracted visitors from all over the world. It cost £2.5 million to build, and when it opened in 1890 the bridge was described as the eighth wonder of the world.

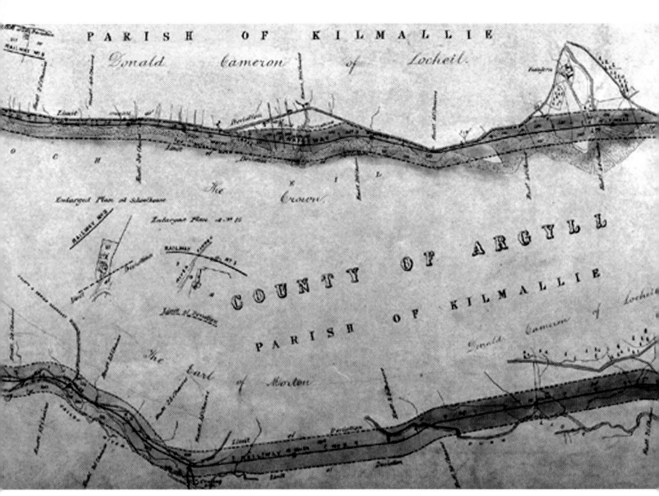

83. West Highland Railway, 1888, by Simpson & Wilson
(RHP 47781. British Railways copyright).

The West Highland line passed through some of the most remote areas of Scotland and went where no roads did. The object of the line was to link the Western Isles, Fort William and Lochaber with the south. Before the railway was built, the mail and newspapers did not arrive in Fort William until late in the afternoon, and anyone who wished to catch a train had to travel by coach fifty miles north-east to Kingussie to do so. Plans for a route through the west Highlands had been considered in the railway mania of the 1840s, but it was not until concern was being expressed over the state of the Highlands in the 1880s that the project came to fruition. Like roads and canals earlier, the speedy transport connections that a railway provided were seen as the answer to all the area's ills: 'At present there is great destitution in some parts of the West Highlands, but there is none near where there is a railway. Destitution flies away from within a considerable distance of a railway.'[14]

The route from the Clyde up Loch Long to the north end of Loch Lomond and Bridge of Orchy was impressive enough in terms of scenery, but in crossing

Rannoch Moor the railway reached new heights in drama. This stretch of the line ran through thirty miles of country devoid of population. In January 1889 a survey party who set out to walk across the moor almost perished – an object lesson in the hostility of the landscape through which they proposed to build a railway. Construction started in 1889 and the contractors offered to pay the fares of destitute Highlanders to encourage them to work on the line. Two years later 5,000 men were employed on the route. The engineering problems presented by Rannoch Moor were solved by floating the line across the bog on a carpet of turf and brushwood.

The railway opened in 1894 and did wonders for the tourist industry of Fort William. The route also encouraged shooting and stalking on the estates through which it passed, and a special chute for loading deer carcasses was built at Rannoch. In 1901 an extension to Mallaig opened, allowing the railway to realise one of the main reasons for its existence – the linking of the Western Isles with the south of Scotland. This stretch of the line took passengers through some of the most magnificent scenery Scotland has to offer. As well as assisting the fishing industry by providing a speedy route to southern markets, the extension fostered tourism in the islands.

The plan shows the route to the west of Fort William with the names of landowners through whose property the line passed. The West Highland Railway was a boon to many estate owners: for example, the earl of Breadalbane negotiated free first-class passes for himself and his factor in return for a water supply from his land.[15] At least one impoverished laird was quite open in his view of the railway as a cash cow: 'There is no doubt but all the Lairds about here whether friends or foes will in time follow our disinterested example and get as much out of the Railway Company as they possibly can! I only wish there were a dozen more Railways running through this poverty stricken part of the country.'[16]

84a & b. (*Overleaf*) **Steamer excursions on the Clyde, 1907**
(BR/TT(S) 3/2/6. British Railways).

Railways provided the general public with the first real opportunity for leisure travel, and Scotland's tourist industry grew rapidly as a result. Railway companies built hotels all over Scotland, offering a high standard of accommodation to travellers. Several companies also ran steamers which provided links with the islands, as well as tours for longer holidays and day trips. Going 'doon the watter' became a very popular pastime, particularly at the Glasgow Fair.

The Glasgow and South Western Railway Company offered a variety of destinations, including Arran, Loch Lomond, Ayr, Rothesay and Dunoon. The coming of the railway and the related steamer services resulted in the rapid growth of settlements such as Dunoon and Rothesay from seaside villages into full-blown tourist resorts.

GLASGOW & SOUTH WESTERN
RAILWAY
STEAMERS
PROGRAMME
of Popular Excursions

DIRECT
ROUTE TO **CLYDE**
WATERING PLACES

July
1907
VIA GREENOCK · PRINCES · PIER
ARDROSSAN & FAIRLIE

JUPITER
Leaving Princes Pier.

DAVID COOPER, General Manager.

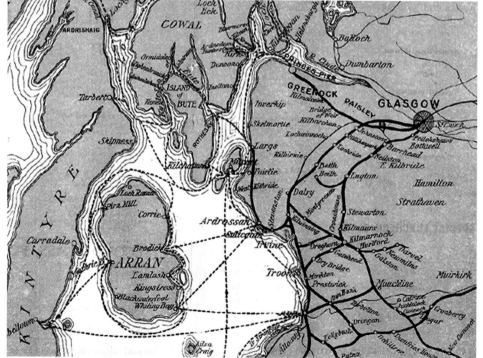

17

Land Settlement

New forests are rising up like mushrooms . . . Houses, roads, enclosures, cattle, men,
– every work of time and progress . . . are all extirpated by a word, in order that deer
may enjoy the luxury of solitude, and sportsmen monopolise the pleasures of the chase
. . . The deer forests and the people cannot co-exist. One or other of the two must
yield. Let the forests be increased in number . . . and the Gael will perish from their
native soil.[1]

ONE writer's comments on the growth of deer forests in the Highlands illustrate the
history of the area in the second half of the nineteenth century. Railways had opened
up the country not only to tourists but to sportsmen as well. The spread of railway
routes across the west Highlands coincided with the conversion of many Highland
sheep farms to deer forests. These were not woods, but areas of land used exclusively
for deer-stalking. Hunting, shooting and fishing had gone on in the Highlands for
centuries but, starting in the early nineteenth century, the sporting assets of estates
became marketable. When sheep farming became less profitable in the second half of
the century because of imports of wool and frozen mutton from abroad, many estates
changed their emphasis to sport. It became difficult to let sheep farms, but sporting
tenants were willing to pay high rents.

The extent of some of these sporting estates was vast: for example, the Park
deer forest on Lewis ran to 80,000 acres. The setting aside of so many acres exclusively
for leisure had serious consequences for crofters, who were desperately short of land.
Despite emigration, there was too little cultivated land in the Highlands and islands
available to support the numbers living there. Crofters had subdivided the small plots
that they had been cleared onto earlier in the century into tiny pieces of ground to
accommodate their families. By the 1880s conditions in some parts of the west
Highlands and islands were critical, with many crofter families trying to exist on as little
as half an acre of ground. Their congested townships were often surrounded by huge
sterile tracts used solely for sport. Some crofters had their common grazings taken away
and also had to contend with damage to their crops by deer.

When the Napier Commission visited Kintail, the local minister left them in
no doubt about how badly deer forests were affecting the Highlands: 'this land is wholly

withdrawn from contributing to the supply of any of the needs of the human race, except the need of Highland lairds for cash . . . The general effect on the Highlands of the forest system I believe to be in a very great degree an evil one . . . the land is being denuded of all capital, skill, industry, stock and everything that gives it true value.'[2]

Discontent at the land shortage boiled over in the early 1880s when the Highlands were hit by poor harvests, potato blight and a disastrous herring fishing. Conditions were almost as bad as during the potato famine of the 1840s. Faced with rising rents at a time when all their means of subsistence had failed, crofters followed the example of the Irish Land League and took to rent strikes and land seizures. The Crofters' War began in Skye and spread rapidly throughout the crofting counties. In 1883 the Highland Land Law Reform Association (later known as the Highland Land League) was formed, and the same year the government set up a commission of inquiry into conditions in the Highlands and islands under Lord Napier.

The Napier Commission toured the north and west hearing evidence from almost 800 witnesses, including crofters, factors and estate owners. Its recommendations included giving crofters security of tenure (previously they could be evicted at forty days' notice), increasing the size of crofts to an economic level and providing assistance to emigrate for those with little or no land. Landowners found these recommendations revolutionary, as they interfered in the relationship between landlord and tenant, while crofters felt they did not go far enough and opposed emigration as a solution to land shortages. The government felt the recommendations were impractical, and when they failed to act on the report unrest continued. Sheriffs and police trying to serve eviction notices were attacked and driven off, and the government sent in troops to restore order. The election of four crofting MPs in the 1885 general election ensured that the Highland land question remained at the top of the political agenda. The following year the Crofters Holdings (Scotland) Act was passed, giving crofters security of tenure and establishing the Crofters Commission to set fair rents.

The act, however, did nothing for cottars, those who had no land, of whom there were thousands in the Highlands and islands – Lewis alone had over 800 cottar families. This resulted in a further period of protest in the late 1880s, which started with a raid on the Park deer forest on Lewis. In response to the publicity the raid received, the government ordered an investigation into conditions for cottars on the island. The inquiry found widespread destitution and overcrowding: 'On all sides, not only among the cottars, but among the crofters also, we observed evidence of the deepest poverty and dejection; the soil is of the poorest quality; everywhere the potato crop is nearly consumed . . . crofts, already too small to maintain one individual, are made the home of three or even four families.'[3]

The government responded with initiatives targeted on the usual staples for Highland development – communications and fishing. They also attempted to deal with congestion by setting up assisted emigration schemes. None of these policies assuaged the land hunger that was by now endemic in the north and west. In 1895 a further Royal Commission on the Highlands and Islands (the Deer Forest Commission) reported, identifying 1.75 million acres of land which might be used for crofts or grazings. Two years later the Congested Districts Board was set up to increase the quantity of land available to crofters, pursue economic development through public works such as harbours, roads and bridges, and raise the standard of agriculture and housing.

With a restricted budget and no compulsory purchase powers, the Congested Districts Board was severely limited in its ability to buy and break up estates for redistribution. Continuing land raids in Barra, Vatersay and the Uists emphasised the inadequacy of the board's powers. In 1911 the Small Landholders (Scotland) Act replaced the Congested Districts Board with the Board of Agriculture for Scotland. The new board had stronger powers to carry out land settlement schemes but they still stopped short of compulsory purchase. Although the board was inundated with applications for crofts, its limited powers, combined with estate owners' reluctance to provide land, meant that in its first seven years the board was able to create only 502 new holdings.[4]

Protests ceased temporarily during the First World War, but the land question was given renewed impetus at the end of the conflict by returning servicemen demanding that the government keep its promise of land for volunteers. With desperate cottars seizing farms across the Highlands and islands, and the Russian Revolution fresh in their minds, in 1919 the government passed the Land Settlement (Scotland) Act, which finally gave the Board of Agriculture compulsory purchase powers. Progress was now more rapid and in the next seven years the board established 1,571 new crofts.[5] The Highland land-settlement programmes managed to restore some of the land that was the subject of clearances in the nineteenth century to the descendants of those who had been evicted.

The creation of new crofts and the security of tenure provided by the Crofters Act brought much-needed improvements in housing. Living conditions in the Highlands had been a cause for concern for some time. Most families lived in single-roomed black houses, which were often shared with livestock, people living at one end of the building and the beasts at the other. These were low buildings with thatched roofs, the poorest of which had walls of turf rather than stone. The houses had earthen floors and a fire in the middle of the room, from which the smoke escaped through the thatch. Damp was a constant problem and brought with it diseases such as tuberculosis. The Napier Commission was blunt in its assessment of the black house, though it was careful to report that not all such houses were hovels: 'These humble dwellings are by no means uniform in character; in the lowest stage there is the sordid hovel, in which horses, cows, and pigs occupy one end of the undivided tenement, while the human inhabitants, accompanied by dogs and poultry, are immersed in obscurity and dirt at the other.'[6]

Land settlement was not purely a Highland phenomenon. In the early twentieth century there was concern at the loss of the rural population to towns and cities, and the government hoped that the provision of smallholdings in the Lowlands would encourage people to stay on the land. The First World War emphasised the consequences of the drift away from rural life and had a major effect on land settlement policy. The conflict highlighted Britain's lack of self-sufficiency in food and the poor state of health of recruits from urban areas. It was felt that getting people out of towns and back to the land was the best way to encourage a healthy population and improve the food supply. In the 1920s and 1930s land settlement was also used to alleviate unemployment. Schemes were set up in the Lowlands providing holdings of a sufficient size to allow holders to practise market gardening, small-scale dairy farming, and poultry and pig rearing.

Land settlement projects had a marked effect on the appearance of the countryside. In the Highlands, the empty acres of sheep farms and deer forests were turned back into productive and inhabited crofting townships. In the Lowlands, large farms were broken up into small settlements. By the late 1930s land settlement projects accounted for 4.5 per cent of the Scottish countryside, and the Board of Agriculture had become a major landowner in the Highlands with almost half a million acres to its name.[7] These projects also resulted in a significant improvement in rural housing. New crofts and smallholdings required new houses, and the dwellings for these schemes were strictly controlled to improve standards of living in the countryside. Many of the houses built as a result of the land settlement policy are still inhabited today.

In the late twentieth century an era of radical change in land ownership in the Highlands started when the Assynt Crofters managed to buy out the estate of North Assynt in Sutherland. Since their achievement in 1993, several other Highland communities have purchased the estates on which they live. One aim of these acquisitions of land by communities is to reverse the trend of depopulation which has long blighted the Highlands.

85. (*Opposite*) **Deer forests in Scotland, 1891** (RHP 6576).

Deer-stalking grew rapidly in popularity during the nineteenth century, encouraged by the royal family's adoption of the Highlands in the 1840s. Owning or renting a sporting estate became fashionable among both the aristocracy and rich industrialists: 'Nowadays as soon as a man has amassed a fortune in any way his first desire seems to be to buy or hire a deer forest in Scotland and there to gather his friends to enjoy hospitality and sport.'[8]

Consequently the number of deer forests in Scotland doubled between 1873 and 1891. This map, which is taken from a sportsmen's and tourists' guide to Scotland, shows 124. By this time over 2.5 million acres of land in Scotland were devoted to deer-stalking.

86. Loch Rosque lodge, 1880 (RHP 3306).

As sporting rents could account for over half an estate's income, it was important to provide a good standard of accommodation for shooting tenants. New lodges were built throughout the Highlands, often, like this one, in the Scots baronial style. The development of estates for sport also involved building new roads and paths, which made many estates more accessible.

Loch Rosque is near Achnasheen in Ross-shire. It was owned by Sir Arthur Bignold MP. In 1880 he had the estate's 11,000 acres converted to a deer forest. He also planted 8 million trees on the property. During the twenty years he owned the estate, Sir Arthur increased the deer population from 0 to 2,000.[9] One sportsman praised him for his efforts with Loch Rosque and the two adjoining estates: 'The three properties are excellent examples of what can be done with deer in a short time, for when Mr Bignold first bought the property there was nearly as good a chance of meeting with a Red Indian as of coming across a red deer.'[10] As well as stalking and grouse shooting, the tenant also had fishing rights on the loch and on the river Bran. The lodge had twelve bedrooms and 'all modern requirements'.

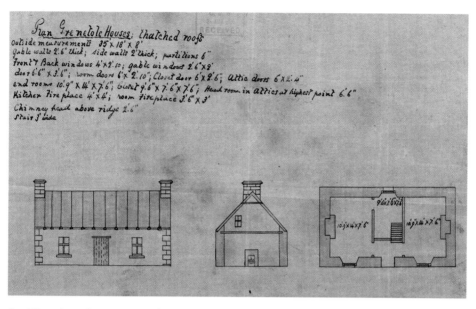

87. Housing for new crofts at Grenitote, 1898 (AF 42/379).

This was one of the areas of North Uist cleared in 1849 (see Fig. 55). A few years later Lord Macdonald sold the estate to the Campbell Orde family. By the 1880s the shortage of land for crofting on North Uist had become acute. John Morrison, one of the crofters who had been evicted from Sollas in 1849, told the Napier Commission of the difficulties he and his neighbours had in trying to wrest a living from poor and desperately overcrowded land at Locheport: 'The inferiority of the soil of the place we live in, and its unsuitableness for human existence, is indescribable . . . We have laboured for the last thirty years and our crofts will not yield us today as much food on an average as will support our families for two months of the year . . . The place is overcrowded, there being thirty-four crofts, on which live forty families where formerly there were only three.'[11]

The Congested Districts Board brought the crofters of North Uist some hope. Sir Arthur Campbell Orde co-operated with the board in their first land-settlement scheme. In 1898 he agreed to divide the farms of Grenitote and Sollas into thirty-four crofts. The land that had been cleared for a sheep farm was returned to crofting again.

Plans for houses for the new crofts were submitted to the medical officer of health. He agreed that the house illustrated was suitable, 'taking into consideration the circumstances of the people and the climatic conditions'. The estimated cost of the house was £63, and the board provided loans of £50 to enable the crofters to build. This type of cottage was very different from old black houses criticised by the Napier Commission. The houses had two rooms downstairs measuring 14 feet by 10 feet 9 inches, with a ceiling height of 7½ feet, a fireplace, an attic and a thatched roof.

88. Gress smallholdings scheme, 1915 (RHP 44256/1. Crown copyright).

The Board of Agriculture's lack of compulsory purchase powers meant that unwilling landowners could hold up land-settlement schemes for years. This happened on Lewis, where the shortage of land for cottars was particularly serious. The First World War added to the islanders' sense of grievance. They felt they had provided a disproportionate number of men to the war effort, and wanted promises of land made during the conflict to be kept. They had considerable justification for their claims: the township of North Tolsta alone, with 77 crofts, had sent 210 men to the trenches.[12]

  The farms of Coll and Gress near Stornoway were owned by the millionaire soap-maker Lord Leverhulme. He was opposed to crofting, preferring large-scale development of the fishing industry to provide employment on the island. A scheme to divide the two farms had been proposed in 1913, but the government agreed to allow Leverhulme time to try out his plans for the island. Because of financial problems caused by the war, nothing came of his proposals. Even after the Board of Agriculture acquired compulsory purchase powers, Leverhulme continued to stall plans for the farms, claiming they were essential to Stornoway's milk supply.

In 1919 nearby cottars ran out of patience and occupied the farms, dismissing the landowner's employment plans as 'the jingling of his money bags'.[13] The farms were raided on several occasions before they were divided. Some of those who seized the farms in 1920 were ex-servicemen, who felt their desperate living conditions justified their actions:

> our action in taking possession of parts of the farms of Coll and Gress was dictated by dire necessity and not by any disregard for the law . . . we were squatting under revolting conditions in hovels situated on other men's crofts. Into one of these hovels, containing two apartments, no fewer than 25 people were crowded. Our families were suffering unspeakably, not only from insufficient accommodation, but also from want of milk and other food while hundreds of acres of good land were lying untilled at our doors . . . Long before the War, land was promised to us. During the early months of the War these promises were repeated.[14]

In 1922 the farms were finally settled. Between them, Coll and Gress provided eighty-eight new crofts.[15] The following year Leverhulme abandoned his plans for Lewis and left the island to concentrate his efforts on Harris. Ironically it is through him that Stornoway parish can claim the oldest community-owned estate in Scotland. In a startling about-turn, in view of his opposition to land reform, Lord Leverhulme donated his home, Lews Castle, and his 69,000 acre estate to the local community. Since then it has been run by the Stornoway Trust.

89a & b. Thorntonloch smallholdings scheme, 1922
(AF 83/1286. Crown copyright).

Thortonloch was one of three smallholding schemes set up in East Lothian after the First World War. The Board of Agriculture for Scotland bought the land in 1920 and proposed that a central farm of 150 acres should be set up employing five or six families, while the rest of the land was to be divided into small plots for disabled soldiers and larger holdings of about 50 acres: 'The situation of the cothouses and steading near the sea afford an excellent site for the settlement of disabled soldiers on small areas of land, and I think 10 or so of such holdings of say 5–10 acres might be settled at the steading. Their holdings could be devoted largely to poultry, fruit, pigs and the keep of a cow or two on the soiling system. The Central Farm would be able to buy and deal with the milk.'[16]

The plan shows 11 smallholdings of between 6 and 13 acres, and 14 larger

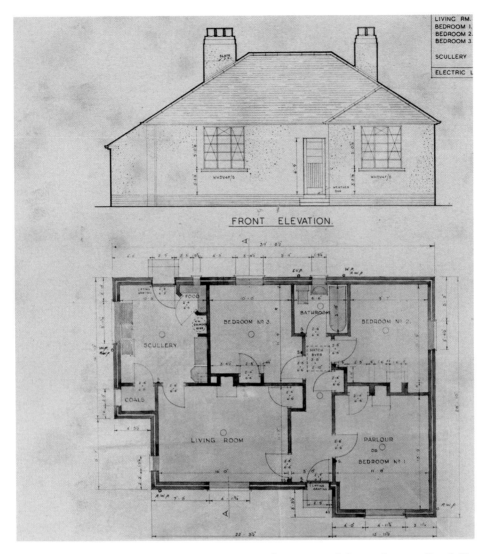

FRONT ELEVATION.

holdings ranging from 25 to almost 50 acres. The names of the settlers are listed. By 1927 there were 95 people living at Thorntonloch, along with 182 cattle, 95 sheep, 126 pigs and over 2,200 domestic fowls. Those in the smaller holdings included two railway porters, a gamekeeper, a joiner and a wireless operator. The most successful smallholder devoted all his efforts to dairying and sold the milk locally. Thorntonloch was a great success, but by 1930 concern was being expressed about the effect on the environment of some of the smaller tenants' revenue-raising activities. Several were renting out plots for summer homes and selling holidaymakers produce from their smallholdings. The summer homes in question were converted buses.

The houses at Thorntonloch are typical of those built on smallholdings all over the Lowlands. Many bungalows like this can still be seen today with their plots of land around them. They provided a good standard of living, with three bedrooms, living room, kitchen, bathroom and electricity.

18

Water, Electricity and Forestry

Thus, year by year, the old face of the Highlands is changing, as dam, tunnel, aqueduct, pipe-line and power-station appear in one glen after another, while, side by side with these, distribution lines change living conditions in isolated crofts and farms.[1]

MAJOR landscape change continued into the twentieth century as the development of water and electricity services and the spread of modern forestry all affected the appearance of the countryside. The bringing of sewerage services and safe water-supplies to cities and towns was one of the greatest achievements of Victorian municipal effort. Previously, in urban areas, water was only available from town wells, which were often polluted by sewage. As Scotland's towns and cities expanded during the nineteenth century, water supplies could not keep pace with demand, and public health problems worsened. Cholera epidemics in the 1830s, 1840s and 1850s brought home forcefully the necessity for clean water. However, because water supplies were often in the hands of private companies, municipal schemes to improve matters were regularly opposed by commercial interests, and it was not until the later decades of the nineteenth century that many areas had clean water.

Glasgow was the first city in Britain to provide its inhabitants with a comprehensive water supply. In 1859 water from Loch Katrine was brought fifty miles through tunnels and aqueducts to the city at a cost of £1.5 million to the public purse, bringing immeasurable benefits to the citizens' health. Aberdeen obtained a proper water supply in 1862 and Dundee in 1875. Edinburgh had water from reservoirs in the Pentlands from the late 1840s. In 1869 the Edinburgh Water Trust was formed, and set up schemes to improve supplies by bringing water from the Moorfoot hills to the city. Other towns and cities followed and, during the rest of the nineteenth century and into the twentieth, lochs were turned into reservoirs, and aqueducts and pipelines built to carry water from the countryside to the towns.

In the twentieth century the advent of electricity left indelible marks on the face of the country with pylons, power stations, reservoirs and dams. Hydro-electricity in particular had major effects, altering the appearance of many glens. The first hydro-electric scheme in Scotland was a pilot project which opened at Greenock in 1885. Five years later the monks of Fort Augustus Abbey were the first to use hydro-electric power in the Highlands and over the next few years a handful of small, mostly privately financed schemes followed. The first major projects were built to provide power to the aluminium industry. Aluminium production required a substantial electricity supply, and so the British Aluminium Company sought a cheap method of producing the fuel. It opened its first hydro-electric power station at Foyers, on Loch Ness, in 1896. By 1909 it had built an aluminium works at Kinlochleven, powered by water from the Blackwater lochs.

In 1928 the Grampian Electricity Supply Company started work on the first large-scale hydro scheme in the Highlands to provide a domestic supply of electricity. It was based on Lochs Ericht and Rannoch. In the south of Scotland the Falls of Clyde were utilised in a project which opened in 1926, and five years later the Galloway Water Power Company started work on a scheme using Loch Doon and Clatteringshaws Loch. This was the last hydro project to get approval for some time. Although the construction of these huge works provided employment for thousands of men during the Depression of the 1920s and 1930s, there was great concern over the effects such projects were having on the countryside, and by 1930 proposals for further hydro-electric schemes were being refused. Opposition came from diverse groups: miners and pit owners concerned at a rival energy source; landowners trying to protect the amenity value of their estates, and in particular their fishings; and a variety of people opposed to the building of dams, power stations and pipelines in some of Scotland's wildest areas.

However, Tom Johnston, secretary of state for Scotland from 1941 to 1945, believed hydro-electricity was essential for the regeneration of the Highlands, and in 1943 the North of Scotland Hydro-Electric Board was set up. Its Gaelic motto, *Neart nan Gleann* (power of the glens), reflected the ambitious aims of the new body. Like earlier initiatives with roads, canals and railways, politicians saw hydro-power as both a means of job creation and a vehicle to boost the Highland economy and infrastructure. By the end of 1947 parliament had approved twelve projects, though the level of opposition was such that some had to go through public inquiries before they could proceed. The three largest projects approved were the Loch Sloy scheme in Dunbartonshire, the Tummel–Garry scheme in Perthshire and the Affric–Mullardoch scheme in Inverness-shire. The hydro projects in the Highlands were some of Europe's largest post-war construction schemes and attracted workmen from Poland, Ukraine and Ireland, as well as ex-servicemen from Scotland.

There is no doubt that the Hydro Board did much for the Highlands. At the height of construction work during the 1950s and 1960s the board was the main employer in the area. By 1961 it was supplying 400,000 homes with electricity – an achievement which did much to raise the standard of living in the Highlands and in doing so gave a boost to the tourist industry. It is thanks to the 400 miles of roads built or improved for these projects that today we have easy access to some of the remotest glens in Scotland. The board took its social and environmental duties very seriously. Fish ladders were provided at dams to ensure fish stocks did not suffer. The board took considerable care to ensure its power stations blended in with the environment as much as possible. It used local stone to face the buildings and in doing so was responsible for rejuvenating quarrying in the Highlands. New, high quality housing was provided for employees, built in appropriate local styles.

Despite the huge benefits they brought to the area, hydro-electric schemes altered the Highland landscape irrevocably. They required storage reservoirs, dams, tunnels, pipelines and power stations, and levels of lochs had to be raised. Much of this construction took place in highly scenic areas. We need only think of the very visible pipelines stretching 600 feet down the flank of Ben Nevis to Fort William, or the pylons striding along beside the A9 at Drumochter to realise how intrusive these developments must have appeared when first built. In the 1930s one writer confessed to being 'numb with horror' at the effects of the Tummel scheme in Perthshire, but accepted the price to be paid for progress with considerable pragmatism:

> We ought to be pleased now that the hydro-electric enterprises and their frightful works are realities. It had to be, and one accepts the spoliation of the country about Loch Tummel and Loch Rannoch as the toll levied for progress. But it is difficult, when you have come down through the singing Tummel birchwoods, not to feel numb with horror at your first sight of the black pipes that lance the loins of Schiehallion. Nor is that all. There is the power-station across the river, dwarfing the pitiful span of the Wade bridge below it, a glass-fronted hulk galvanised by the soundless shudder of its transformers. Far and wide over the hills deploy armies of pylons.[2]

Ironically some hydro-electric works, such as Loch Faskally at Pitlochry, are now tourist attractions. The Cruachan project, which involved building a power station inside the mountain, now attracts some 50,000 visitors a year to its visitor centre. In recent decades electricity supply has continued to cause controversy, with the advent of nuclear power and the arrival of wind farms. In addition to objections to the effect wind farms have on the landscape, there is now heated debate over the necessity for pylons fifty metres tall to carry this 'green' energy from the Highlands to the south. The conflict identified in the 1950s of 'reconciling our need for power with our need for a landscape fit to live in' continues in the present day.[3]

Large-scale commercial forestry has also played a large part in recent landscape development. In the twentieth century new fast-growing forests were planted to meet the needs of industry. The huge demands of railway building in the nineteenth century, followed by the First World War, took a severe toll on the country's forests. As timber could not be imported during the war, native forests were ravaged in an attempt to keep up with demand. About 149,000 acres of trees were felled in Scotland during the conflict. It was clear that private forestry could not provide timber supplies at such a level, and a national forestry policy was developed. In 1919 the Forestry Commission was set up to improve Britain's timber supplies.

The government also saw forestry as a means of retaining the rural population on the land. Like hydro-power, forestry was regarded as a way of providing jobs for returning servicemen and, during the Depression, for the unemployed. Like the Hydro Board, the Forestry Commission fostered the growth of villages by providing housing for its employees. It went one step farther and set up new forest villages: the first was established at Ae in Dumfriesshire in 1947. Altogether the commission started forty such villages, many built with two-storey, semi-detached timber houses, which still survive today. The Forestry Commission realised the importance of woodlands for leisure purposes at an early stage and opened its first forest park at Argdarten in Argyll in 1936.

From the 1950s huge planting programmes took place to try to restore the ravages caused by the Second World War when 230,000 acres of trees were felled in Scotland. As well as planting its own forests, the commission worked with landowners to encourage private forestry. In 1947 a dedication scheme was introduced under which landowners received financial assistance to plant areas which they had to dedicate to forestry in perpetuity. Such programmes resulted in Scotland's forest cover quadrupling during the twentieth century,[4] and by the new millennium it stood at 17 per cent of the landscape. However, this huge expansion in Scotland's forests resulted in the planting of non-native species to achieve a quicker return on investment. By the 1980s this was causing concern among environmentalists, as was the related problem of using forestry to gain tax breaks. The spread of Sitka spruce, lodge-pole pine and Douglas fir over landscapes such as the Flow Country of Caithness provoked particular criticism. The tax loophole was closed in 1988, and in the same year the Forestry Commission started giving grants to landowners to restore native woodlands.

The drive to encourage Scotland's native trees has recently speeded up with the start of the Millennium Forest for Scotland project. This scheme gives lottery support for the creation and restoration of native woods. It encourages community-managed woodlands, where commercial, leisure and cultural concerns coexist to the benefit of local people and visitors. Many of Scotland's forests now serve the same purpose as the woods planted by eighteenth-century improvers – 'a source of pleasure to the eye and spirit'.[5]

90. (*Overleaf*) **Dundee water supply area, 1834, by William Blackadder** (RHP 5024/1: courtesy of the countess of Airlie).

Until 1845 water in Dundee came from the town's wells and was supplied to the public by water caddies at a price of around a penny per bucket. The quality of the water was poor: the supply from one well was described as 'nothing but a very purified sewage'.[6]

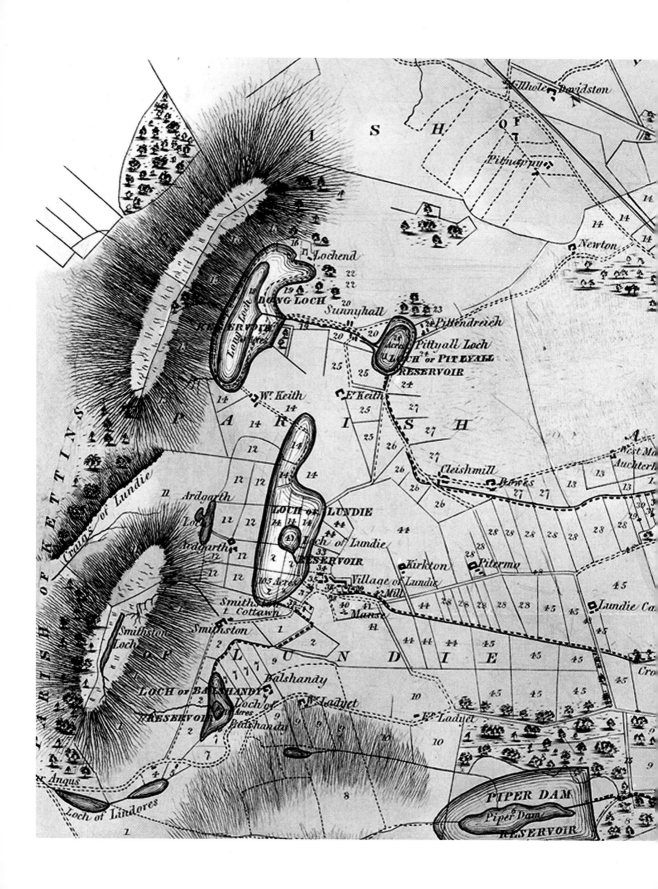

In 1831 the town council started attempts to bring clean water to the city. It commissioned a report, of which this plan is a part, which recommended utilising several lochs in a large catchment area and building dams and aqueducts. Unfortunately for the citizens, the scheme was opposed by a private company and the Guildry and Nine Trades of Dundee, who were not in favour of people receiving from the council what they regarded as a saleable commodity. It took the council forty years to achieve its goal.

In 1845 a private company gained the right to supply water to the city. It used the Monikie and Crombie reservoirs, but the supply proved inadequate. In 1869 the council took over the works and drew up a scheme to improve matters. A proper supply was ensured when the Loch of Lintrathen was brought into use and its level raised by twenty feet. The plan indicates the scale of a municipal water works: numerous lochs were to be changed into reservoirs, and miles of aqueducts and piping built.

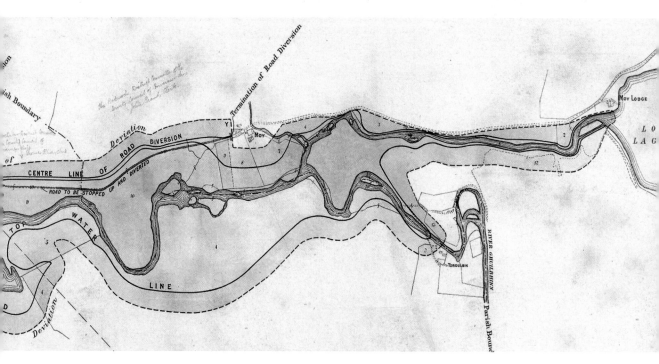

91. Lochaber hydro-electric scheme, 1917 (RHP 47683).

In order to meet the post-war demand for aluminium, the British Aluminium Company decided to build another factory, near Fort William. Supplying the new works involved a huge hydro-electric project to harness the waters of Loch Laggan and Loch Treig. At the time it was the biggest engineering project ever seen in the Highlands.

It had a catchment area of about 350 square miles and involved diverting the waters of the Spey. Construction work included building a dam 700 feet long across Loch Laggan, altering the line of the railway, raising the level of Loch Treig by 35 feet, and constructing a 15-mile-long tunnel to carry water to the pipeline at Inverlochy. The tunnel was the longest in the world at the time. Three thousand men worked on the project, which started in 1924 and took until 1943 to complete, at a cost of £5 million.

92. Mullardoch dam, 2004 (R.M Gibson).

Proposals to use Loch Affric for a hydro project were turned down by parliament in 1928 and 1941 because of concerns over damaging one of Scotland's most scenic areas. The original scheme planned to create one huge area of water by raising the level of Loch Beinn a'Mheahoin to join that of Loch Affric.

A new project was approved in 1947 which left the pristine beauty of Loch Affric untouched by using Loch Mullardoch in the neighbouring glen instead. Its level was raised by over 100 feet and a tunnel built to connect it to Loch Beinn a'Mheahoin. The Mullardoch dam is 160 feet high and still dominates the north end of the glen.

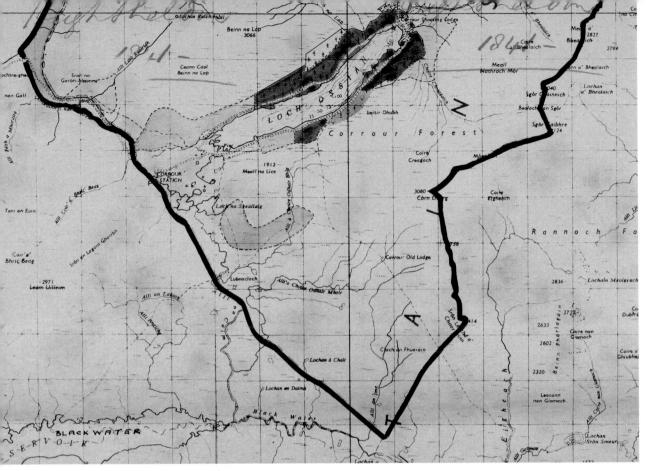

93. Corrour forest, 1965 (FC7/60. Annotations Crown copyright. Underlying mapping reproduced by permission of Ordnance Survey on behalf of HMSO. © Crown copyright 2007. All rights reserved. Licence number 100041103).

Corrour estate lies north-west of Loch Rannoch in some of the most inhospitable landscape in Scotland, which was made accessible only by the West Highland Railway. The 50,000 acres of moorland had been used purely for deer-stalking until Sir John Stirling Maxwell bought the estate in 1891 and started to plant trees.

The peaty soil and high altitude (1,200–1,700 feet) were a challenge. After a visit to Belgium in 1906 Sir John started a new method known as turf planting, where seedlings were put into turfs cut from drains in the peat. He planted Scots pine to start with, but it did not do well, and by experimenting he found he had more success with Sitka spruce, Norway spruce and European larch. He created a forest around Loch Ossian and a garden around the lodge out of a bare wilderness.

Sir John's pioneering work led others, including the Forestry Commission, to plant trees in upland areas. By the late 1940s almost 450 acres of Corrour had been planted. These and a further 223 acres above Loch Ossian became part of the Forestry Commission's dedication scheme in the 1950s. The map shows the extent of the planting in the mid-1960s.

Notes

Introduction

1 E 769/79/74.
2 Cockburn, H., *Circuit Journeys* (Edinburgh, 1975), 268.

1. The Old Face of the Country

1 Stuart, J., ed., 'Monymusk Papers', *Miscellany of the Spalding Club* II (Aberdeen, 1842), 96–7.
2 Devine, T., *The Transformation of Rural Scotland: Social Change and the Agrarian Economy, 1660–1815* (Edinburgh, 1994), 7–8; Whyte, I.D., *Scotland before the Industrial Revolution: An Economic & Social History, c.1050–c.1750* (Harlow, 1995), 161; Dodgshon, R.A., *Land and Society in Early Scotland* (Oxford, 1981), 215–17.
3 *OSA* XII, 287.
4 RHP1423, surveyor's notes.
5 *OSA* XIV, 386.

2. Homes and Gardens

1 *General Report* II, 45.
2 Reid, J., *The Scots Gard'ner*, ed. A. Hope (Edinburgh, 1988), 26.
3 Stewart, M.C.H., 'Lord Mar's Gardens at Alloa, *c.*1700–1732', in Frew, J., and Jones, D., eds, *Aspects of Scottish Classicism: The House and Its Formal Setting, 1690–1750* (St Andrews, 1989), 33.
4 GD 124/15/440.
5 GD 124/15/897/2.
6 Mackay, J., *A Journey through Scotland* (London, 1723), 182.
7 Cited in McKean, C., *The Scottish Chateau: The Country Houses of Renaissance Scotland* (Stroud, 2001), 247.
8 Neill, P., *On Scottish Gardens* (Edinburgh, 1813), 165.
9 Crawford, G. and Semple, W., *A History of the Shire of Renfrew* (1782; reprinted Paisley, 1991), 59–60.
10 *NSA* VII, 506.
11 Mitchell, A. and Clark, J., eds, *Geographical Collections relating to Scotland Made by W. Macfarlane*, 3 vols, SHS 51–3 (Edinburgh, 1906–8), III, 202.
12 Defoe, D., *A Tour through the Whole Island of Great Britain*, ed. P.N. Furbank, W.R. Owens and A.J. Coulson (London, 1991), 324.

3. Division of Commonty

1 *OSA* XX, 65.
2 Cited in Handley, J.E., *Scottish Farming in the Eighteenth Century* (London, 1953), 172.

3 *APS*, 1647, ch. 430.
4 *APS*, 1695, ch. 69.
5 Statistics calculated from Adams, I.H., *Directory of Former Scottish Commonties*, Scottish Record Society, new series, 2 (Edinburgh, 1971).
6 Ibid., 1, 7.
7 Callander, R.F., *The History of Common Land in Scotland* (2003), 8.
8 SC 67/83/1.

4. *Enclosure*

1 *OSA* XI, 152.
2 *APS*, 1661, ch. 284.
3 *APS*, 1685, ch. 49.
4 *APS*, 1695, ch. 36.
5 Whyte, I., *Agriculture and Society in Seventeenth Century Scotland* (Edinburgh, 1979), 12.
6 Aitchison, P. and Cassell, A., *The Lowland Clearances: Scotland's Silent Revolution, 1760–1830* (East Linton, 2003), 39.
7 GD 18/1483a/2.
8 E 777/23/3.

5. *Drainage*

1 *General Report* II, 366.
2 Fenton, A., *Scottish Country Life* (East Linton, 1999), 22; *NSA* V.
3 GD 1/1008.

6. *Tree Planting*

1 *General Report* II, 279.
2 Smout, T.C., *People and Woods in Scotland* (Edinburgh 2003), 41.
3 Fowler, J., *Landscapes and Lives: The Scottish Forest through the Ages* (Edinburgh 2002), 63.
4 Millar, A.H., ed., *The Glamis Book of Record, 1684–1689*, SHS (Edinburgh, 1890), 33.
5 *General Report* II, 209.
6 Anderson, M.L., *A History of Scottish Forestry* (London, 1967), II, 560.
7 *OSA* XIII, 135.
8 GD 44/43/35/25.
9 GD 44/51/393; GD 44/51/392.
10 Grant, E., of Rothiemurchus, *Memoirs of a Highland Lady* (Edinburgh, 1988), 269–75.
11 *OSA* XIII, 135; *NSA* XIII, 52, Elginshire section.
12 E 783/84/1, p. 8.
13 Steven, H.M. and Carlisle, A., *The Native Pinewoods of Scotland* (Edinburgh, 1959), 139.
14 GD 307/15, p. 18.
15 Cox, E.H.M., *A History of Gardening in Scotland* (London, 1935), 116; Rogers, B.M.H., 'Andrew Heron and his Kinsfolk', *Transactions of the Dumfriesshire and Galloway Natural History and Antiquarian Society*, 3rd series, 5 (1916–18), 215.

7. *Rural Housing*

1 *General Report* I, 127.
2 Pennant, T., *A Tour in Scotland* (London, 1774; reprinted Perth, 1979), 117.
3 Fenton, A. and Walker, B., *The Rural Architecture of Scotland* (Edinburgh, 1981), 73.

4   *General Report* I, 130, plate II.
5   GD 51/16/29/1 and GD 51/16/40.
6   GD 51/16/29/4; RHP 6768; RHP 6770.
7   GD 224/508/1/4.
8   GD 305/2/1854, f. 372v.

8. *The New Face of the Country*

1   *OSA* XVIII, 388.
2   Gray, *Scottish Emigration*, 149.
3   Lynch, M., *The Oxford Companion to Scottish History* (Oxford, 2001), 322.
4   Gray, M., 'The Social Impact of Agrarian Change in the Rural Lowlands', in Devine, T.M., and
    Mitchison, R., eds, *People and Society in Scotland* I, *1760–1830* (Edinburgh, 1988), 60.
5   Symon, J., *Scottish Farming, Past and Present* (Edinburgh, 1959), 139.
6   *OSA* XV, 338.
7   Cited in Handley, *Scottish Farming*, 123.
8   Fenton, *Scottish Country Life*, 41.
9   Devine, T.M., *The Scottish Nation, 1700–2000* (London, 1999), 153.
10 C. Whatley, cited in Aitchison and Cassell, *Lowland Clearances*, 62.
11 *OSA* V, 315.
12 Defoe, *Tour*, 339.
13 GD 40/2/xiv, no. 2; printed in Laing, D., ed., *Correspondence of Sir Robert Kerr, First Earl of Ancram
    and His Son William, Third Earl of Lothian*, 2 vols (Edinburgh, 1875), I, 69, 71.
14 GD 65/213.
15 Smout, T.C., 'The Improvers and the Scottish Environment: Soils, Bogs and Woods', in Devine,
    T.M., and Young, J.R., eds, *Eighteenth Century Scotland: New Perspectives* (East Linton, 1999), 215.
16 *General Report* I, 552–3.

9. *Mining*

1   *General Report* I, 65.
2   Smout, 'Improvers', 125.
3   Hamilton, H., *The Industrial Revolution in Scotland* (Oxford, 1932), 168.
4   Whatley, Christopher A., 'New light on Nef's numbers: coal mining and the first phase of
    Scottish industrialisation, *c.*1700–1830', in Cummings, A.J.G. and Devine, T.M., eds, *Industry,
    Business and Society in Scotland since 1700* (Edinburgh, *c.*1994), 7.
5   *General Report* III, addenda, 6, cited in Hamilton, *Industrial Revolution*, 172.
6   Butt, J., *The Industrial Archaeology of Scotland* (Newton Abbot, 1967), 90.
7   *Scots Magazine* 33 (1771), 24–6.
8   Donnachie, I., 'A Tour of the Works: Early Scottish Industry Observed, 1790–1825', in
    Cummings, A.J.G., and Devine, T.M., eds, *Industry, Business and Society in Scotland since 1707*
    (Edinburgh, 1994), 51.
9   CB 27/3, p. 278.
10 Bremner, D., *The Industries of Scotland* (1868; reprinted Newton Abbott, 1969), 6.

10. *Rural Industries*

1   *NSA* X, 1239.
2   *OSA* IX, 428, cited in Butt, J., and Ponting, K., eds, *Scottish Textile History* (Aberdeen, 1987), 20.
3   *General Report* III, 312, 317.
4   Devine, T.M., 'Urbanisation', in Devine, T.M., and Mitchison, R., eds, *People and Society in*

Scotland I, *1760–1830* (Edinburgh, 1988), 36.

5 Cooke, A. and Donnachie, I., 'Aspects of Industrialisation before 1850', in Cooke, A., Donnachie, I., MacSween, A. and Whatley, C., eds, *Modern Scottish History, 1707 to the Present* I, *Transformation of Scotland, 1707–1850* (East Linton, 1998), 151.

6 *Resolutions of the Landed Interest of Scotland respecting the Distillery* (Edinburgh, 1786), cited in Turnock, D., *The Historical Geography of Scotland since 1707* (Cambridge, 1982), 103.

7 Brown, D.J., 'The Politicians, the Revenue Men and the Scots Distilleries, 1780–1800', *Review of Scottish Culture* 12 (1999–2000), 50.

8 Bremner, *Industries of Scotland*, 446.

9 Irving, J., *Book of Dumbartonshire: A History of the County, Burghs, Parishes, and Lands, Memoirs of Families, and Notices of Industries Carried on in the Lennox District,* (Edinburgh and London, 1879), vol. I, 357.

10 Bremner, *Industries of Scotland*, 158.

11 Campbell, R.H., *Scotland since 1707: The Rise of an Industrial Society* (Oxford, 1965), 103.

12 *OSA* XVIII, 395.

13 Brown, 'Politicians', 53.

11. *The Highland Landscape*

1 E 705/8/3, pp. 7–8.

2 Cited in Devine, T.M., 'A Conservative People? Scottish Gaeldom in the Age of Improvement', in Devine, T.M., and Young, J.R., eds, *Eighteenth Century Scotland: New Perspectives* (East Linton, 1999), 232.

3 Macinnes, A.I., 'Scottish Gaeldom: The First Phase of Clearance', in Devine, T.M., and Mitchison, R., eds, *People and Society in Scotland* I, *1760–1830* (Edinburgh, 1988), 74.

4 Devine, T.M., *Exploring the Scottish Past: Themes in the History of Scottish Society* (East Linton, 1995), 138.

5 Mitchell, J., *Reminiscences of My Life in the Highlands*, 2 vols (1883; reprinted Newton Abbot, 1971), II, 114.

6 AF 49/6, cited in Devine, T.M., 'Highland Landowners and the Highland Potato Famine', in Leneman, Leah, ed., *Perspectives in Scottish Social History: Essays in Honour of Rosalind Mitchison* (Aberdeen, 1988), 161.

7 Devine, 'Highland Landowners', 173.

8 Mitchell, *Reminiscences*, II, 110.

9 E 746/78/2.

10 Pennant, *Tour*, 83, 92.

11 GD 112/11/1/31.

12 RH 2/8/24, pp. 131–2.

13 GD 403/1, p. 16.

14 Hunter, J., *The Making of the Crofting Community* (Edinburgh, 2000), 68.

15 McKay, M., ed., *The Rev Dr John Walker's Report on the Hebrides of 1764 and 1771* (Edinburgh, 1980), 65.

16 Bangor-Jones, M., 'Sheep Farming in Sutherland in the Eighteenth Century', *Agricultural History Review* 50, part II (2002), 197.

17 Devine, T.M., 'The Emergence of the New Elite in the Western Highland and Islands, 1800–1860', in Devine, T.M., ed., *Improvement and Enlightenment* (Edinburgh, 1989), 125.

12. *Planned Villages*

1 Sinclair, Sir John, *General View of the Agriculture of the Northern Counties and Islands of Scotland* (London, 1795), xvii–xviii.

2   Turnock, *Historical Geography*, 91.

3   Lockhart, D., 'Nuts and Bolts: Planned Villages, A Review of Sources', *Scottish Local History* 39 (1997), 34–8.

4   Pennant, *Tour*, 145.

5   GD 44/32/7/40.

6   GD 44/52/40, p. 180.

7   E 777/243, p. 5.

8   E 729/8, p. 55.

9   GD 345/1014/53; GD 345/1015/17.

10 E 728/17/2.

11 GD 9/4/371.

13. *Roads and Bridges*

1   GD 124/15/1569, memorial of James Erskine of Grange, 1746.

2   Irvine, A., *An Inquiry into the Causes and Effects of Emigration from the Highlands of Scotland* (Edinburgh, 1802), 118.

3   *Report from the Committee on the Survey of the Coasts and Central Highlands of Scotland* (London, 1803), 4.

4   Smout, T.C. and Wood, S., eds, *Scottish Voices, 1745–1960* (London, 1990), 268.

5   Sinclair, *Agriculture*, 211.

6   Pennant, *Tour*, 92.

7   Highland Roads and Bridges, 15th Report (London, 1829), Appendix B, 8–9.

8   E 783/84/1, pp. 4, 10, printed in Scottish Record Office, *Reports on the Annexed Estates, 1755–1769*, ed. V. Wills (Edinburgh, 1973), 31, 33.

9   PA 2/20, p. 394: Register of the Privy Council, VI, 498.

10 Rolt, L.T.C., *Thomas Telford* (London, 1958), 73.

11 E 728/30/2.

12 Bishop Forbes' journal, CH 12/18/1, p. 799: printed in Craven, J.B., *Journal of Episcopal Visitations of Right Rev. Robert Forbes* (London, 1886).

13 Mitchell, *Reminiscences*, II, 128.

14 GD 44/42/4/27.

15 GD 44/42/3/10.

16 GD 44/42/4/27.

17 *OSA* V, 506.

18 Glen, A., *The Cairngorm Gateway* (Dalkeith, 2002), 67, 90.

14. *Harbours and Lighthouses*

1   E 728/33/2(1).

2   Lenman, B., *From Esk to Tweed: Harbours, Ships and Men of the East Coast of Scotland* (Glasgow, 1975), 23.

3   Morris, R. and Morris, F., *Scottish Harbours* (Sandy, 1983), 4.

4   E 728/33/2(1).

5   GD 9/3, pp. 639–40.

6   GD 9/376/2.

7   Ibid.

8   GD 45/16/1432.

15. *Canals*

1 *General Report* III, 346.
2 NG 1/7/6, p. 109.
3 E 728/32/1.
4 *Report on the Survey of the Coasts*, 46.
5 BR/FCN 1/2.
6 GD 24/1/566/6.
7 Ransom, P.J.G., *Scotland's Inland Waterways* (Edinburgh, 1999), 29.
8 MT 1/209.
9 MT 1/156.
10 MT 1/156/17.
11 *Inverness Courier* report: MT 1/209.
12 BR/CRI/1/8, p. 321.

16. *Railways*

1 Cockburn, *Circuit Journeys*, 268.
2 Scottish Record Office, *The Scottish Railway Story* (Edinburgh, 1992), 8.
3 Campbell, *Scotland since 1707*, 93.
4 Cited in Gordon, A., *To Move with the Times: The Story of Transport and Travel in Scotland* (Aberdeen, 1988), 141.
5 GD 18/3733.
6 GD 416/85.
7 GD 135/2393.
8 BR/LIB(S) 18/14, pp. 31–2.
9 Cited in Robertson, C.J.A., *The Origins of the Scottish Railway System* (Edinburgh, 1983), 24.
10 BR/CJR 1/1.
11 Jackson, D., *Royal Deeside's Railway: Aberdeen to Ballater* (Perth, 1999), 5.
12 Farr, A.D., *The Royal Deeside Line* (Newton Abbot, 1968).
13 CS 249/3281.
14 Cited in Thomas, J., *The West Highland Railway* (Newton Abbot, 1984), 35.
15 GD 112/53/116.
16 GD 176/2737/23.

17. *Land Settlement*

1 Somers, R., *Letters from the Highlands in the Famine of 1846* (Inverness, 1985), 25–6.
2 Napier Commission Report, 435–7.
3 *Report on the Condition of the Cottar Population in the Lews*, Parliamentary Papers (1888), vol. 80, 5.
4 Hunter, *Crofting Community*, 263.
5 Cameron, E., *Land for the People? The British Government and the Scottish Highlands, c.1880–1925* (East Linton, 1996), 188.
6 Napier Commission Report, 49.
7 Leneman, L., *Fit for Heroes? Land Settlement in Scotland after World War I* (Aberdeen, 1989), 51.
8 Crealock, H.H., *Deer Stalking in the Highlands of Scotland* (London, 1892; reprinted 1981), 2.
9 McConnochie, A.I., *The Deer and Deer Forests of Scotland: Historical, Descriptive, Sporting* (London, 1923), 194, 260.
10 Grimble, A., *The Deer Forests of Scotland* (London, 1896), 219.
11 Napier Commission Evidence I, 797.
12 AF 83/363.

13 AF 67/328.
14 AF 67/254.
15 AF 67/331.
16 AF 3/1286, no. 102

18. *Water, Electricity and Forestry*

1 *Scottish Industrial Guide* (Edinburgh, 1956), 129.
2 Nairne, C., 'Perthshire', in Scott Moncrieff, G., ed., *Scottish Country* (London, 1935), 242–3.
3 Crowe, S., *The Landscape of Power* (London, 1958), 10.
4 Smout, T.C., *Nature Contested* (Edinburgh, 2000), 59.
5 Forestry Commission annual report 1960, cited in Turnock, *Historical Geography*, 257.
6 Cited in Jones, S.J., ed., *Dundee and District* (Dundee, 1968), 279.

Bibliography

Manuscript sources in the National Archives of Scotland

AD 14	Lord Advocate's Department: precognitions
AF 42	Department of Agriculture and Fisheries: Congested Districts Board files
AF 66	Land settlement files
AF 67	Crofting files
AF 83	Estate management files
BR/CCL	Caledonian Canal
BR/CJR	Clydesdale Junction Railway
BR/CRL	Crinan Canal
BR/FCN	Forth and Clyde Canal
BR/FOR	Forth Bridge
BR/LIB	British Rail library
BR/TT(S)	British Rail timetables (Scotland)
BR/WEH	West Highland Railway
CB	Coal Board
CH12/18	Bishop Robert Forbes
CR	Crown Estates Commissioners
CS	Court of Session
E 700–788	Forfeited Estates papers
FC	Forestry Commission
GD 1/1008	The Moss of Kincardine
GD 1/321	Census of inhabitants of Blair Drummond Moss
GD 3	Earls of Eglinton
GD 9	British Fisheries Society
GD 16	Earls of Airlie
GD 18	Clerk of Penicuik
GD 24	Stirling Home Drummond Murray of Abercairney
GD 30	Shairp of Houston
GD 40	Marquesses of Lothian
GD 44	Dukes of Richmond and Gordon
GD 45	Marquess of Dalhousie
GD 51	Viscounts Melville
GD 58	Carron Company
GD 105	Duff of Fetteresso
GD 112	Breadalbane papers
GD 124	Mar and Kellie
GD 128	Fraser Mackintosh
GD 129	Ross of Balnagown
GD 135	Earls of Stair

GD 176	Mackintosh of Mackintosh
GD 219	Murray of Murraythwaite
GD 224	Dukes of Buccleuch and Queensberry
GD 225	Hay of Leith Hall
GD 236	Dundas and Wilson CS
GD 237	Tods, Murray and Jamieson WS
GD 244	Skene, Edwards and Garson WS
GD 247	Brodies WS
GD 248	Earls of Seafield
GD 298	Weir and MacGregor WS
GD 305	Earls of Cromartie
GD 307	Heron of Heron and Kiroughtree
GD 345	Grant of Monymusk
GD 403	Mackenzie collection (Skye and North Uist)
GD 416	Captain Sir Samuel Brown, RN
JC	High Court of Justiciary
MT	Ministry of Transport
NG	Board of Trustees for Fisheries, Manufactures and Improvements in Scotland
PA	Parliament (to 1707)
RH 2/8/24	Report by John Blackadder on agriculture of Skye and North Uist
RHP	Register House plans
RT	Register of Entails
SC 2	Banff Sheriff Court
SC 67	Stirling Sheriff Court

Printed sources

GENERAL

Checkland, S. and Checkland, O., *Industry and Ethos: Scotland, 1832–1914* (London, 1984)

Cooke, A., Donnachie, I., MacSween, A. and Whatley, C., eds, *Modern Scottish History 1707 to the Present*, 5 vols (East Linton, 1998)

Devine, T.M., *The Scottish Nation, 1700–2000* (London, 1999)

—— and Mitchison, R., eds, *People and Society in Scotland* I, *1760–1830* (Edinburgh, 1988)

—— and Young, J.R., eds, *Eighteenth Century Scotland: New Perspectives* (East Linton, 1999)

Ferguson, W., *Scotland 1689 to the Present* (Edinburgh, 1868)

Fraser, W.H. and Morris, R.J., *People & Society in Scotland* II, *1830–1914* (Edinburgh, 1990)

Gray, M., *Scots on the Move: Scots Migrants, 1750–1914* (Edinburgh, 1990)

——, 'Scottish Emigration: The Social Impact of Agrarian Change in the Rural Lowlands, 1775–1875', *Perspectives in American History* 7 (1973), 95–174

Houston, R.A. and Knox, W.W.J., eds, *The New Penguin History of Scotland from the Earliest Times to the Present Day* (London, 2001)

Lenman, B., *Integration and Enlightenment: Scotland, 1746–1832* (Edinburgh, 1992)

Lynch, M., *The Oxford Companion to Scottish History* (Oxford, 2001)

New Statistical Account of Scotland 15 vols (Edinburgh, 1845)

Sinclair, Sir John, *Statistical Account of Scotland* 21 vols (Edinburgh, 1791–1799).

Smout, T.C., *A History of the Scottish People* (London, 1969)

——, 'Scottish Landowners and Economic Growth', *Scottish Journal of Political Economy* 11 (1964), 218–34

—— and Wood, S., eds, *Scottish Voices, 1745–1960* (London, 1990)

——, *Nature Contested* (Edinburgh, 2000)

Whatley, C.A., *Scottish Society, 1700–1830: Beyond Jacobitism, Towards Industrialisation* (Manchester, 2000)

HISTORICAL GEOGRAPHY

Adams, I.H., *Agrarian Landscape Terms: A Glossary for Historical Geography* (London, 1976)
Caird, J.B., 'The Making of the Scottish Rural Landscape', *SGM* 80 (1964), 72–80
Dodgshon, R.A., *Land and Society in Early Scotland* (Oxford, 1981)
Kay, G., 'The Landscape of Improvement: A Case Study of Agricultural Change in North East Scotland', *SGM* 78, no. 2 (1962), 100–11
Lebon, J.H.G., 'The Face of the Countryside in Central Ayrshire during the Eighteenth and Nineteenth Centuries', *SGM* 62, no. 1 (1946), 7–15
——, 'The Process of Enclosure in the Western Lowlands', *SGM* 62, no. 3 (1946), 100–10
Millman, R.N., *The Making of the Scottish Landscape* (London, 1975)
Mitchell, A. and Clark, J., eds, *Geographical Collections relating to Scotland Made by W. Macfarlane*, 3 vols, SHS 51–3 (Edinburgh, 1906–8)
Morrison, I., 'Evidence of Climatic Change before and during the Age of Agricultural Improvement', *Scottish Archives* 1 (1995), 3–16
Parry, M.L. and Slater, T.R., eds, *The Making of the Scottish Countryside* (London, 1980)
Turnock, D., *The Historical Geography of Scotland since 1707* (Cambridge, 1982)
Whyte, I.D., 'Before the Improvers: Agricultural and Landscape Change in Lowland Scotland c.1660–c.1750', *Scottish Archives* 1 (1995), 31–42
Whyte, I. and Whyte, K., *The Changing Scottish Landscape, 1500–1800* (London, 1991)
Whittington, G. and Whyte, I.D., *An Historical Geography of Scotland* (London, 1983)
Wickham-Jones, C.R., *The Landscape of Scotland: A Hidden History* (Stroud, 2001)

CARTOGRAPHY

Adams, I.H., 'Large Scale Manuscript Plans in Scotland', *Journal of the Society of Archivists* 3 (1965–9), 286–90
——, 'The Land Surveyor and his Influence on the Scottish Rural Landscape', *SGM* 84 (1968), 248–55
——, *Papers on Peter May, Land Surveyor, 1749–1793*, SHS, 4th series, 15 (Edinburgh, 1979)
Geddes, A., 'The Changing Landscape of the Lothians, 1600–1800, as Revealed by Old Estate Plans', *SGM* 54 (1938), 129–43
International Conference on the History of Cartography, *The Mapping of Scotland* (Edinburgh, 1971)
MacLeod, F., ed., *Togail Tir. Marking Time: The Mapping of the Western Isles* (Stornoway, 1989)
Moore, J.N., *The Mapping of Scotland: A Guide to the Literature of Scottish Cartography prior to the Ordnance Survey* (Aberdeen, 1983)
Royal Scottish Geographical Society, *The Early Maps of Scotland*, 2 vols (Edinburgh, 1973, 1983)
Scottish Record Office, *Descriptive List of Plans in the Scottish Record Office*, ed. I.H. Adams, 4 vols (Edinburgh, 1966–74 [vols 1–3], 1988 [vol. 4])
Third, B.M.W., 'The Significance of Scottish Estate Plans and their Associated Documents', *Scottish Studies* 1 (1957), 39–64
——, 'The Changing Landscape and Social Structure in the Scottish Lowlands as Revealed by Eighteenth Century Estate Plans', *SGM* 71 (1955), 83–93

TOURS OF SCOTLAND

Cockburn, H., *Circuit Journeys* (Edinburgh, 1975)
Defoe, D., *A Tour through the Whole Island of Great Britain*, ed. P.N. Furbank, W.R. Owens and A.J. Coulson (London, 1991)
Mackay, J., *A Journey through Scotland* (London, 1723)
McKay, M., ed., *The Rev Dr John Walker's Report on the Hebrides of 1764 and 1771* (Edinburgh, 1980)
Pennant, T., *A Tour in Scotland* (London, 1774; reprinted Perth, 1979)

Buxbaum, T., *Scottish Garden Buildings: From Food to Folly* (Edinburgh, 1989)

Campbell, R.H., *Carron Company* (Edinburgh, 1961)

Clackmannanshire Field Studies Society and Friends of Alloa Tower, *Alloa Tower and the Erskines of Mar* (Alloa, 1996)

Cockburn-Hood, T.H., *The Rutherfords of that Ilk* (Edinburgh, 1884)

Connachan-Holmes, J.R.A., *Country Houses of Scotland* (Colonsay, 1995)

Countryside Commission for Scotland, *Inventory of Gardens and Designed Landscapes in Scotland* (Perth, 1983)

Cox, E.H.M., *A History of Gardening in Scotland* (London, 1935)

Crawford, G. and Robertson, G., *A General Description of the Shire of Renfrew* (Paisley, 1818)

Crawford, G. and Semple, W., *A History of the Shire of Renfrew* (1782; reprinted Paisley, 1991)

Cummings, A.J.G., 'The Business Affairs of an Eighteenth Century Lowland Laird: Sir Archibald Grant of Monymusk, 1696–1778', in Devine, T.M., ed., *Scottish Elites* (Edinburgh, 1994)

Dingwall, C., *Researching Historic Gardens in Scotland: A Guide to Information Sources* (Perth, 1995)

Dunbar, J.G., *The Historic Architecture of Scotland* (London, 1966)

Erskine, S., *The Earl of Mar's Legacies to Scotland and to His Son, Lord Erskine, 1722–1729*, SHS, 1st series, 36 (Edinburgh, 1896), 139–257

Eyre-Todd, G. and Guy, W., *The Princess Louise Scottish Hospital* (1917)

Fraser, W., *Memorials of the Montgomeries, Earls of Eglinton* (Edinburgh, 1859)

Gifford, J., *The Buildings of Scotland: Dumfries and Galloway* (London, 1996)

Glendinning, M., MacInnes, R. and MacKechnie, A., *A History of Scottish Architecture from the Renaissance to the Present Day* (Edinburgh, 1996)

Gow, I. and Rowan, R., eds, *Scottish Country Houses, 1600–1914* (Edinburgh, 1995)

Grant, I.D., 'Landlords and Land Management in North-Eastern Scotland, 1750–1850', PhD thesis, University of Edinburgh, 1978

Gray, J.M., *Memoirs of the Life of Sir John Clerk of Penicuik*, SHS 13 (Edinburgh, 1892)

Hamilton, H., *Selections from the Monymusk Papers, 1713–1755*, SHS, 3rd series, 39 (Edinburgh, 1945)

Holloway, J. and Errington, L., *The Discovery of Scotland* (Edinburgh, 1978)

Horn, B.L.H., 'Domestic Life of a Duke: Cosmo George, 3rd Duke of Gordon', PhD thesis, University of Edinburgh, 1977

Howard, D., *Scottish Architecture from the Reformation to the Restoration* (Edinburgh, 1995)

Hynd, N., 'Towards a Study of Gardening in Scotland', in Breeze, D., ed., *Studies in Scottish Antiquity* (Edinburgh, 1984)

Jamieson, F., *Drumlanrig Castle Gardens* (1996) Typescript in RCAHMS

Jeffrey, A., *The History and Antiquities of Roxburghshire and Adjacent Districts*, vol. 3 (Edinburgh, 1859)

Kyle and Carrick District Library and Museum Services, *Eglinton Tournament, 1839* (Ayr, 1992)

Laing, D., ed., *Correspondence of Sir Robert Kerr, First Earl of Ancram and His Son William, Third Earl of Lothian,* 2 vols (Edinburgh, 1875)

Little, G.A., ed., *Scotland's Gardens* (Edinburgh, 1981)

Macaulay, J., *The Classical Country House in Scotland, 1600–1800* (London, 1987)

Mackay, S., *Early Scottish Gardens: A Writer's Odyssey* (Edinburgh, 2001)

McKean, C., *The Scottish Chateau: The Country Houses of Renaissance Scotland* (Stroud, 2001)

Millar, A.H., *The Castles and Mansions of Renfrewshire and Buteshire* (Glasgow, 1889)

Murray, P, *Leith Hall* (Edinburgh, 1991)

Neill, P., *On Scottish Gardens* (Edinburgh, 1813)

Omond, G., *The Arniston Memoirs* (Edinburgh, 1887)

Reid, J., *The Scots Gard'ner*, ed. A. Hope (1683; reprinted Edinburgh, 1988)

Robertson, F.W., *Early Scottish Gardeners and their Plants, 1650–1750* (East Linton, 2000)

Royal Institute of Architects of Scotland, illustrated architectural guides to Scottish districts (Edinburgh, 1984 onwards)

Smout, T.C., 'The Erskines of Mar and the Development of Alloa, 1689–1825', *Scottish Studies* 7 (1963), 57–74

Stewart, M.C.H., 'Lord Mar's Plans, c.1700–1732', 2 vols, MLitt thesis, University of Glasgow, 1988

——, 'Lord Mar's Gardens at Alloa, c.1700–1732', in Frew, J., and Jones, D., eds, *Aspects of Scottish Classicism: The House and Its Formal Setting, 1690–1750* (St Andrews, 1989)

Strawhorn, J., *Ayrshire: The Story of a County* (Ayr, 1975)

——, *The History of Irvine* (Edinburgh, 1985)

Stuart, J., ed., 'Monymusk Papers', *Miscellany of the Spalding Club* II, 91–100 (Aberdeen, 1842)

Tait, A.A., *The Landscape Garden in Scotland, 1735–1835* (Edinburgh, 1980)

Tayler, A. and Tayler, H., *The Book of the Duffs* (Edinburgh, 1914)

Watson, J.W., *Morayshire Described* (Elgin, 1868)

AGRICULTURE

Adams, I.H., 'Division of Commonty in Scotland', PhD thesis, University of Edinburgh, 1967

——, *Directory of Former Scottish Commonties,* Scottish Record Society, new series, 2 (Edinburgh, 1971)

Aitchison, P. and Cassell, A., *The Lowland Clearances: Scotland's Silent Revolution, 1760–1830* (East Linton, 2003)

Brien, R.J., *The Shaping of Scotland: Eighteenth Century Patterns of Land Use and Settlement* (Aberdeen, 1989)

Cadell, H.M., *The Story of the Forth* (Glasgow, 1913)

Callander, R.F., *A Pattern of Landownership in Scotland* (Finzean, 1987)

——, *The History of Common Land in Scotland* (2003)

Campbell, R.H., 'The Scottish Improvers and the Course of Agrarian Change in the Eighteenth Century', in Cullen, L.M., and Smout, T.C., eds, *Comparative Aspects of Scottish & Irish Economic and Social History, 1600–1900* (Edinburgh, 1977)

Devine, T.M., *Lairds and Improvement in the Scotland of the Enlightenment* (Glasgow, 1978)

——, *Farm Servants and Labour in Lowland Scotland, 1770–1914* (Edinburgh, 1984)

——, *The Transformation of Rural Scotland: Social Change and the Agrarian Economy, 1660–1815* (Edinburgh, 1994)

Dodgshon, R.A., 'Farming in Roxburghshire and Berwickshire on the Eve of Improvement', *Scottish Historical Review* 54 (1975), 141–54

Fenton, A., *Scottish Country Life* (East Linton, 1999)

——, 'How did the Pre-Improvement Landscape and Society Work? Reconstructing the Past through its Material Culture', *Review of Scottish Culture* 15 (2002–3), 13–24

Gray, M., 'The Social Impact of Agrarian Change in the Rural Lowlands', in Devine, T.M., and Mitchison, R., eds, *People and Society in Scotland* I, *1760–1830* (Edinburgh, 1988)

Handley, J.E., *Scottish Farming in the Eighteenth Century* (London, 1953)

——, *The Agricultural Revolution in Scotland* (Glasgow, 1963)

Hood, A.N.L., 'Runrig on the Eve of the Agricultural Revolution in Scotland', *SGM* 90 (1974), 130–3

Knox, S., *The Making of the Shetland Landscape* (Edinburgh, 1985)

McKerracher, A., *Perthshire in History and Legend* (Edinburgh, 1988)

Megaw, B.R.S., 'Farming and Fishing Scenes on a Caithness Plan, 1771', *Scottish Studies* 6 (1962), 218–23

——, 'The Moss Houses of Kincardine, Perthshire, 1792', *Scottish Studies* 6 (1962), 87–93

Sinclair, J., ed., *General Report of the Agricultural State and Political Circumstances of Scotland* (Edinburgh, 1814)

Sinclair, J, *General View of the Agriculture of the Northern Counties and Islands of Scotland* (London, 1795)

Smith, B., *Touns and Tenants: Settlement and Society in Shetland, 1299–1899* (Lerwick, 2000)

Smout, T.C., 'Scottish Landowners and Economic Growth, 1650–1850', *Scottish Journal of Political Economy* 11 (1964), 218–34

——, 'The Improvers and the Scottish Environment: Soils, Bogs and Woods', in Devine, T.M., and
Young, J.R., eds, *Eighteenth Century Scotland: New Perspectives* (East Linton, 1999)

Sprott, G., *Farming*, Scotland's Past in Action (Edinburgh, 1995)

Symon, J., *Scottish Farming, Past and Present* (Edinburgh, 1959)

Transactions of the Society of Improvers of Agriculture in Scotland (Edinburgh, 1743)

Whittington, G., 'The Problem of Runrig', *SGM* 86 (1970), 69–73

Whyte, I., *Agriculture and Society in Seventeenth Century Scotland* (Edinburgh, 1979)

——, 'Rural Transformation and Lowland Society', in Cooke, A., Donnachie, I., MacSween, A. and
Whatley, C., eds, *Modern Scottish History, 1707 to the Present* I, *Transformation of Scotland, 1707–1850*
(East Linton, 1998)

Wight, A., *The Present State of Husbandry in Scotland* (Edinburgh, 1784)

FORESTRY

Anderson, M.L., *A History of Scottish Forestry* (London, 1967)

Dixon, G., 'Forestry in Strathspey in the 1760s', *Scottish Forestry* 30 (1976), 38–60

Fenton, A., 'The Currach in Scotland with Notes on the Floating of Timber', *Scottish Studies* 16 (1972),
61–81

Fowler, J., *Landscapes and Lives: The Scottish Forest Through the Ages* (Edinburgh, 2002)

Grant, E., *Abernethy Forest: Its People and Its Past* (Nethy Bridge, 1994)

Grant, E., of Rothiemurchus, *Memoirs of a Highland Lady* (Edinburgh, 1988)

Lindsay, J.M., 'Some Aspects of the Timber Supply in the Highlands', *Scottish Studies* 19 (1975), 39–53

Millar, A.H., ed., *The Glamis Book of Record, 1684–1689*, SHS (Edinburgh, 1890)

Nairne, D., 'Notes on Highland Woods, Ancient and Modern', *Transactions of the Gaelic Society of
Inverness* 17 (1890–91), 170–221

Rogers, B.M.H., 'Andrew Heron and his Kinsfolk', *Transactions of the Dumfriesshire and Galloway
Natural History and Antiquarian Society*, 3rd series, 5 (1916–18), 212–23

Smout, T.C., 'The History of the Rothiemurchus Woods in the Eighteenth Century', *Northern Scotland*
15 (1995), 19–31

——, *Scottish Woodland History* (Edinburgh, 1997)

——, *People and Woods in Scotland* (Edinburgh, 2003)

—— and Lambert, R.A., eds, *Rothiemurchus: Nature and People on a Highland Estate, 1500–200* (Dalkeith,
1999)

Steven, H.M. and Carlisle, A., *The Native Pinewoods of Scotland* (Edinburgh, 1959)

Stewart, M., *Loch Tay: Its Woods and Its People* (Scottish Native Woods, Aberfeldy, 2000)

RURAL HOUSING

Beaton, E., *Scotland's Traditional Houses: From Cottage to Tower-house* (Edinburgh, 1997)

Fenton, A. and Walker, B., *The Rural Architecture of Scotland* (Edinburgh, 1981)

Naismith, R.J., *Buildings of the Scottish Countryside* (London, 1989)

Whyte, I.D., 'Rural Housing in Lowland Scotland in the Seventeenth Century: The Evidence of Estate
Papers', *Scottish Studies* 19 (1975), 55–68

MINING AND RURAL INDUSTRIES

Bremner, D., *The Industries of Scotland* (1868; reprinted Newton Abbott, 1969)

Brown, D.J., 'The Politicians, the Revenue Men and the Scots Distilleries, 1780–1800', *Review of
Scottish Culture* 12 (1999–2000), 46–58

Butt, J., *The Industrial Archaeology of Scotland* (Newton Abbot, 1967)

——, 'The Scottish Cotton Industry during the Industrial Revolution, 1780–1840', in Cullen, L.M., and Smout, T.C., eds, *Comparative Aspects of Scottish & Irish Economic and Social History, 1600–1900* (Edinburgh, 1977)

—— and Ponting, K., eds, *Scottish Textile History* (Aberdeen, 1987)

Cadell, P.M., *The Iron Mills at Cramond* (Edinburgh, 1973)

Cameron, A., 'A Page from the Past: The Lead Mines at Strontian', *Transactions of the Gaelic Society of Inverness* 38 (1937–41), 444–52

Campbell, A.B., *The Lanarkshire Miners: a Social History of Their Trade Unions, 1775–1974* (Edinburgh, 1979)

Campbell, R.H., *Scotland since 1707: The Rise of an Industrial Society* (Oxford, 1965)

Cooke, A. and Donnachie, I., 'Aspects of Industrialisation before 1850', in Cooke, A., Donnachie, I., MacSween, A. and Whatley, C., eds, *Modern Scottish History, 1707 to the Present* I, *Transformation of Scotland, 1707–1850* (East Linton, 1998)

Craig, H.C., *The Scotch Whisky Industry Record* (Dumbarton, 1994)

Cummings, A.J.G. and Devine, T.M., eds, *Industry, Business and Society in Scotland since 1707* (Edinburgh, 1994)

Devine, T.M., 'Urbanisation', in Devine, T.M., and Mitchison, R., eds, *People and Society in Scotland* I, *1760–1830* (Edinburgh, 1988)

Dingwall, C., 'The Scots Mining Company's House, Leadhills', *Garden History Society Newsletter* 36 (1992), 11–12

Donnachie, I., 'A Tour of the Works: Early Scottish Industry Observed, 1790–1825', in Cummings, A.J.G., and Devine, T.M., eds, *Industry, Business and Society in Scotland since 1707* (Edinburgh, 1994)

Duckham, B.F., *A History of the Scottish Coal Industry* I, *1700–1815* (Newton Abbot, 1970)

Dumfriesshire and Galloway Natural History and Antiquarian Society, *Transactions*, 3rd series, 54, *Wanlockhead and Leadhills* (1979)

Durie, A.J., 'Saltoun Bleachfield, 1746–1773', *Transactions of the East Lothian Antiquarian and Field Naturalists' Society* 14 (1974), 49–74

——, 'The Scottish Linen Industry in the Eighteenth Century: Some Aspects of Expansion', in Cullen, L.M., and Smout, T.C., eds, *Comparative Aspects of Scottish & Irish Economic and Social History, 1600–1900* (Edinburgh, 1977)

——, *The Scottish Linen Industry in the Eighteenth Century* (Edinburgh, 1979)

Gauldie, E., *Spinning and Weaving*, Scotland's Past in Action (Edinburgh, 1995)

Halliday, R., *The Disappearing Scottish Colliery* (Edinburgh, 1990)

Hamilton, H., *The Industrial Revolution in Scotland* (Oxford, 1932)

Hay, G.D., and Stell, G., *Monuments of Industry: An Illustrated Historical Record* (Edinburgh, 1986)

Hutton, G., *Mining from Kirkintilloch to Clackmannan & Stirling to Slamannan* (Ochiltree, 2000)

Joseph Irving, *The Book of Dumbartonshire: A History of the County, Burghs, Parishes, and Lands, Memoirs of Families, and Notices of Industries Carried on in the Lennox District*, 3 vols (Edinburgh and London, 1879)

Lenman, B., *An Economic History of Modern Scotland* (London, 1977)

Macleod, D., *Dumbarton, Vale of Leven and Loch Lomond* (Dumbarton, 1883)

Megaw, B.R.S., 'Women Coal-Bearers in a Midlothian Mine: a Contemporary Drawing of 1786', *Scottish Studies* 10 (1966), 87–89

Moss, M.S., and Hume, J.R., *The Making of Scotch Whisky: A History of the Scotch Whisky Distilling Industry* (Edinburgh, 1981)

National Coal Board, Scottish Division, *A Short History of the Scottish Coal-mining Industry* (1958)

Nef, J., *The Rise of the British Coal Industry* (London, 1932)

Scottish Record Office, *The Coalminers* (Edinburgh, 1983)

Shaw, J., 'The New Rural Industries: Water Power and Textiles', in Parry, M.L., and Slater, T.R., eds, *The Making of the Scottish Countryside* (London, 1980)

——, *Water Power in Scotland, 1550–1870* (Edinburgh, 1984)

Smout, T.C., 'Lead-mining in Scotland, 1650–1850', in Payne, P.L., ed., *Studies in Scottish Business History* (London, 1967)

Wanlockhead Museum Trust, *All about Wanlockhead: A Brief History of Scotland's Highest Village* (Wanlockhead, 1989)

Whatley, C.A., *The Industrial Revolution in Scotland* (Cambridge, 1997)

Whatley, C.A. 'New light on Nef's numbers: coal mining and the first phase of Scottish industrialisation, c.1700–1830', in Cummings, A.J.G. and Devine, T.M.eds., *Industry, business and society in Scotland since 1700* (Edinburgh, c.1994), 2–23.

Whyte, I.D., *Scotland before the Industrial Revolution: An Economic & Social History c.1050–c.1750* (Harlow, 1995)

Wright, L., *Historical Sources for Central Scotland: The Coal Industry* (Stirling, 1978)

HIGHLANDS AND LAND SETTLEMENT

Bangor-Jones, M., 'Sheep Farming in Sutherland in the Eighteenth Century', *Agricultural History Review* 50, part II (2002), 181–202

Buchanan, J., *The Lewis Land Struggle: Na Gaisgich* (Stornoway, 1996)

Caird, J.B., 'Land Use in the Uists since 1800', *Proceedings of the Royal Society of Edinburgh* 77B (1979), 505–26

——, *Sollas, 1799–1999: A Short History* (Dundee University Press, 1999)

Cameron, A.D., *Go Listen to the Crofters: The Napier Commission and Crofting a Century Ago* (Stornoway, 1990)

Cameron, E., *Land for the People? The British Government and the Scottish Highlands, c.1880–1925* (East Linton, 1996)

——, 'The Scottish Highlands: From Congested District to Objective One', in Devine, T.M., and Finlay, R.J., eds, *Scotland in the 20th Century* (Edinburgh, 1996)

——, 'The Highlands since 1850', in Cooke, A., Donnachie, I., MacSween, A. and Whatley, C., eds, *Modern Scottish History, 1707 to the Present* II, *Modernisation of Scotland, 1850 to the Present* (East Linton, 1998)

Carrell, C. and MacLean, M., *As an Fhearann/From the Land: Clearance, Conflict and Crofting* (Edinburgh, 1986)

Christie, J., *The Lairds and Lands of Loch Tayside* (Aberfeldy, 1892)

Crealock, H.H., *Deer Stalking in the Highlands of Scotland* (London, 1892; reprinted 1981)

Devine, T.M., 'Highland Landowners and the Highland Potato Famine', in Leneman, L., ed., *Perspectives in Scottish Social History: Essays in honour of Rosalind Mitchison* (Aberdeen, 1988), 140–162.

——, 'The Emergence of the New Elite in the Western Highland and Islands, 1800–1860', in T.M. Devine ed., *Improvement and Enlightenment* (Edinburgh, 1989)

——, 'Social Responses to Agrarian "Improvement": The Highland and Lowland Clearances in Scotland', in Houston, R.A., and Whyte, I.D., eds, *Scottish Society, 1500–1800* (Cambridge, 1989)

——, *Clanship to Crofters War: The Social Transformation of the Scottish Highlands* (Manchester, 1994)

——, *Exploring the Scottish Past: Themes in the History of Scottish Society* (East Linton, 1995)

——, 'A Conservative People? Scottish Gaeldom in the Age of Improvement', in Devine, T.M., and Young, J.R., eds, *Eighteenth Century Scotland: New Perspectives* (East Linton, 1999)

Dodgshon, R.A., 'West Highland and Hebridean Settlement prior to Crofting and the Clearances: A Study in Stability or Change?', *Proceedings of the Society of Antiquaries of Scotland* 123 (1993), 419–38

——, *From Chiefs to Landlords: Social and Economic Change in the Western Highlands and Islands, c.1493–1820* (Edinburgh, 1998)

Gailey, R.A., 'Agrarian Improvement and the Development of Enclosure in the South-west Highlands of Scotland', *Scottish Historical Review* 42 (1963), 105–25

Gibson, R.M., *The Crofters* (Edinburgh, 1994)

Gillies, W.A., *In Famed Breadalbane* (Perth, 1938)

Glen, A., *The Cairngorm Gateway* (Dalkeith, 2002)

Gray, M., *The Highland Economy, 1750–1850* (Edinburgh, 1957)

Grimble, A., *The Deer Forests of Scotland* (London, 1896)

Hunter, J., 'Sheep and Deer: Highland Sheep Farming, 1850–1900', *Northern Scotland* 1, no. 2 (1973), 199–222

——, *The Making of the Crofting Community* (Edinburgh, 2000)

Leneman, L., *Fit for Heroes? Land Settlement in Scotland after World War I* (Aberdeen, 1989)

Macdonald, D., *Lewis: A History of the Island* (Edinburgh, 1978)

Macdonald, I.S., 'Alexander Macdonald of Glencoe: Insights into Early Highland Sheep Farming', *Review of Scottish Culture* 10 (1996–97), 55–66

Macinnes, A.I., 'Scottish Gaeldom: The First Phase of Clearance', in Devine, T.M., and Mitchison, R., eds, *People and Society in Scotland* I, *1760–1830* (Edinburgh, 1988)

——, *Clanship, Commerce and the House of Stuart, 1603–1788* (East Linton, 1996)

MacKay, D., 'The Congested Districts Boards of Ireland and Scotland', *Northern Scotland* 16 (1996), 141–73

MacPhail, I.M.M., *The Crofters' War* (Stornoway, 1989)

McArthur, M., *Survey of Lochtayside, 1769*, SHS, 3rd series, 27 (Edinburgh, 1936)

McCleery, A.M., 'The Role of the Highland Development Agency, with Particular Reference to the Work of the Congested Districts Board, 1897–1912', PhD thesis, University of Glasgow, 1984

McConnochie, A.I., *The Deer and Deer Forests of Scotland: Historical, Descriptive, Sporting* (London, 1923)

Mitchell, J., *Reminiscences of My Life in the Highlands*, 2 vols (1883; reprinted Newton Abbot, 1971)

Moisley, H.A., 'North Uist in 1799', SGM 77, no. 2 (1961), 89–92

O'Dell, A.C., and Walton, K., *The Highlands and Islands of Scotland* (Edinburgh, 1962)

Orr, W., *Deer Forests, Landlords and Crofters: The Western Highlands in Victorian and Edwardian Times* (Edinburgh, 1982)

Report of Her Majesty's Commissioners of Inquiry into the Condition of the Crofters and Cottars in the Highlands and Islands of Scotland, etc., Parliamentary Papers (1884) vol. 32

Evidence taken by Her Majesty's Commissioners of Inquiry into the Condition of the Crofters and Cottars in the Highlands and Islands of Scotland [Napier Commission], Parliamentary Papers (1884) vols 33–36.

Report on the Condition of the Cottar Population in the Lews, Parliamentary Papers (1888), vol. 80

Richards, E., *A History of the Highland Clearances: Agrarian Transformation and the Evictions, 1746–1886* (London, 1982)

——, *Patrick Sellar and the Highland Clearances* (Edinburgh, 1999)

Scottish Record Office, *Reports on the Annexed Estates, 1755–1769*, ed. V. Wills (Edinburgh, 1973)

Scottish Vernacular Buildings Working Group, proceedings of Uists Conference (privately printed, 1991)

Smith, A., *Jacobite Estates of the Forty-Five* (Edinburgh, 1982)

Somers, R., *Letters from the Highlands in the Famine of 1846* (Inverness, 1985)

Watson, J., 'The Rise and Development of the Sheep Industry in the Highlands', *Transactions of the Highland and Agricultural Society of Scotland* 45 (1932), 1–25

Willis, D., *The Story of Crofting in Scotland* (Edinburgh, 1991)

PLANNED VILLAGES

Dunbar, J.G., *The Historic Architecture of Scotland* (London, 1966)

Dunlop, J., *The British Fisheries Society, 1786–1893* (Edinburgh, 1978)

Gibson, R.M., *The '45 and After* (Edinburgh, 1995)

Gordon, G., *The Last Dukes of Gordon and the Consorts, 1743–1864* (Aberdeen, 1980)

Lockhart, D., 'The Planned Villages', in Parry, M.L., and Slater, T.L., eds, *The Making of the Scottish Countryside* (London, 1980)

——, 'Scottish Village Plans: a Preliminary Analysis', *SGM* 96, no. 3 (1980), 141–57

——, 'The Construction and Planning of New Urban Settlements in Scotland in the Eighteenth Century', in Màczak, A., and Smout, C., eds, *Gründung und Bedeutung kleinerer Städte im nördlichen Europa der frühen Neuzeit* (Wiesbaden, 1991)

——, 'Nuts and Bolts: Planned Villages, A Review of Sources', *Scottish Local History* 39 (1997), 34–8

Munro, J., *The Founding of Tobermory* (Coll, 1976)

Omand, D., ed., *The Moray Book* (Edinburgh, 1976)

Simpson, A. and Simpson, J., 'John Baxter, Architect, and the Patronage of the Fourth Duke of Gordon', *Bulletin of the Scottish Georgian Society* 2 (1973) 47–57.

Smout, T.C., 'The Landowner and the Planned Village in Scotland', in Phillipson, N., and Mitchison, R., eds, *Scotland in the Age of Improvement* (Edinburgh, 1970)

ROADS AND BRIDGES

Barron, J., *The Northern Highlands in the Nineteenth Century* (Inverness, 1903–13)

Calder, J.T., *History of Caithness* (Inverness, 1978)

Coleman, R. and Dennison, E.P., *Historic Dumbarton: The Archaeological Implications of Development* (East Linton, 1999)

Craven, J.B., *Journal of Episcopal Visitations of Right Rev. Robert Forbes* (London, 1886)

Gordon, A., *To Move with the Times: The Story of Transport and Travel in Scotland* (Aberdeen, 1988)

Grant, J.G., *Banffshire Roads during the First Half of the Eighteenth Century* (Banff, 1905)

Haldane, A.R.B., *New Ways Through the Glens* (Colonsay, 1995)

——, *The Drove Roads of Scotland* (Edinburgh, 1997)

Institution of Civil Engineers, *Thomas Telford*, bicentenary exhibition catalogue (London, 1957)

Irvine, A., *An Inquiry into the Causes and Effects of Emigration from the Highlands of Scotland* (Edinburgh, 1802)

Macleod, D., *Ancient Records of Dumbarton and Glasgow* (Dumbarton and Glasgow, 1896)

MacPhail, I.M.M., *Dumbarton Through the Centuries* (Dumbarton, 1972)

Miller, R., 'The Road North', *SGM* 83 (1967), 78–88

Mitchison, R., *Agricultural Sir John: The Life of Sir John Sinclair of Ulbster* (London, 1962)

Nelson, G., *Highland Bridges* (Aberdeen, 1990)

Report from the Committee on the Survey of the Coasts and Central Highlands of Scotland (London, 1803)

Reports of the Royal Commissioners for Highland Roads and Bridges, nos 1–49 (1804–1863)

Report of the Commissioners for Inquiring into Matters Relating to Public Roads in Scotland (Edinburgh, 1859)

Rolt, L.T.C., *Thomas Telford* (London, 1958)

Salmond, J.B., *Wade in Scotland* (Edinburgh, 1938)

Taylor, W., *The Military Roads in Scotland* (Colonsay, 1996)

Whetstone, A., *Scottish County Government in the 18th and 19th Centuries* (Edinburgh, 1981)

HARBOURS AND LIGHTHOUSES

Allardice, K. and Hood, E., *At Scotland's Edge* (Glasgow, 1986)

Coull, J.R., *The Sea Fisheries of Scotland: A Historical Geography* (Edinburgh, 1996)

Hume, J., *Harbour Lights in Scotland* (Edinburgh, 1997)

Lavery, B., *Maritime Scotland*, Historic Scotland (London, 2001)

Lenman, B., *From Esk to Tweed: Harbours, Ships and Men of the East Coast of Scotland* (Glasgow, 1975)

Miller, J., *Salt in the Blood: Scotland's Fishing Communities, Past and Present* (Edinburgh, 1999)

Morris, R. and Morris, F., *Scottish Harbours* (Sandy, 1983)

Munro, R.W., *Scottish Lighthouses* (Stornoway, 1979)

Skempton, A.W., ed., *John Smeaton FRS* (London, 1981)

CANALS

Allan, J.K., *Their is a Cannal* (Falkirk, 1977)
Cameron, A.D., *The Caledonian Canal* (Edinburgh, 1994)
Duff, D., *Queen Victoria's Highland Journals* (Exeter, 1990)
Hutton, G., *Scotland's Millennium Canals: The Survival and Revival of the Forth & Clyde and Union Canals* (Catrine, 2002)
Lindsay, J., *The Canals of Scotland* (Newton Abbot, 1968)
Ransom, P.J.G., *Scotland's Inland Waterways* (Edinburgh, 1999)
Ross, A., 'The Caledonian Canal and its Effects on the Highlands', *Transactions of the Gaelic Society of Inverness* 13 (1886–87), 313–35

RAILWAYS

'Deeside Line', *Railway Magazine*, January 1957, p. 3; February 1957, p. 92
Farr, A.D., *The Royal Deeside Line* (Newton Abbot, 1968)
Jackson, D., *Royal Deeside's Railway: Aberdeen to Ballater* (Perth, 1999)
Jones, K.G., *The 'Subbies': the Story of Aberdeen's Suburban Trains, 1887–1987* (Aberdeen, 1987)
Kirkpatrick, G., 'The Kilmarnock and Troon Railway', *Backtrack* 6, no. 1 (Jan–Feb 1992), 41–8
Mackay, S., *The Forth Bridge: A Picture History* (Edinburgh, 1990)
Paxton, R., *100 Years of the Forth Bridge* (London, 1990)
Robertson, C.J.A., *The Origins of the Scottish Railway System* (Edinburgh, 1983)
Scottish Record Office, *The Scottish Railway Story* (Edinburgh, 1992)
Smith, W.A.C. and Anderson, P., *An Illustrated History of Glasgow's Railways* (1993)
Thomas, J., *Regional History of the Railways of Great Britain* VI, *Scotland: The Lowlands and Borders* (Newton Abbot, 1984)
——, *The West Highland Railway* (Newton Abbot, 1984)
Wood, J.L., *Building Railways*, Scotland's Past in Action (Edinburgh, 1996)

WATER AND ELECTRICITY SUPPLY

Adams, I.H., *The Making of Urban Scotland* (London, 1978)
Birrell, J.F., *An Edinburgh Alphabet*, (Edinburgh, 1980)
Crowe, S., *The Landscape of Power* (London, 1958)
Ferguson, T., *The Dawn of Scottish Social Welfare* (Edinburgh, 1948)
Gibson, J.S., *The Thistle and the Crown: A History of the Scottish Office* (Edinburgh, 1985)
Gow, W., *The Swirl of the Pipes: A History of Water and Sewerage in Strathclyde* (Glasgow, 1996)
Hill, G., *Tunnel and Dam: the Story of the Galloway Hydros* (Glasgow, 1994)
Jones, S.J., ed., *Dundee and District* (Dundee, 1968)
Lea, K.J., 'Hydro-Electric Power Developments and the Landscape in the Highlands of Scotland', *SGM* 84 (1968), 239–47
Logan, J.C., 'Electricity Supply. Electrical Engineering and the Scottish Economy in the Inter-War Years', in Cummings, A.J.G., and Devine, T.M., eds, *Industry Business and Society in Scotland since 1700* (Edinburgh, 1994)
Nairne, C., 'Perthshire', in Scott Moncrieff, G., ed., *Scottish Country* (London, 1935)
Payne, P., *The Hydro* (Aberdeen, 1988)
Scottish Industrial Guide (Edinburgh, 1956)
Smith, A.M., Swinfen, D.B. and Whatley, C.A., *The Life and Times of Dundee* (Edinburgh, 1993)
Smout, T.C., *The Highlands and the Roots of Green Consciousness*, Scottish Natural Heritage Occasional Paper 1 (Perth, 1992)

Index

The Home Office Reimagined

The Home Office Reimagined

Spaces to Think, Reflect, Work, Dream, and Wonder

Oscar Riera Ojeda & James Moore McCown

RIZZOLI
NEW YORK

New York · Paris · London · Milan

Table of Contents

Introduction
"The Home Office and Its Splendid, Varied Roots"
James Moore McCown

James Moore McCown is a Boston-based architectural jour-
nalist who writes for numerous design publications including
Metropolis, Architect's Newspaper and *AD PRO Architectural Digest.* He has collaborated with Oscar Riera Ojeda on
several books including the Architecture in Detail series that
comprised four volumes: *Elements, Materials, Colors* and
Spaces. McCown studied journalism at Loyola University
New Orleans and holds an ALM (Master's Degree) in the
history of art and architecture from Harvard University, where
his thesis on modern Brazilian architecture received an Honorable Mention, Dean's Award, Best ALM Thesis (2007). He
lives in Newton, Massachusetts.

It's 1960. A confident man of 35 in a Brooks Brothers suit steps off a train at Grand Central Terminal in New York and makes his way through the new PanAm Building onto Park Avenue. It's a brisk fall day. After the lull of summer, there is a spring in New Yorkers' steps as they race to work. Our "junior executive," bedecked in a crisp white shirt with a thin blue silk tie, has just begun a family back in New Canaan, Connecticut, and is on a fast track at his job as a marketing director at a large real estate concern. He walks briskly up the steps of 277 Park and into one of the elevators, getting out at the 46th floor.

"Good morning, Mr. Sheldrake," comes the welcome from the receptionist as our hero returns the greeting, walks into his private office and hangs up his hat and coat. His first meeting begins at 9:30, so he begins to prepare. The economy is booming, the world is largely at peace and all is well at this mid-point of the American century.

This scenario has repeated itself uncounted millions of times. "Going to work" meant, well, going to work. You were the Man in the Grey Flannel Suit. You left the wife and kids back in Connecticut and got on the 7:45 to Grand Central. You returned home that evening—it all seemed divinely ordained that this paradigm would continue forever.

But that was then. This is now. Remote working and telecommuting in a home office, egged on by the COVID-19 pandemic, is now a firmly entrenched business concept practiced widely throughout the United States. This book deals in the jaunty and creative ways in which architects have responded to this trend, creating, as the subtitle says, "Pavilions, shacks and extensions for optimum inspiration and productivity."

What is the origin of the concept of "office"? It is a fairly recent invention. According to Brie Weiler Reynolds, "during Medieval times, most working-class English people lived in work-homes. The single-story, one-room houses were a combination of kitchen and spinning/weaving/dressmaking workshop, bedroom and dairy, dining room, butchery, tannery and byre."[1]

The Renaissance
The Renaissance was a turning point. Reynolds continues: "The Renaissance's focus on administration [led] to 'Offices' . . . a growing interest in keeping historical archives, administering state business and creating a centralized location for these activities led to some of the first administrative buildings. One of the most notable examples is the Uffizi [which literally means 'Offices'], built by the Medici family in Florence in 1581. This process required the administration, archives and a state court to come together in the same building."[2]

The mental shift during this time toward free thinking and education created a growing need for centralized learning in the form of schools. And the Industrial Revolution was just around the corner, bringing even more administrative oversight to the working world.

The Industrial Revolution
According to Reynolds, the Industrial Revolution "pull[ed] workers out of the house." She elaborates:

---

1 Brie Weiler Reynolds, *The Complete History of Working from Home,*
flexjobs.com/blog/post, accessed on September 16, 2022.
2 Ibid.

From upper to lower Victorian England was the site of the East India House, one of the first office buildings; New York's Grand Central Terminal epitomized the life of the modern commuter; a secretary greets a junior executive; women, especially, were deeply affected by the rise in office culture.

The industrial age birthed a new movement of skilled workers and set up a working-outside-the-home model that many employers still follow today . . . That model (the precursor of the 9-to-5 work schedule) meant working an inflexible schedule from an employer-provided environment, with employer-provided tools or equipment. The means of production were transferred from the work-home to the work-site . . . the first commercial spaces were hugely transformative, thanks largely to some new-fangled inventions: the telephone, the telegraph, widespread public electricity and the typewriter.[3]

No one was more deeply affected by all this than women: "Women, in particular, moved into a new realm of professionalism that took them beyond craft-based or domestic work. The job of secretary, still a leading position among so-called 'pink collar workers,' required trading off home for the office."[4]

The profession of architecture was of course indelibly affected by all of these changes. One of the first structures that we would now call an "office building" was the East India House, built in 1729 in London in a Georgian baroque style to the designs of Theodore Jacobsen.

At the height of the Victorian era, and at the zenith of Colonialism, the East India House was the nerve center of Britain's far-flung empire, with no place more important than India. What had begun as a trading company in the 1600s was by the mid-nineteenth century a humming bureaucracy overseeing virtually every detail of what was happening in Bombay, Dehli and Calcutta, to use the traditional names for those cities. Even though it was located in the heart of London, it was administering trade and business thousands of miles away, enriching Britain immeasurably with little benefit accruing to the locals.

As the decades passed, more and more "office buildings" were constructed in London, New York, Chicago and other major business centers. But it was left to legendary Chicago engineer William LeBaron Jenney to build the first office skyscraper, the Home Insurance Building, in 1885 at the corner of Adams and LaSalle Streets in the Windy City. It was ten stories high and had a revolutionary steel frame that allowed much greater height and stability without the greater weight of traditional masonry construction.[5]

It took less than half a century for the modest ten-story "skyscraper" in Chicago to evolve into the concrete and steel canyon of Park Avenue where our hero "junior executive" goes to work each morning.

3 Ibid.
4 Ibid.
5 History.com Editors, "Home Insurance Building," accessed on September 16, 2022.

Two movies, *The Man in the Grey Flannel Suit* and *The Apartment*, aptly pictured the stance of the office design in the heady 1950s and 1960s. Morgan Lovell discusses:

> The dawn of the 1950s brought with it further advances in constructions, with modern materials such as steel and glass. The smart, clinical architecture of the international modern movement was adopted as the new image of corporate business. With the widespread use of more advanced air-conditioning and fluorescent lighting, these new high-rise buildings had very little need for natural light or ventilation through opening windows. With these technological developments, the 1950s saw the corporate office become completely autonomous from the outside world—as well as allowing for wider, more open plan floors where workers could be placed virtually anywhere. This formula enjoyed worldwide influence.[6]

Later disparaged as "soulless glass boxes," there were actually early architectural triumphs that epitomized this era. Chief among these is Skidmore, Owings & Merrill's Lever House on Park Avenue in New York and Ludwig Mies van der Rohe's Seagram House, just across the street. Morgan Lovell continues the discussion:

> The Lever House's modernist image of efficiency and standardisation [*sic*] started a trend in the 1950s and 60s that saw a number of glass boxes spring up across the New York skyline, expressing the city's commercial and cultural dominance. These skyscrapers allowed for even more natural light to flood the wide office floors.[7]

The era following John F. Kennedy's assassination could be pinpointed as the beginnin of the social and sexual revolution of the 1960s. Standardized open plans in pristine glass edifices, whatever their visual appeal, started to lose steam in favor of the "Action Office," as promoted by the modernist furniture firm Herman Miller. The idea had its infancy in Germany in the 1950s with a concept known as *Bürolandschaft,* which translates literally as "office landscape." Morgan Lovell explains:

> Office Landscape consisted of free and open plans of furniture scattered in large, loose and undivided spaces with different environments. These were divided less rigidly, with creative use of partitions and plants, the natures of them often dictated by the type, and function of workers inhabiting them. For example, workers in creative fields (like advertising, or media) could be grouped loosely where they could easily interact more frequently, whereas

From upper to lower The Uffizi (meaning "office" in Italian) in Florence was another early administrative office, meant to manage the Medicis' vast holdings; the "glass and steel canyons" of Park Avenue in New York marked the quintessence of the office culture of the 1950s and onward.

---

6 Morgan Lovell, "The Evolution of Office Design, accessed on October 19, 2022.
7 Ibid.

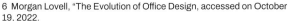

bureaucratic, corporate management staff were situated in more regimented, subdivided areas.[8]

The action office was perfectly in step with the freedom and "swinging" zeitgeist of the 1960s. Morgan Lovell:

> Out of the socio-democratic principles of *Büro-landschaft* rose Herman Miller's Action Office, a series of desks, workspaces, and other modular furniture designed to allow freedom of movement, and flexibility to work in a position suitable for the work being done. Action Office was developed and marketed under the supervision of George Nelson and Robert Propst, who were among the first designers to argue that office work was mental work and that mental effort was tied to a suitable working environment.[9]

But it was not to last. Bean counters, pencil pushers and various assorted other bureaucrats conspired to create the infamous cubicle farms of the 1980s. One final note from Morgan Lovell:

> The cubicle farm is the manifestation of the Action Office of the 1960s taken to its absolute dystopian limits. It was born out of the reality that human resource departments, supervisors, senior managers, and directors were less interested in the wellbeing of their workers than they were in their profitability. Robert Propst may have envisioned the Action Office as a means of freeing workers from the dull, mechanical nature of the open plan . . . office floor, but even he soon realized that 'not all organisations [*sic*] are intelligent and progressive. Lots are run by crass people who can take the same kind of equipment and create hellholes. They make little bitty cubicles and stuff people in them. Barren, rat-hole places.[10]

Out of these places, it is no wonder that very notion of going to the office every day might come under question. Change was afoot. Work-from-home guru Andy Stofferis explains:

> . . . in 1973, the oil embargo against the United States by OPEC due to its support of Israel in the Arab-Israeli War began. And it lasted until March 1974. The Oil Crisis of 1973 forced the United States to confront its significant dependence on foreign oil and the negative impact it can have on the economy.[11]

Suddenly, going to work was not just tedious and exhausting due to traffic, it was bad for the environment. Stofferis continues:

The events that occurred played a pivotal role in demonstrating to the wider public the potential pitfalls of depending on oil as the main source of energy. This then led to the expansion of the idea of reducing or eliminating the job commute that became an integral part of American life with the post-World War II creation of suburbs and expanded vehicle ownership. The concept of "telecommuting" was introduced into the world and it challenged the notion of commuting that was since ingrained into American Society. Specifically, we have Jack Nilles to thank for that. He is considered to be the father of telecommuting as he coined both terms *telecommuting* and *teleworking.* His cardinal work is a book in which he is the lead author is called *The Telecommunications-Transportation Tradeoff.* The book was published in 1973 and it recommended: "either the jobs of the employees must be redesigned so that they can still be self-contained at each individual location, or sufficiently sophisticated telecommunications and the information-storage system must be developed to allow the information transfer to occur as effectively as if the employees were centrally collocated."[12]

The introduction of the first personal computers changed everything, and added fuel to the telecommuting fire. Wrkfrce.com elaborates:

> In 1975, the first personal computers became available. However, it wasn't until 1977 that the PC became widely accessible, thanks to the Apple computer and Tandy Radio Shack TRS-80. In 1979, as the oil embargo continued, the work-from-home movement gained momentum when tech giant IBM moved five employees fully remote. In the 1980s, companies began experimenting more with remote work.
>
> 'If 10 percent of those who commute to work each weekday were to start working at home two days each week, this would reduce the volume of such travel by 4 percent,' Frank Schiff, the vice president and chief economist of the Committee for Economic Development wrote in a 1979 *Washington Post* article titled 'Working at Home Can Save Gasoline.'
>
> Only four years after IBM [which introduced its own PC in 1981] moved . . . five employees to remote work, about 2,000 of its staff were telecommuting; that made IBM one of the earliest major companies to move large numbers of employees to remote work. By 1987, about 1.5 million Americans were working remotely. Companies like J. C. Penney, American Express, and General Electric were all experimenting with telecommuting programs.[13]

---

8 Ibid.
9 Ibid.
10 Ibid.
11 https://andysto.com/the-history-of-remote-working/, accessed on October 22, 2022.

---

12 Ibid.
13 Accessed on October 23, 2022.

Management grandees large and small began to hype remote work. Wrkfrce continues:

> By the early 1990s, renowned management authority Peter Drucker called working from the office obsolete. "It is now infinitely easier, cheaper, and faster to do what the 19th century could not do: move information, and with it office work, to where the people are," Drucker wrote in 1993. "The tools to do so are already here: the telephone, two-way video, electronic mail, the fax machine, the personal computer, the modem, and so on."[14]

Fast forward a generation and a half. Today, with global warming a reality and COVID-19 having upended the go-to-work-every-day paradigm, work at home is a permanent fixture of American life. Perversely, around the globe, real estate developers and governments continue to build higher and higher and more luxurious skyscrapers, from Seattle to Shanghai. Who or what is going to fill all of this space? Stay tuned.

But, apropos of this book, there have for centuries been home offices both modest and grand, places where men and women of great consequence were at their experimenting, decision-making and creative best. These included Thomas Jefferson at Monticello, Winston Spencer Churchill at Chartwell Manor and Eleanor Roosevelt at Val-Kill Cottage, among countless others.

Significantly, the home office is the place to deal with money. Anthony Lawlor avers: "Handling money and doing accounts play an essential role in a home for the soul. The roots of the word "economy" mean "Household Management"—from the Greek *oikos* (house) and *nemein* (manage).[15]

Lawlor continues:

> The place for managing money can also be a setting for creating it. With the current trend toward corporate downsizing and the "have skill will travel" approach to work, home offices are growing in importance. Working at home also provides the opportunity to conduct business in styles that are personal and soulful. We can work at a pace that responds to our individual needs in environments that delight and inspire us.[16]

Delight and inspiration! That's what this book is about. It's no surprise that architects worldwide have begun to design innovative home offices in the form of pavilions, shacks and extensions. The interpretations of this project type are as varied as the people who use them and the sites from which they spring. The latter is an apt term because virtually all are designed to "sit softly" on their respective plots of land, whether it be a sharp hillside, an urban backyard or an exurban garden.

The examples are small, one virtually a micro-building of about 100 square feet and most about the size of an average Manhattan studio apartment. The one thing they seem to have in common, except being ecologically advanced, is large windows so the occupants can enjoy the surrounding verdure, be it in bustling London, the Vienna Woods or tropical São Paulo.

Examples of Pavilions, Shacks and Extensions

In northern California's Marin County, the Mill Valley Cabins, by Feldman Architecture, are two small structures of 56 and 35 square meters, respectively. One is a painter's studio, the other a yoga studio. The architects describe them as being "perched lightly between existing pines and redwoods." The description continues:

> The wooded site had served as the client's home for many years, and the cabins provided them with the opportunity to become even more intimate with their natural surroundings. While the studios are only a stone's throw away from the main house, they stand independently from the larger structure, offering pockets of seclusion among the trees. They nestle into the steeply sloping site, offering two distant perspectives of the surrounding forest and creating a quiet space for reflection in a woodland setting.

Who says California is no longer a paradise?

Thousands of miles away, on the outskirts of Buenos Aires, is a 17.82-square-meter extension to an existing house by Almoznivila office studio. The working architecture office is made of rugged, board-formed concrete. The architect's brief is as follows:

> This little office is situated at the same terrain as a house in a small town in the middle of the Pampas in Buenos Aires Province. Functionally, we needed a worktable and a library with a sitting place to read. As we had few meters to build the work was synthesized into a pure concrete prism. We pierced the facade with a floating volume which allows seating without adding area.

In the Kensal Rise section of London, a 15-square-meter extension with a weathered steel-clad structure is humorously dubbed Brexit Bunker. RISE Design Studio describes its work:

---

14 Ibid.
15 Lawlor, Anthony, *Home for the Soul*, Clarkson Potter Publishers, 1997.
16 Ibid.

Above Studio Ben Allen, a Room in the Garden.

Hot-rolled steel, the same material used in the railway track directly behind the site, was installed as cladding to the entire exterior of the garden room and then left to rust naturally. Featuring a pyramidal roof with an oriel window, it faces the main house from the other end of a paved garden and it is sandwiched between two reclaimed London stock brick walls.

Just when we thought examples of these structures couldn't get any smaller, along comes Watershed by FLOAT architecture research and design in Willemette Valley, Oregon. It is a miniscule 9 square meters. Not only does it push the limits of smallness, it continues a great architectural tradition of a young practitioner designing for a parent. In this case the parent is a philosophy professor and well-known nature writer.

The architect describes the writing studio:

> . . . it is on a small piece of land along the Marys

River about 20 minutes from [my mother's] home in town. The studio sits just uphill from riparian wetlands that are part of a project to restore hydrological and ecological function to the whole Marys River watershed . . . Two major intentions underlie careful design detailing: 1) That the studio be able to be constructed without road access, without electricity on site, and without major excavation and 2) that the building be removable and recyclable at the end of its useful life.

Back in London, there is a pavilion proving that architects can have a sense of humor. Studio Ben Allen dubs this folly a Room in the Garden. The firm explains:

> A Room in the Garden is part garden folly, part "other space." It is intended to relieve the congestion of an urban home and provide a space for family members to "work, play, read, sleep or just enjoy a moment of peace and quiet." Packed with innovation, it is

designed as both product and building. It is intended to be simple enough for self-build assembly and reassembly, coming as a flat pack kit of parts. . . . it is ultra low VOC both in assembly and use.

The Dutch are known for their innovative design of small abodes. This was needed for a 30-square-meter shack in Bussum, just southeast of Amsterdam, which has to do triple duty: serve as a study, provide guest accommodations and be a storage unit. Architect Serge Shoemaker elaborates:

> The aim was to design a contemporary, well-crafted studio that fit with the traditional surroundings. The use of materials, detailing and exceptional craftsmanship in the construction play an important role here. Durable black-varnished red cedar shingles envelop the structure from the walls to the roof, the color recalling black wooden sheds found in the region. The use of shingles enabled the application of a uniform material to minimize the roof line, thereby accentuating the studio's sculptural quality. Approximately 2,000 shingles were sanded and painted by hand and individually mounted on the structure.

A writer's studio in Los Angeles is dubbed Black Box and is by ANX / Aaron Neubert Architects. It is 200 square feet and serves as a studio for a technology author and columnist. Neubert discusses:

> Entry to the structure is obtained by ascending the hillside stairs and passing below the tree canopy enveloping the studio. A custom fabricated steel fenestration system opens to the entry platform through a pair of telescoping doors. The assembly turns the corner and terminates in a picture window, directing the occupant to expansive views. The position of the studio and the arrival sequence create the desired separation between home life and work life.

The next shack is Down Under in a suburb of Melbourne, Australia. It too is a writer's shed and was designed by Matt Gibson Architecture + Design. The verdure around the structure is so thick as to suggest that it is camouflaged, as if its occupants don't want to be discovered and their peace disturbed. The architect gives some details:

> Masquerading itself amongst the garden landscape and boundary fences, the shed is one with the landscape—a living part of the garden rather than an imposition on it. The successful coverage of Boston Ivy, accompanied by a collection of lush, verdant plantings was developed in collaboration with Landscape Garden Designer Ben Scott.

Latin American architects are known for their structural daring—Lina Bo Bardi and Oscar Niemeyer in Brazil, Pedro Ramirez Vasquez and Rafael Mijares at the National

Museum of Anthropology in Mexico City are just four examples. An 18-square-meter photographer's studio in São Paulo continues this tradition. Architect Teresa Mascaro explains the structure of Studio 4x4:

> The new building comes down to a 4m x 4m square plant which is big enough to accommodate the workspace. Only two main metal supports (columns) maintain the construction and are held together by two "rings" made of two beams and two pillars each which involved the volume. That is, the seals do not rely on the structure which was intentionally and completely exposed.

Appropriately called the Enchanted Shed, an 80-square-meter shack in the Vienna Woods in lower Austria recalls the villas that became typical weekend retreats for Austrians as the country rebuilt after World War II. Architect Franz&Sue:

> We inserted a large pane of glass into the front of the attic floor and carefully insulated the trusses. The walls were paneled with varnished grey fir, and an elevated section at the rear was upholstered so that the attic can also be used as a guest room. An elegant brass trapdoor closes off this enchanted place, from where you can watch the squirrels play in the treetops.

Finally, a Scholar's Library in upstate New York reduces a shack down to its most spartan modernist roots, in the words of architects Gluck+ "a pure and elegant Platonic cube." The architects elaborate:

> The first floor is completely closed and contains stacks for a library of books. The second floor, which is entirely open, is a scholar's working study . . . the structure expresses the dual character, with the floating roof cantilevered off the second floor to highlight the distinction between the solid and the void. The windows (standard-issue sliding doors) open on all four sides, stacking in opposite corners, to create the feeling of an aerie in the woods.

These are just eleven off the twenty-five case studies contained herein. They are splendidly diverse by geography, usage and tectonics. They are a long way, practically and conceptually, from the hero "young executive" in the early 1960s we met at the beginning of this essay. Work may never be the same, and these works of architecture are living proof. Each indeed is designed for optimum inspiration and productivity.

Twenty-Five Projects

SHOFFICE /
Platform 5 Architects

Architects: Platform 5 Architects
Location: London, United Kingdom
Year: 2012
Built area: 7 m²
Photography: Alan Williams Photography
Structural Engineer: Morph Structures
Contractor: Millimetre

'Shoffice' (shed + office) Designed to appear as if it is rising from the ground naturally, Shoffice (shed + office) is a free-form garden pavilion containing a small office alongside garden storage space located to the rear of a 1950s terraced house in St. John's Wood.

An innovative use of wood, plywood and steel, the pavilion is conceived as a sculptural object that flowed into the garden space.

A glazed office space nestles into an extruded timber elliptical shell, which curls over itself like a wood shaving, and forms a small terrace in the lawn.

The interior is oak lined and fitted out with storage and a cantilevered desk. Two roof lights—one glazed above the desk with another open to the sky outside the office—bring light into the workspace.

The project was a close collaboration between architect, structural engineer and contractor. The lightweight structure, formed with two steel ring beams, timber ribs and a stressed plywood skin, sits on minimal pad foundations. Much of the project was prefabricated to reduce the amount of material that needed to be moved through the house during construction.

In 2013 Shoffice won the NLA Don't Move, Improve! Awards in the small office category.

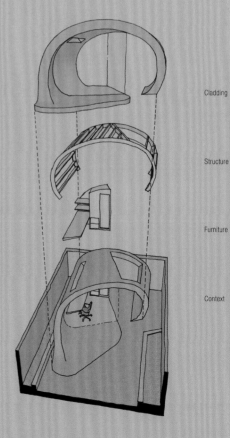

Cladding

Structure

Furniture

Context

shed + office = Shoffice

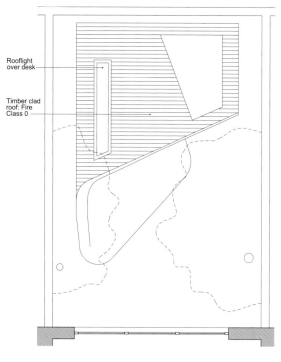

Rooflight over desk

Timber clad roof: Fire Class 0

Roof plan

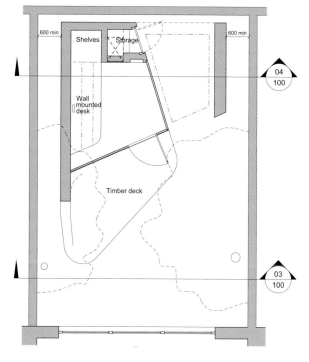

600 min

Shelves   Storage

Wall mounted desk

Timber deck

600 min

04
100

03
100

Floor plan

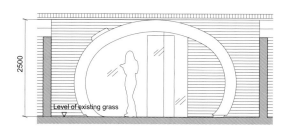

2500

Level of existing grass

West elevation

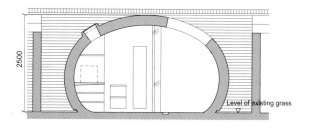

2500

Level of existing grass

Section

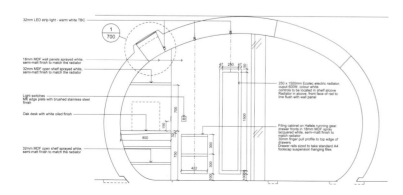

32mm LED strip light - warm white TBC

18mm MDF wall panels sprayed white,
semi-matt finish to match the radiator
32mm MDF open shelf sprayed white,
semi-matt finish to match the radiator

Light switches
MK edge plate with brushed stainless steel
finish

Oak desk with white oiled finish

32mm MDF open shelf sprayed white,
semi-matt finish to match the radiator

250 x 1500mm Ecolec electric radiator,
output 600W, colour white
controls to be located in shelf alcove
Radiator in alcove, front face of rad to
line flush with wall panel

Filing cabinet on Hafele running gear,
drawer fronts in 18mm MDF spray
lacquered white, semi-matt finish to
match radiator
30mm finger pull profile to top edge of
drawers
Drawer rails sized to take standard A4
foolscap suspension hanging files

Internal elevation

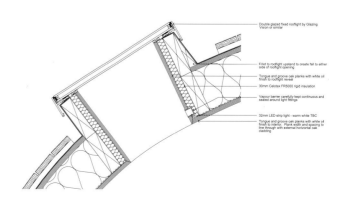

Rooflight detail

MILL VALLEY CABINS /
Feldman Architecture

Architects: Feldman Architecture
Location: Mill Valley, California, USA
Year: 2010
Built area: 46.45 m2 Upper, 35 m2 Lower
Photography: Joe Fletcher
Green Roof and Landscape Architecture: Jori Hook
Engineer: Strandberg Engineering
Contractor: JP Builders

The Mill Valley Cabins make extraordinary use of their steeply sloping site in Northern California. The cabins are nested into the hillside and accommodate the retirement needs of their owners, an artist and an avid gardener. The owners were intent on situating their active retirement pursuits in spaces that would inspire the imagination. Feldman Architecture responded with a sensible design that met the challenges posed by the slope of the site: two small cabins, 46.45 square meters and 35 square meters in size, that take the form of an artist's studio and a yoga studio and allow the structure to perch lightly between existing pines and redwoods with minimal re-grading. This wooded site had served as the client's home for many years, and the cabins provided them with the opportunity to become even more intimate with their natural surroundings.

While the studios sit only a stone's throw away from the site's main house, they stand independently from the larger structure, offering pockets of seclusion among the trees. They offer two distinct perspectives of the surrounding forest and create a quiet space for reflection in a woodland clearing. The lower building's planted roof provides a quilt-like garden for the artist to look down upon from his studio and blends into the hillside to create a canvas for the clients' gardening amusement. The green roof also plays an integral role in the site's stormwater management solution; along with onsite dissipaters, the roof collects, diverts and releases stormwater back onto the sloped site in a controlled manner to prevent erosion. The low- and no-VOC materials used in the cabins' construction further reduce the homes' impact on its sylvan surroundings. The site's landscape design made only subtle shifts in the site's vegetative composition, implementing wildfire resistant species and landscaping techniques to ultimately reduce the risk of wildfire.

Mill Valley Cabins' innovative form and sustainable practices allow the creative couple to exist not only in the forest but as a part of it, as well, building on the concept of biophilia, the theory that an intrinsic bond connects human beings to the living systems around them.

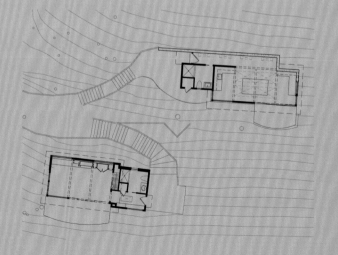

Floor plan

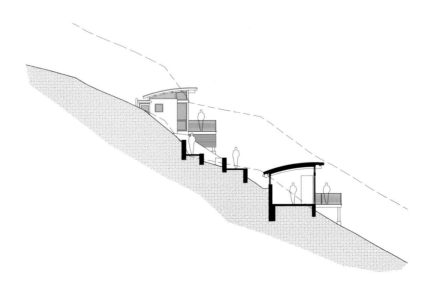

Section

ARCHITECTURE OFFICE STUDIO / Almoznivila

Architects: Agustina Vila & Damián Almozni
Location: Agustin Roca, Junin, Argentina
Year: 2019
Built area: 17.82 m²
Photography: Walter Gustavo Salcedo
Interior: Almoznivila

This little office is an annex to a house in a small town in the middle of the pampas plain in Buenos Aires Province, Argentina. Functionally an architecture office, the annex needed a worktable and a library with a sitting place to read. There were only a few square meters to build on and the annex was synthesized into a pure concrete prism. The facade was pierced with a floating volume, which allows window seating without adding area.

The exterior of the office, shown with a raw concrete facade, has a house-like shape protrusion with wood-framed windows. By having the windows protrude away from the building, it gave us a bit more space, allowing designers to create a deep window seat.

The window seat is surrounded by dark wood shelving, while the interior of the window seat is lined with raw concrete, complementing the exterior of the building. To make the concrete surface more comfortable, a large cushion and a sheepskin rug have been added.

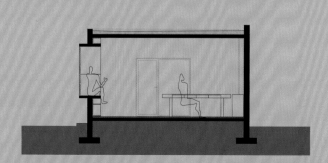

Section

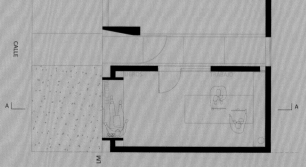

Plan

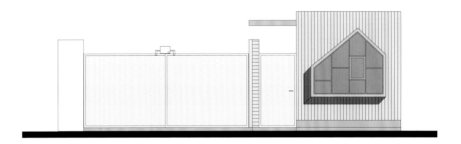

Elevation

THE BUNKER /
RISE Design Studio

Architects: Sean Ronnie Hill, Natsuka Muto
Location: Kensal Rise, London, United Kingdom
Year: 2019
Built area: 15 m²
Photography: Edmund Sumner
Interior: RISE Design Studio
Landscape: Daniel Shea Garden Design
Manufacturers: Black metal installed by Contractor, Pavers
by Vande Moortel
Consultants: Osprey Building Consultants
Structural Engineer: CAR Ltd
Contractor: CBC London

This pavilion uses hot-rolled steel as a prominent protruding window to form an extension of the main house in suburban London. Conceived as a sanctuary from the hustle and bustle of London and inclement weather, and dubbed the Bunker, the small studio provides a place to work or relax. Hot-rolled steel, the same material used in the construction of the railway track directly behind the site, was installed as cladding to the entire exterior of the garden room then left to rust naturally.

Featuring a pyramidal roof with an oriel window, it faces the main house from the other end of a paved garden and is sandwiched between two reclaimed London Stock brick walls. The garden studio is nestled at the rear of a small garden connected by a patio clad in clay pavers, a contemporary addition that is still reminiscent of the reclaimed bricks used for the garden walls. Steps lead down from this patio to the Brexit Bunker's door next to a projecting window box providing seating overlooking the garden.

At the back, where it faces the railway tracks, the only views are upwards through the skylight. Plywood provides a surprising contrast to the rough exterior, lining the walls and ceiling to create a warm and light-filled space. Built-in storage has been arranged to provide a niche for seating below. A set of steps lead over the niche and up to create an accessible platform area directly beneath the skylight.

The client can relax surrounded by the sounds of birds without any visual hint that they are in the city instead of the country; it is a place of sanctuary. The walls and roof of the studio have been highly insulated to offer both thermal and acoustic protection. A hanging light fixture also made from weathered steel illuminates the patio. Its shape is designed to emulate the pyramid-shape of the Bunker, connecting the house and the studio.

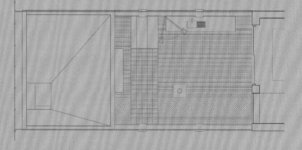

Roof plan

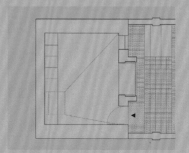

Floor plan

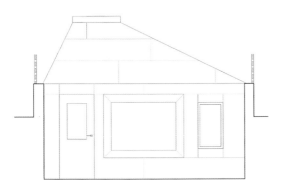

Elevation

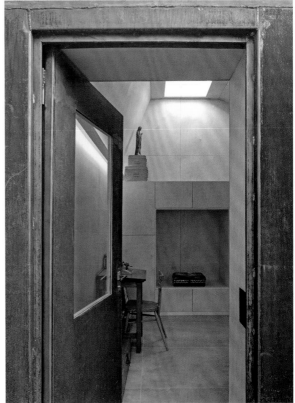

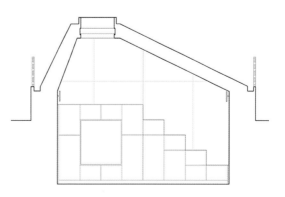

Section

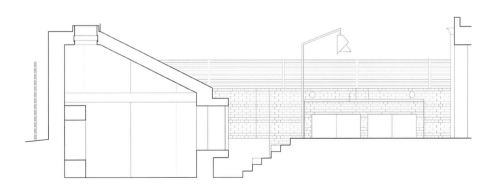

Section

WATERSHED /
FLOAT architecture research and design

Architect: FLOAT architecture research and design
Location: Willamette Valley, Oregon, USA
Year: 2008
Built area: 9 m²
Photography: J. Gary Tarleton
Interior: FLOAT architecture research and design
Fabrication: FLOAT architecture research and design
Engineering: FLOAT architecture research and design

This tiny studio in Oregon is miniscule by design, a small writing studio (just 100 square feet) in the Willamette Valley that the owner calls her Watershed, 2008.

The owner is a philosophy professor and a well-known nature writer. She commissioned the studio as a retreat for herself and for visiting writer friends. Her first request was for a roof that would let her hear rain falling.

The designer is the owner's daughter. Erin Moore is a faculty member at the University of Oregon where she works in teaching, research and practice on lifecycle thinking in ecology, design and construction. She uses her own small firm, FLOAT, to conduct small-scale projects that engage architecture with ecology. The writing studio site is a small piece of land along the Marys River about 20 minutes from the owner's home in town. The studio sits just uphill from riparian wetlands that are part of a project to restore hydrological and ecological function to the whole Marys River watershed.

The writing studio is designed to reveal the ecological complexity of the site to visitors and in this way it is successful: Small tunnels under the studio bring rare reptiles and amphibians into view through the floor-level window. The water collection basin that doubles as the front step draws in birds and deer. At midday, the silhouettes of these animals project from the water onto the interior ceiling. Windows on the west and north sides frame different bird habitats—the tops of fence row trees and the patch of sky at a hilltop updraft. The roof diaphragm amplifies rain sounds, and the collection basin is a measure of past rainfall.

Two major intentions underlie careful design detailing: 1) that the studio be able to be constructed without road access,

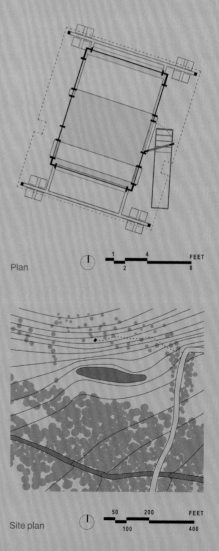

Plan

1 2 4 8 FEET

Site plan

50 100 200 400 FEET

without electricity on site and without major excavation and 2) that the building be removable and recyclable at the end of its useful life. The way the studio is designed in three separate construction stages made it possible to shop fabricate most of it and then to walk the parts to the site for assembly. The first stage of construction was the site-poured foundation piers that are cast to spread the weight of the building on the ground and to drain water away from the steel frame. The second stage, the steel frame, was shop fabricated and dropped in a single piece onto the piers by a track drive front loader. Stainless steel bolts connect dado-grooved cedar two-by-sixes to the frame and the final tongue-in-groove cedar and glass enclosure layer floats in those grooves and on rubber engine seats. There are no irreversible connections. The wood enclosure can be updated or recycled piece-by-piece as necessary. The steel frame can be removed the same way it arrived and can be reused or recycled.

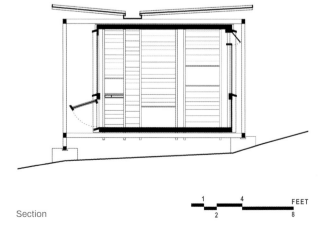

Section

| 1 | | 4 | | FEET |
| 2 | | | 8 | |

A ROOM IN THE GARDEN /
Studio Ben Allen

Architects: Studio Ben Allen
Team: Ben Allen, Omar Ghazal, Marco Nicastro,
Arthur Wong, Massine Yallaoui
Location: Putney/South West London, United Kingdom
Year: 2019
Built area: 15 m²
Photography: Ben Tynegate
Landscape Design: Daniel Bell Landskap
Structural Engineer: Format Engineers
Installer: Sullivan and Company
CNC cutting: Hub Workshop

In the great tradition of eccentric English architecture, a Room in the Garden is an architectural folly, recalling in a small way the architecture of John Nash's Royal Pavilion at Brighton. It is pure fantasy, intended to relieve the congestion of the urban home and provide a space for family members to work, play, read, sleep or to enjoy a moment of peace and quiet. Packed with innovation, it is designed as both product and building. It is intended to be simple enough for self-build assembly and reassembly, coming as a flat pack kit of parts, fully fabricated on a CNC machine. It is ultra-low VOC both in assembly and use and embraces the principals of circular design in that it can be fully demounted and re-erected.

As well as being driven by the desire to innovate in terms of the construction approach, the architects strove to make a Room in the Garden, above all, a work of architecture. Architecturally it is designed to exude playfulness, with the patterned green cladding intended to partially and surreally camouflage the building in its natural surroundings.

The geometry of the architecture is an interplay of changing geometric forms. The octagonal wall structure rises to form a hexagonal roof, which then frames a square skylight. The main timber columns that support the walls converge to form a truss like structure that supports the roof. The interior is designed to adapt with the seasons; providing a sense of tactile warmth during the winter months, the large double doors enable it to be opened to the garden in summer. The exposed timber structure, which rises to the ceiling converging and framing the skylight, gives a central focal point and top light, ideal when seeking a place to read or for quiet contemplation.

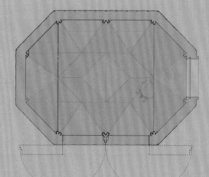

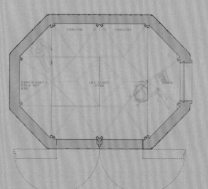

Plans

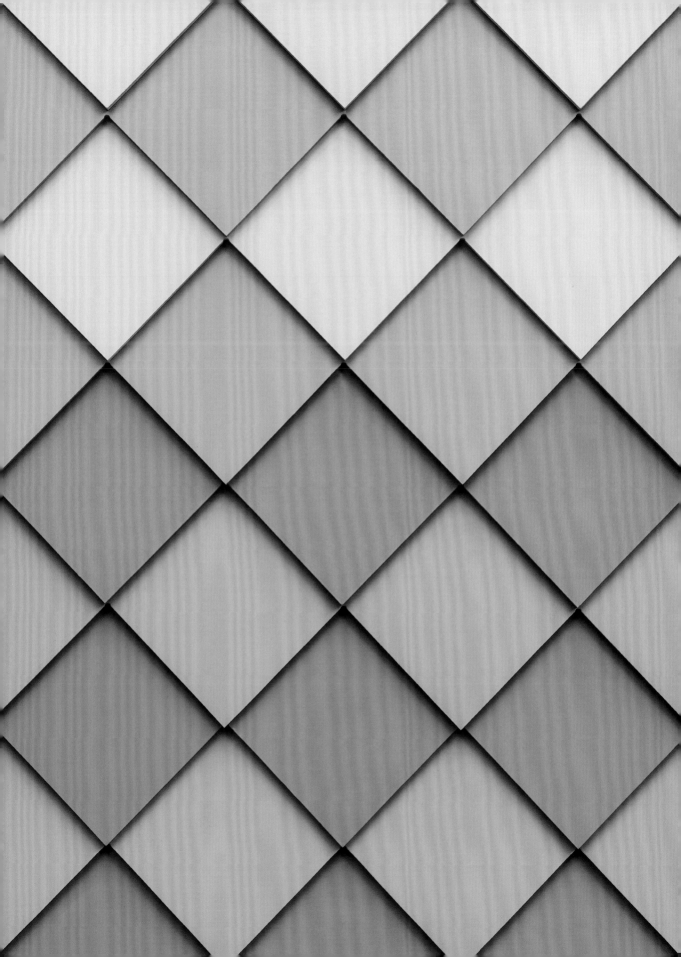

Elevation

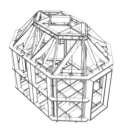

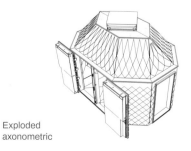

Exploded
axonometric

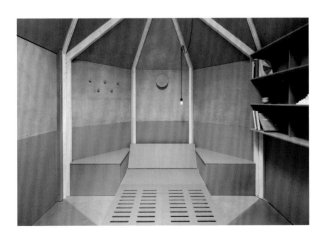

BUSSUM GARDEN STUDIO /
Serge Schoemaker Architects

Architects: Serge Schoemaker, Beatrice Nespega
Location: Bussum, Netherlands
Year: 2014
Built area: 30 m²
Photography: Raoul Kramer
Interior: Serge Schoemaker Architects

Ever inventive, Dutch architects seem to have a knack for making the most of limited space and challenging building conditions. The Garden Studio in Bussum involves the design and construction of a freestanding shed in a private garden that functions as a study, guest accommodation and storage. The challenge — to fit a relatively large structure in a long, narrow garden—resulted in an elongated plan. A geometric form entirely clad in shingles, combined with the transparent corner and rotated siting at the rear of the garden lends the studio a distinct presence and identity.

The aim was to design a contemporary, well-crafted studio that fit with the traditional surroundings; the use of materials, detailing and exceptional craftsmanship in the construction play an important role here. Durable black-varnished red cedar shingles envelop the structure from the walls to roof, the color recalling black painted wooden sheds found in the region. The use of shingles enabled the application of a uniform material to minimize the roof line, thereby accentuating the studio's sculptural quality. Approximately 2,000 shingles were sanded and painted by hand, and individually mounted onto the structure.

The windows lend the studio a characteristic appearance. Extending full-height over two facades, the largest window opens up the corner of the structure, its sharp lines forming a striking contrast with the irregular textured facade. Careful attention was required for the construction of this window as the glass panes meet here at a non-perpendicular angle without a window frame under the cantilevered roof corner. A second full-height opening views onto the garden, complemented by a built-in desk. Deeply recessed to highlight the thick walls and sculptural volume, the openings are expressed in black plywood reveals that frame views of the garden.

Contrasting with the dark, rough textured exterior, the interior appears seamless and light. Extending continuously from the floor,

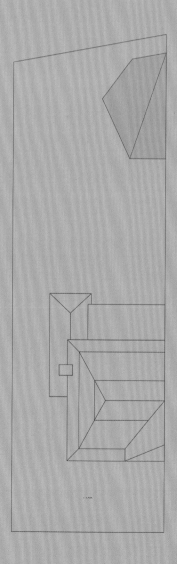

Site plan

walls and joinery to the ceiling, its entire surface is fashioned from transparent white-lacquered birch plywood. The interior is composed of various plywood pieces cut precisely to size and carefully pieced to fit seamlessly like a jigsaw puzzle, a task made more challenging by the structure's geometric form. The lightness of the material creates a calming atmosphere and its restrained, continuous finish emphasizes the sculptural quality of the space.

The built-in furniture is composed of three linear elements: a floating table in front of the window, a long bench with drawers and a vertical cabinet. Bicycle storage is concealed behind large sliding birch plywood doors. From the interior, the open corner and garden window both greatly increase the sense of space. The house further appeals to the senses through the smell of the wood, and sunlight that falls beautifully into the interior. The careful attention to detail in the design and craftsmanship results in a cherished place for the family to retreat from the everyday.

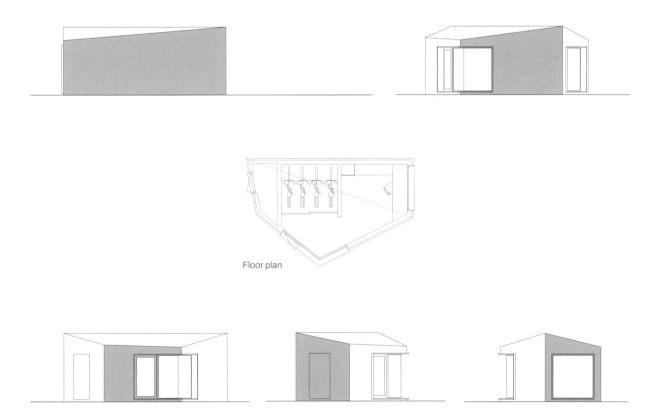

Floor plan

Elevations

BLACK BOX /
ANX / Aaron Neubert

Architect: ANX / Aaron Neubert Architects
Project Team: Aaron Neubert (Principal), Jeremy Limsenben,
David Chong, Xiran Zhang
Location: Los Angeles, USA
Year: 2015
Built area: 18.5 m²
Photography: Brian Thomas Jones
Structural Engineer: FJ Engineering
General Contractor: Doug Dalton
Steel Windows and Doors: John Dunne
Millwork: Dan Taron

Los Angeles, with its tradition of architectural excess, seems a million miles away from the reductive architecture of the Dutch masters like Rietveld and the art of Mondrian and Van Doesburg. But this elegant and spare structure fits firmly within that minimalist tradition.

A steeply sloping property in a hillside neighborhood is the site for this 200-square-foot writer's studio, labeled the Black Box for its sparse geometry and dark stained cladding. Floating above an existing residence and capturing a panoramic view of Griffith Park and its famed Observatory, the Black Box serves as the office for a technology author and columnist.

Entry to the structure is obtained by ascending the hillside stairs and passing below the tree canopy enveloping the studio. A custom fabricated steel fenestration system opens to the entry platform though a pair of telescoping doors. The assembly turns the corner and terminates in a picture window, directing the occupant to the expansive views. The position of the studio and the arrival sequence creates the desired separation between home life and work life.

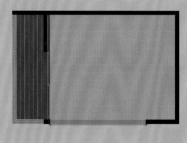

Plan

Site plan

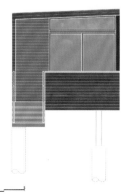

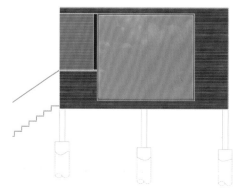

Elevations

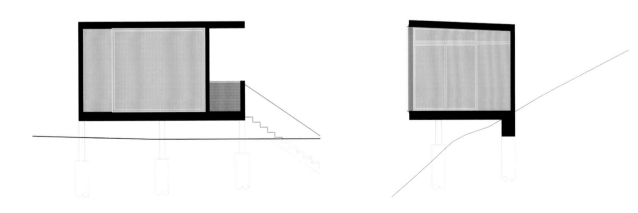

WRITERS SHED /
Matt Gibson
Architecture + Design

Architects: Matt Gibson Architecture + Design
Project Team: Matt Gibson, Wei-an Lim, Cassie Southon
Location: Elsternwick, Australia
Year: 2017
Built area: 10 m²
Photography: Shannon McGrath
Interior: Matt Gibson Architecture + Design
Landscape: Ben Scott
Manufacturers: AutoDesk, Trimble
Builder: Warwick Constructions

Camouflaged and nestled into a modest residential garden, the Writer's Shed provides an isolated workspace for a creative scribe. It is set in a corner of a triangular-shaped garden, located in a quiet, leafy residential suburb in Melbourne's South East. Masquerading itself among the garden landscape and boundary fences the shed is one with the landscape— a living part of the garden rather than an imposition on it. The successful coverage of Boston Ivy, accompanied by a collection of lush, verdant plantings was developed in collaboration with Landscape Garden Designer Ben Scott.

Stepping inside, a generous and simple plywood-clad workspace reveals itself, with a framed window looking back to the garden. A mirrored doorway opens out to the rear bluestone laneway providing an option for deliveries and access. Sitting inside at the desk there's a certain inherent delight in bunkering down to look out to the garden and house beyond. The 10-square-meter space was sized to fall into a Class 10a structure, allowing economical building and planning methods and a rather simple, low-tech, modestly priced and modestly constructed solution. A concrete slab supports engineered timber flooring, ply clad stud walls, sealed on the exterior with a rolled Butynol© wet-suit that both insulates and waterproofs.

As the ways we work and live continue to adapt and change to our environment and technology, traditional notions are challenged and new opportunities appear. An antidote is often needed to balance the overstimulating, populous and constantly contactable workplaces where we spend much of our modern lives. More people are opting to work from a variety of locations, sometimes rejecting the rigid and sealed open plan office for the benefits of more natural surroundings. As a detached and flexible workspace, the Writer's Shed provides an intimate private space to recoup, reflect and recharge the imagination.

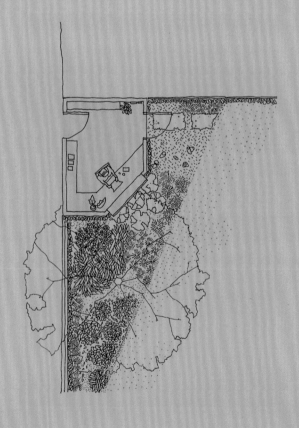

Site plan

5.0m

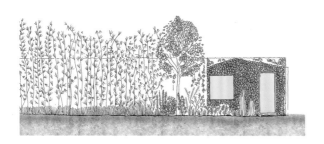

Elevation   Section

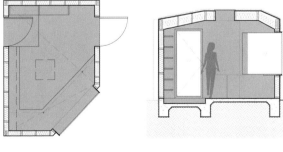

Floor plan   Section

THE LIGHT SHED /
Richard John Andrews

Architects: Richard John Andrews
Location: Forest Gate, London, United Kingdom
Year: 2019
Built area: 12 m²
Photography: Chris Snook
Structural Engineer: Structure Workshop

The brief was to design and fabricate a low-cost bespoke studio space for an emerging architecture practice in East London. With the studio being positioned at the end of a mid-terraced East London garden there were certain constraints that required thorough attention. The material palette was kept lightweight and simple in order to enable full on-site fabrication as well as easy transfer through a recently finished house renovation and extension, the cork house.

The studio aims to create a sustainable approach to work and play, with the flexibility of flipping its function to become an entertaining space for summer gatherings and more intimate functions. The Light Shed offers desk space for two to three people and has the ability for its inhabitants to fluctuate depending on the tasks at hand. The approach is embedded in the studio ethos. The designer enjoys collaborative endeavors and is always on the lookout for new collaborative projects, nomadic freelancers and interesting cross discipline designers to expand his reach as an architectural design studio.

Architecturally the studio has been constructed as a self-build project using cheap and hard-wearing materials, although these have been finessed to create an elegant and cozy workspace measuring in at 12 square meters internally. Bespoke timber sliding doors connect the space to the sounds and vibrancy of a well-kept garden, and diffused polycarbonate roofing panels give the studio its name, the Light Shed, due to the ambient light that is created. These design details create a perfect environment for the use of computers, model making equipment and presentations on its designated studio display screen.

The project has been a refreshing reminder of what can be achieved when scale and budget are limited. By adopting hard-wearing, malleable materials the architects have reaffirmed

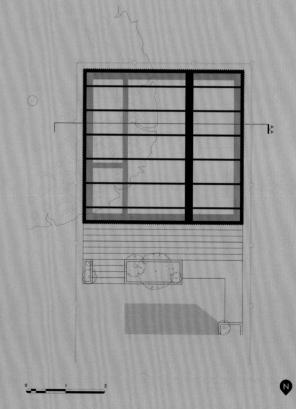

Roof plan

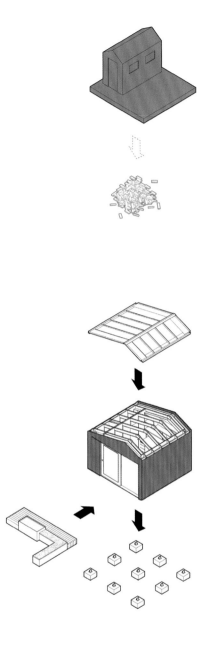

Design development diagram

the possibility of employing a maker's approach to small-scale architectural endeavors; resulting in well-designed, thoroughly thought-out and beautifully crafted small spaces that are more accessible to a wider audience.

For the studio the opal polycarbonate roof was a design breakthrough due to its dual function. The primary function was to create a well-lit space using diffuse natural light in order to operate the required equipment within, as well as provide a healthy and uplifting connection to nature. By its design the polycarbonate heats up in the sun and offers an attractive resting surface for aphids that bloom on the overbearing sycamore tree above.

With current trends showing people's willingness to explore alternatives to creating additional space as a means of maximizing their homelife, the Light Shed offers a superior solution to the common garden shed or summer house at a similar cost. Due to the independent and autonomous nature of the building type that the designers have created, it offers a solution that can utilize the construction methods mirroring well-designed, insulated and soundproofed build-ups of a contemporary timber framing process. This type of building project allows the occupier to enjoy the comfort of their own home in a specific location within their garden that provides an experience the traditional extension cannot offer due to building constraints.

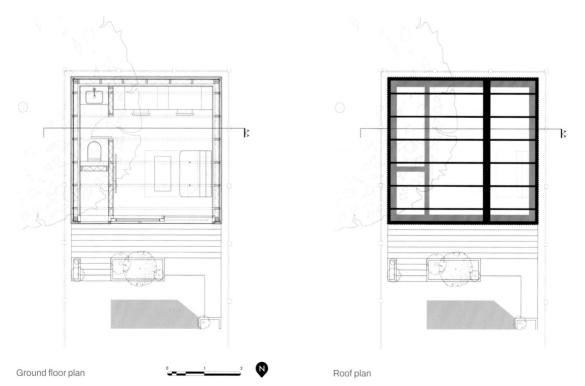

Ground floor plan   0   1   2   N   Roof plan

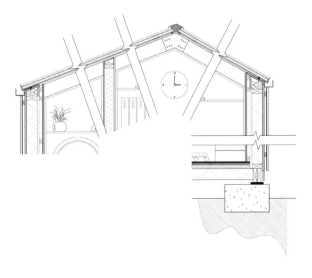

Section details A-A

Section

LOU ROTA'S CERAMIC STUDIO
/ London Garden Studios

Architects: London Garden Studios
Location: London, United Kingdom
Year: 2009
Built area: 9 m²
Photography: Dirk Lindner / Mark Tamer
Interior: built-in furniture by London Garden Studios,
styling by Lou Rota
Landscape: Gerry Murphy
Manufacturers: London Garden Studios
Contractor: London Garden Studios
Interior products: Lou Rota
Decking: London Garden Studios

Part working studio, part playground, this London studio was
designed for Lou Rota, a ceramic artist. She wanted a studio
nestled among the trees and wildlife as her work is very much
influenced by the natural world. She wanted a space that
maximized light and views so the designers fitted double doors
and a picture window and skylight. Maximizing the light was
very important as the space was going to be used for drawing
and designing.

The building, doors and windows are clad in red cedar so it
would all weather uniformly and sit unobtrusively in the natural
environment.

The size of the studio is 3 m x 3 m, external height 2.5 m. The
client did not want the full width of the garden used as the
building site; she wanted to leave a space to the left of the studio
for outdoor seating and a wooden deck and space in front of the
studio for the children to play.

Designers used painted wooden boards for the floor and
installed shelving on one wall of the studio to showcase Lou
Rota's ceramics. The other internal walls were plastered and
painted. On the rear wall we formed an alcove in the plaster-
work as a secondary place for displaying work.

STUDIO 4x4 /
Teresa Mascaro

Architect: Teresa Mascaro
Location: Carapicuiba, São Paulo, Brazil
Year: 2012/2013
Built area: 18 m²
Photography: Cristiano Mascaro
Interior: Teresa Mascaro
Manufacturers: EJC (Electrical), Antoniazzi (Hydraulics), Duar (Air Conditioner), RPS (Concrete treatment), Serralheria GH (Sawmill and Joinery), Artcor (Concrete Slabs painting and treatment), Premium Vidros (Glass), PHd Marcenaria (Wood-work), Reka (Lighting), Walltech Engenharia e Construção
Consultants & Structural Engineer: Yopanan Rebello
Contractor: Cristiano Mascaro

With its millions of German immigrants, Brazil has always had a bit of a Teutonic bent in its architecture. As such this photographer's studio is modernist to the core. The structure was built for a photographer on the grounds of his residence on the outskirts of São Paulo. Having already had a working space in this area for a while it became spatially insufficient due to the growing portfolio of work, boxes of negatives and equipment. Therefore, a new spot was necessary to accom-modate his workspace (desk, workbench, shelves for digital files) in a more comfortable, reserved and inspiring way.

The available location for the new building was a sloping area with lots of greenery; therefore comes the idea of releasing the constructed volume from the soil to bypass unnecessary cuts and deep diggings.

In order to keep a noninvasive concept and avoid damages to the soil, the steel frame solution was adopted because it is easy to assemble and also due to its strength, agility and slenderness.

Similarly, floor slab and seals were assembled on site. The floor slab is formed by a double layer of wall panel, the walls were built by using a steel frame system with internal plaster boards and external concrete boards as well as mineral wool for insulation; the frames are galvanized iron flat glass with large roof tiles and are laminated in thermal-acoustical poly-urethane. Consequently, these materials have made the work "clean" by reducing material waste and rubble, fast assembly and thus saving costs and energy.

The new building comes down to a 4 m x 4 m square plant, which is big enough to accommodate the workspace. Only two main metal supports (columns) maintain the construction

and are held together by two "rings" made of two beams and two pillars each that involve the volume. That is, the seals do not rely on the structure, which was intentionally and completely exposed.

By leveling off the floor it has become aligned with the height of the trees and revealed the sight to beautiful green fields that now naturally match both the interior with the exterior. However, walls are necessary for a photographer and his photographs. Therefore, glass and opaque materials have been balanced by taking into account insolation and functionality.

Southwest elevation

Northeast elevation

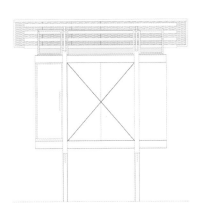

Southeast elevation

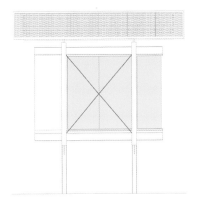

Northwest elevation

0,50m   1,00m   2,00m

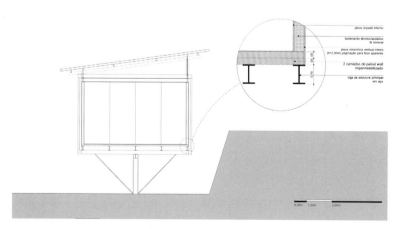

Northeast section and detail

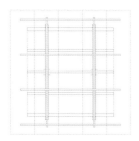

Coverage structure

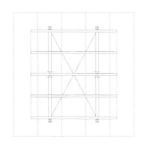

Lower structure

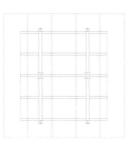

Upper structure

0,50m   1,00m   2,00m

N

Perspective schematic structure

ARTISTS' STUDIO /
Panov-Scott

Architects: Anita Panov & Andrew Scott
Location: Gadigal (indigenous country name)/ Sydney, Australia
Year: 2015
Built area: 35 m²
Photography: Brett Boardman Photography
Structural Engineer: Cantilever Structural Engineering
Contractor: Eris Dufficy

Despite being only 35 square meters, the building has an intriguing public quality, which seems to expand the potential of the owner's artistic practice. The consideration given to the artist's physical habitation and work processes with the building, together with the quality of light and consideration of views and perspectives from and into the workshop, are artfully resolved. This is a work of small architecture with big ideas. —Australian Institute of Architects, New South Wales Jury citation

An unusual hybrid studio/gallery, this structure on the outskirts of Sydney establishes an internal environment for the production, contemplation and display of art. As such the architecture was required to be robust enough to withstand the impacts of production but then also adequately recessive for the favorable display and contemplation of the resultant artwork.

The gallery is associated with, but apart from the domestic life of an active family. In this sense the city-scale impact of the project is the bringing back of production to the suburbs. This act is aligned with archaic patterns of city making, but a challenge to the zoning legacy of the modernist city. The plan mimics the shape of the garden and existing house, in being long and thin. Within, there are three spaces: the first is for the making of photography and small objects, the second is for the production of larger objects, while the third is a small washroom.

The building retains the formal and spatial qualities of a shed. The archetypal silhouette and rudimentary materials belie the sophisticated modulation of natural light relating to each artist's specific practice. The components are assembled with the craftsmanship of a far more substantial endeavor, elevating the building and imbuing the activities undertaken within with even greater purpose. To realize this gallery within such constraints of cost and time requires the commitment and persistence of all involved—a true collaboration between client, architect, engineer and builder.

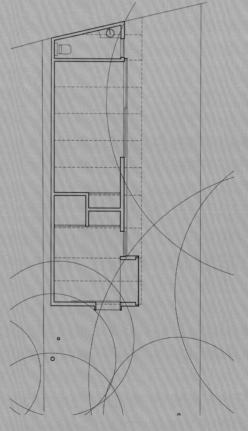

Plan

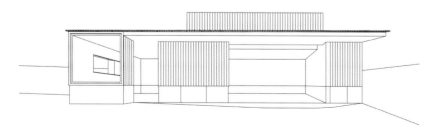

Perspective

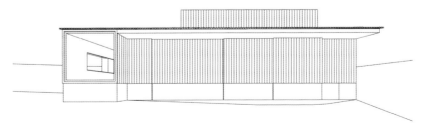

Perspective

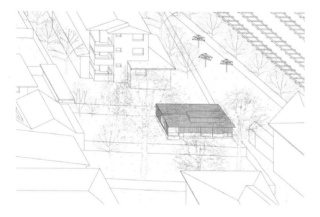

Location diagram

STUDIO BUNKHOUSE /
Cutler Anderson Architects

Architects: James Cutler, FAIA
Location: Bainbridge Island, Washington, USA
Year: 2016
Built area: 80 m²
Photography: Art Grice
Structural Engineer: Jerome Madden of Madden
Baughmann Engineering
Contractor: James Cutler

Located on Bainbridge Island in the Puget Sound across from Seattle, this 80-square-foot studio/bunkhouse was designed to fit carefully into its natural context. It was designed by James Cutler of Cutler Anderson Architects as a means of, according to the architect, showing his (then) 11-year-old daughter "how to build things." Father and daughter built the structure themselves in its entirety.

As a discrete building, the Studio/Bunkhouse allows the family to experience the climate and place in the to-and-fro from the cabin to the main house, located 30 feet away. The building was framed by the 11-year-old and her father out of rough-sawn Douglas fir from a nearby sawmill. The framing lumber and shiplap sheathing were exposed in order to display the nature of the structure. Rigid insulation was applied to the exterior that was then sided with 22-gauge Corten steel "shin-gles" cut from standard-size sheets of the material.

Designed to have two folding bunk beds and one folding desk, the building can function as a bunk house for the 11-year-old, a design studio for her father and, when everything is folded, a poker room for her father's friends.

Because of intermittent power outages on the island, four kilo-watts of batteries and an inverter/charger are hidden behind the rolling file cabinets. The family can then use the building during those events. The building is heated by a highly efficient cast iron woodstove, and a small refrigerator is concealed under the stove.

Since being constructed the building has surprised the design-er/builders by becoming the de facto family/media room for the main residence.

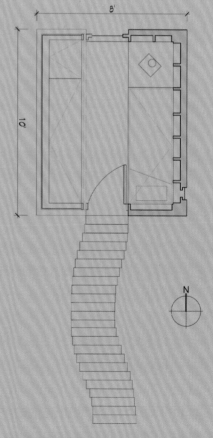

Plan

THE ENCHANTED SHED /
Franz&Sue

Architects: Franz&Sue
Team: Anna Ladurner, Michael Eder, Ulrike Straube
Location: Vienna Woods, Austria
Year: 2016
Built area: 60 m² (shed), 155 m² (house)
Photography: Andreas Buchberger
Structural Engineer: DI Margarete Salzer, Vienna
Building physics: DI Andreas Perissutti

Located in the shadow of the legendary Vienna Woods, the special appeal of this project lies in the appreciation shown for this old outbuilding, converted to modern use. Back in the 1930s, few people could afford a basement, let alone a garage. So they built their own sheds to store wood, raise rabbits or boil laundry. Over the past few decades these structures have lost their original purpose, and many are falling apart. Converted into small, cozy "hideaways," they become affordable, magical retreats for families and their guests.

A large pane of glass was inserted into the front wall of the attic floor, and the trusses were carefully insulated. The walls were paneled with varnished grey fir, and an elevated section at the rear was upholstered so that the attic can also be used as a guest room. An elegant brass trapdoor closes off this enchanted place, from where squirrels play in the treetops.

The ground floor is still used for storing garden tools, the lawn mower and fruit crates, while upstairs it is snug and comfortable. Spotlights illuminate the brass in the evening, creating a warm light—even in freezing winter. The attic is ventilated via an already existing window and small air vents installed along the sides.

After World War II this villa was the typical weekend house of a middle-class family in postwar Austria. We explained that the parlor and tiled stove were just ballast from the past and gently suggested that the house was somewhat overloaded with rustic kitsch. But where should one start with the ceiling construction? Where should the building show respect for the old, where must the new be radically introduced? Together with the clients, the designers felt that, from now on, other elements should shape the character of the building.

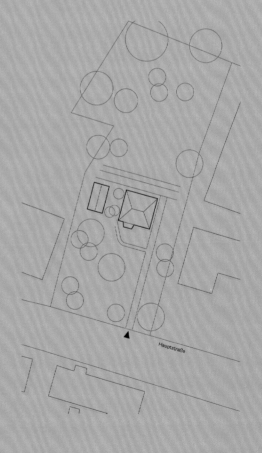

Site plan

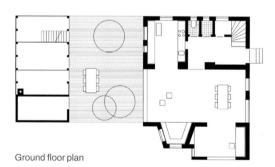

Ground floor plan

Upper level floor plan

For instance, the gnarled apple trees that blossom behind the house, the old terrazzo floors the color of black pudding, the slippery wooden floors and old double windows.

The first sketches showed new routes and visual axes through the orchard and idyllic places that no one had yet discovered. We gave the house a new open structure, a new spatial concept. The designers took only two radical steps: they had an external wall removed and replaced it with a generously sized but economical pane of glass. Out of three dark little rooms we made a big, bright, loft-like space that now revealed a view

of fruit trees and a magnolia, the pool from the 1950s, and the wooden shed treated with carbolineum.

Now children play in small side rooms, the family lounges on an upholstered platform, the kitchen is both open and yet separate. The shed and the house are now connected by an apparently hovering large deck that is like a kind of open living room from where you can look across the garden. Around the old apple trees, circles were cut out of the deck. When the children look out the spectacular window they see the tops of the fruit trees, illuminated from below at night.

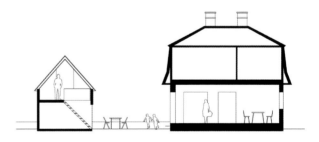

Section

SCHOLAR'S LIBRARY / GLUCK+

Architects: Gluck+
Location: Upstate NY, USA
Year: 2003
Built area: 74.32 m²
Photography: Erik Freeland, Paul Warchol, other image files
"Images courtesy of Gluck+"
Architecture, Construction and Interiors: Peter L. Gluck, David Mabbott, Frederik Rissom
Structural Engineer: Robert Silman Associates P.C.
Mechanical Engineer: Rodkin Cardinale Consulting Engineers P.C.

This jewel of a modernist pavilion in Upstate New York is a pure and elegant Platonic cube. There is a unity to the building's purpose and form, in both programmatic and metaphorical terms. The first floor is completely closed and contains stacks for a library of books. The second floor, which is entirely open, is a scholar's working study. The study sits on the books below much like scholarship rests on the body of work that precedes it.

The structure expresses this dual character, with the floating roof cantilevered off the second floor to highlight the distinction between the solid and the void. The windows (standard-issue sliding doors) open on all four sides, stacking in opposite corners, to create the feeling of an aerie in the woods. The changing seasons provide the context, with the study "walls" green in the summer, orange in the fall and white in the winter. An economy of means in cost, materials and structure result in simplicity and directness with no elaboration.

The study is a serene and solitary haven for quiet work that is at the same time immersed in the natural world around it. In its alignment of use, structure, context and social effect, this library probably comes close to the ever elusive perfect diagram that architects are always seeking.

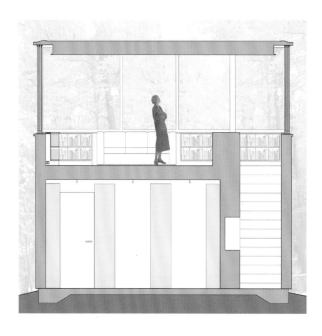

Section

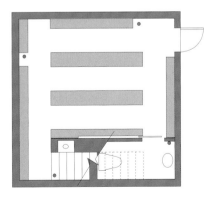

Ground floor plan

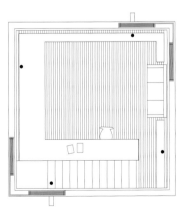

Upper floor plan

GARDEN ROOM /
Atelier Janda Vanderghote

Architect: Indra Janda
Location: Smetlede, Belgium
Year: 2012
Built area: 45 m²
Photography: Tim Van de Velde
Engineering consultancy: Arthur De Roover

This reused barn is meant to replicate the charm of rural Belgium. It recuts an irreparable ruin with scissors of renewal without losing the concept, means and material.

The farmer's house gives place to rebuild an outdoor room with conservation of an indoor feeling. The reused barn becomes a relaxing space.

The garden chamber: A wooden skeleton covered with polycarbonate slates defines the image of a garden chamber. This results in a patio feeling that rises out of this typically Belgian courtyard. The wooden skeleton draws different lines on the slates during daytime. This gives the garden chamber a variety of sights every moment of the day. Solid and fragile. The room shines. Inside it is a cool area during the hot summer, while it gives a pleasing hothouse feeling during wintertime. The courtyard itself has a fresh coolness, by pulling open the angles. All four rhumbs play with the perspectives from inside to outside.

The monumentality of the old barn is totally preserved. It's not just restoration, it's reorientation. Inside the walls are whitewashed like a bleached sheet of stones. Sauna, shower and toilet are somehow hidden in the double-high space. Windows pull the courtyard inside out. The stove reaches high as an exclamation mark. Here is fire.

In the small extension there is a swimming pond. Water, filtered by lava and plants, reflecting the outside on the inside. An energetic bath.

The eclectic feeling of different houses. Old and new. It is the photosynthesis of the Belgian rural feeling.

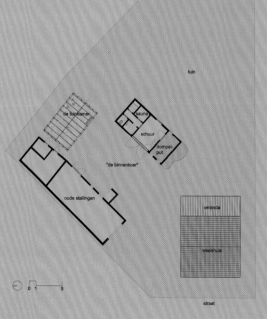

Site plan

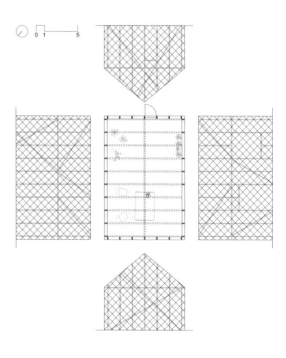

Plan and elevations

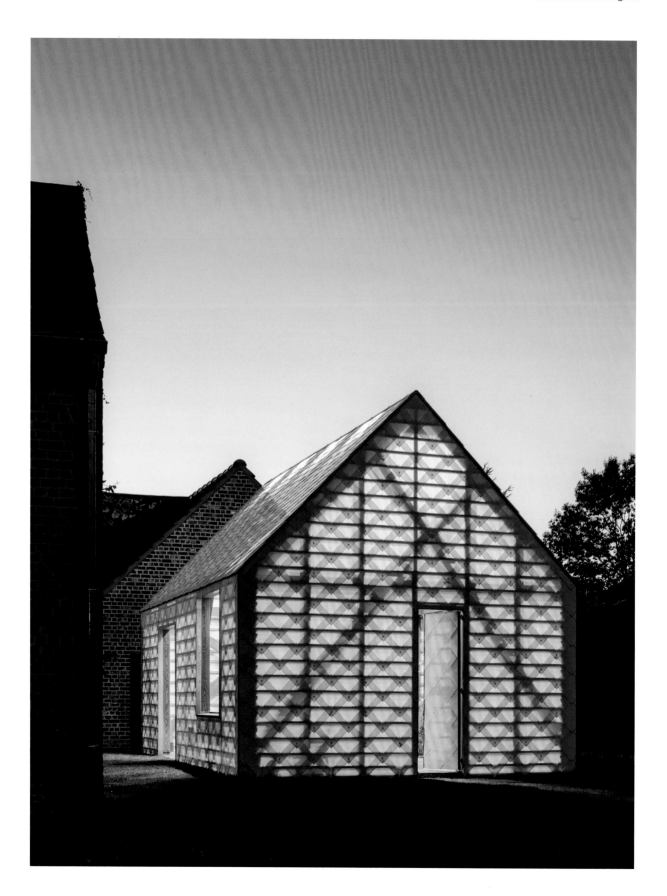

Concept drawing

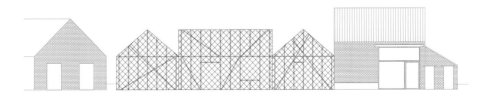

Unfolded profile

THE ESCAPE POD /
Podmakers

Architects: Jeremy Fitter, Dominic Ash (designers and makers)
Location: Gloucestershire, United Kingdom
Year: 2017
Built area: 7 m²
Photography: Tim Brotherton, India Ash
Manufacturers: James Latham, Luctite, Vesta stoves

The ellipsoid Pod, clad in cedar shingles and constructed out of birch ply and European oak, is the podmakers' luxury outdoor-space. The Escape Pod's unique, organic shape and high-quality contemporary interior provides the perfect place to work, meditate, socialize or sleep. It is both a design and a product—it can be adapted to virtually any site worldwide.

The Pod has an aircraft-style plug door and sits on a platform half a meter off the ground, allowing it to be rotated to catch the sun through its curved windows. With an adaptable interior, heating (wood burner or underfloor), electrics and insulation, the Pod has the potential to be used as a garden office, snug or studio. Each Pod is tailored to suit particular needs, from the window placement and internal finish to the fittings and furnishings.

Built with precision in the workshop, the Pod is delivered and installed using a forklift or crane. In a situation of severely restricted access, it can be assembled and clad on site. The Pod adheres to planning laws, so planning permission is not required in most cases.

The Pod includes four popular configurations:
Office: Whether you are writing a novel or looking for a more productive home office environment, the Escape Pod caters perfectly. There is plenty of integrated storage, power sockets and enough room for two people to work; Studio: Used as a studio, the Pod offers a great space for an artist to work or as an escape to indulge a hobbyist. This layout includes a drawing table and day bed; Snug: The comfortable snug has a raised 2.1x2 m mattress to watch the stars through the domed skylight. Alternatively the Escape Pod can be used as the ultimate glamping pod. Storage and clothes hooks can be included; Garden room: Easily seating ten, the circular bench and folding table makes the garden room a great place to socialize. With an upholstered bench and heating options, this is a very comfortable space to entertain or spend time with the family.

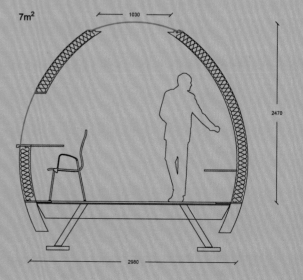

7m²   1030   2470   2980

Section

WRITING PAVILION /
Architensions

Design Principals: Alessandro Orsini & Nick Roseboro
Project designer: Rigo Gonzalez
Project team: Richard W. Off
Location: Brooklyn, New York, USA
Year: 2015
Built area: 10 m^2
Photography: Cameron Blaylock
General Contractor: A-G Home Improvements

Writing and drawing contribute to creating an imaginative parallel world and producing infinite options whenever a condition of isolation or immersive solitude is needed. The small space is located in the lush and protected garden of a creative couple involved in the arts. Nested on a concrete plinth, the pavilion employs black stained cedar for the exterior cladding and natural pine plywood for the interior. The pavilion's sectional shape acts as a device to bring natural light inside and induces optimal conditions for the human eye.

The room is minimally furnished with a chair and a folding writing table; the warm interior wood becomes the unifying element between the interior and exterior. The roof is conceived as a large sloped light well porous toward the trees and the sky; one elevation is dominated by a large opening looking out toward the garden. The specific phenomenological conditions of this retreat space make ideas come to life through a synthesis of material and spatial imagination.

The project, simply titled Writing Pavilion is proof that you don't always need a cabin in the woods to get away from day-to-day life.

The roof acts as partly as a sloping light well, pointing toward the neighboring trees and sky beyond. The window placed above the writing desk frames a view of the tree trunk. The remaining window in the patio door provides plenty of light for the desk area. It also allows you to see if anyone is using the studio from the house.

Over the course of the last few years, garden houses and studios have become increasingly popular due to the instability of the housing market. They're viewed as an affordable alternative that allows expansion of existing living spaces, with less risk compared to moving one's home.

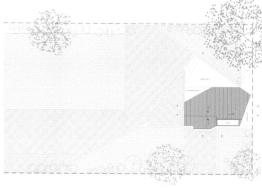

Site plan

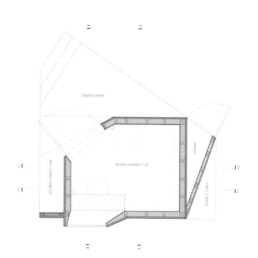

Floor plan

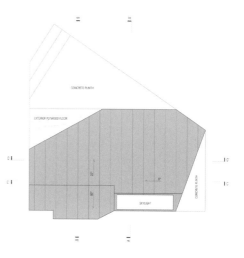

Roof plan

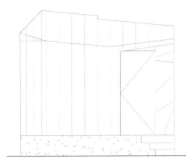

North elevation

Section CC

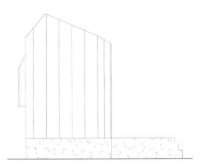

East elevation

Section AA

West elevation

Section BB

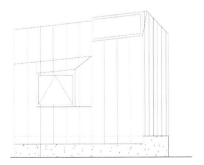

South elevation

Section DD

OFICINA VILA MADALENA / LCAC Arquitetura

Architects: Luis Canepa, André Chukr
Design Team: Ingrid Rosa, Tatiana Meca
Location: Vila Madalena, São Paulo, Brazil
Year: 2021
Built area: 11.40 m²
Photography: Guilherme Pucci
Interior: LCAC Arquitetura
Contractor: LCAC Arquitetura

Brazil has a rich twentieth century architectural history closely tied to the work of Le Corbusier and the Bauhaus. In this tradition, this project was commissioned by an animated film director who needed a space in his home to model pieces that he would use in his films. After walking around the house, the designers came to the conclusion that the roof slab of the house would be the best space to receive the new workshop. To create access to the roof, they continued on an existing spiral staircase.

To ensure that the structure not be overweight in the existing house and also to have a faster construction, the designers opted for prefabricated construction systems. A light metal structure supports the coverage of metal tiles with thermo-acoustic insulation. The walls are made of drywall, externally closed with cement boards for exposure to the weather and internally with naval plywood boards that is a more resistant material than the traditional painted plasterboards, a concern of the customer due to the use of space. Internally the walls are stuffed with pet insulation, a sustainable material produced from the recycling of plastic components, to ensure thermal comfort.

To take advantage of the view, the main facade has floor-to-ceiling windows; on the rear facade we have placed high windows to ensure cross ventilation. The massing and fenestration of the office is pure Bauhaus. On the upper level there is a precise black steel framed window grid, contrasted against light stucco on the lower level. Being in greater São Paulo, known as a concrete jungle, the office features native plantings to add a biophilic touch. Thus it is a sanctuary from the city. The interior is paneled in warm wood to further the natural atmosphere. The windows pivot open to provide fresh air, and they overlook both low-rise, terra-cotta roofed housing and the ubiquitous high-rises for which São Paulo is known. An existing spiral staircase provides easy access to the office from the main house.

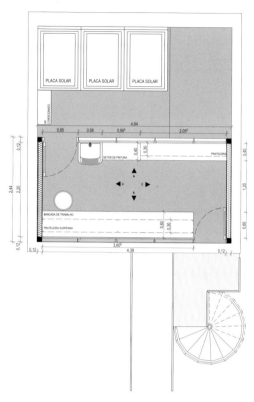

Site plan

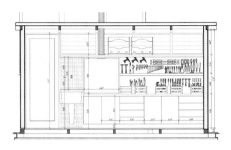

Section AA

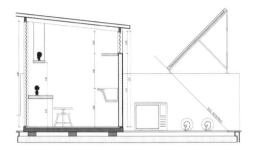

Section DD

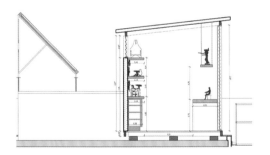

Section CC

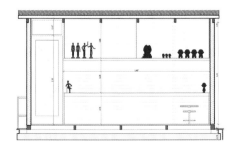

Section BB

LIGHT SHEDS /
FT Architects

Architects: Katsuya Fukushima, Hiroko Tominaga
Location: Kanagawa, Japan
Year: 2014
Built area: 33.12 m²
Photography: Shigeo Ogawa
Structural engineer: Shuji Tada

The Light Sheds are a photographer's studio that stands in the
garden of his existing house, located in the hilly region of greater
Tokyo. The space is solely composed of essential functions
required for a photographic studio, and the result is one single
room of 4.5 meters by 7.2 meters. From the start, the designers
had a concept of creating a simple, pragmatic sheds.

In order to form a large volume out of the limited budget
available, a timber frame, gable roof structure was selected.
However, a gable roof would typically entail horizontal joists,
which would reduce the clear height required for photo shoots.
Following simple geometric rules, the roof was distorted into
a multifacetted, asymmetric form. Three ridge beams at the
folding lines support the roof structure, negating the need for
any horizontal members that may compromise the height of the
room. Logs were selected for the ridge beams, for their ability to
accommodate the complex assembly of timber rafters at various
angles. Translucent polycarbonate panels reveal the "back of
the stage set" timber framework of the walls.

Like artists' ateliers, photographic studios require ample ambient light. Direct sunlight creates overly strong contrasts that
would result in unnatural portraits. A combination of skylights at
45 degrees and a clerestory let in diffused light from two different
angles from above. Together with the wide windows on the side
facing onto the lush garden, the interior, although enclosed, is
always as bright as the external environment. It has the duality
of being both outside and in, blurring the conventional architectural boundaries.

Ever since the practice's first project, C-Office, an office for
a Japanese timber manufacturer, application of pragmatic
structural solutions has been the core of the firm's approach
in all projects.

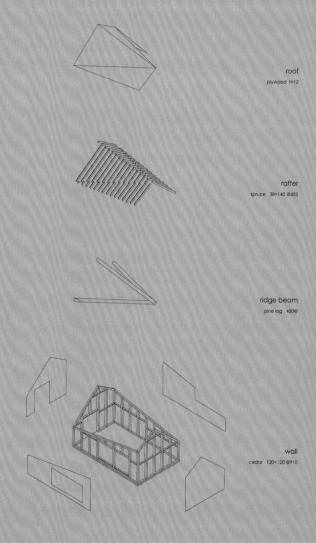

roof
plywood t=12

rafter
spruce 38×140 @455

ridge beam
pine log 450Φ

wall
cedar 120×120 @910

Exploded Axonometric - Composition

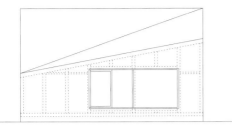

East elevation

South elevation

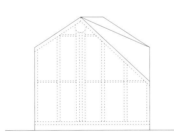

North elevation

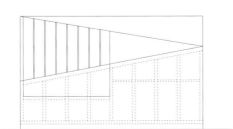

West elevation

The designers have also been continually exploring ways to inherit and translate the purity of traditional Japanese timber compositions into modern construction. Here, while the log beams were employed as pragmatic means to fulfill the brief, they also bring along symbolic associations of being one of the oldest building materials. In this project, designers were able to test the modern significance of this primitive material through using it as a meaningful device to create a man-made enclosure where photographic subjects can be exposed in "natural" light.

Plan

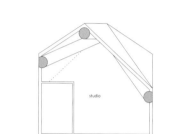

West-east section 01

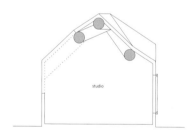

West-east section 02

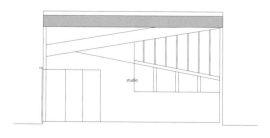

South-north section

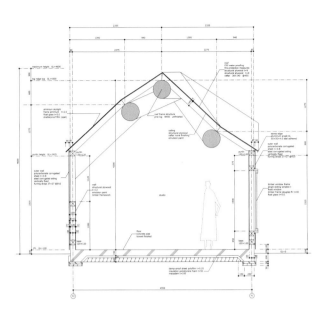

West-east section

gable   transform   reverse

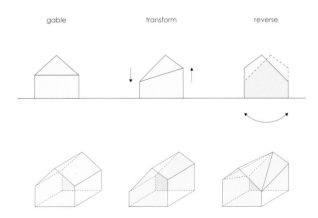

Geometric rule

MY ROOM IN THE GARDEN /
Boano Prišmontas

Design, Manufacturing, Installation: Boano Prišmontas
Location: London, United Kingdom
Year: 2020
Built area: 4 m²
Photography: Dylan Drake
Illustration: Raphaelle Macaron
Metalwork: Canofgas
Birch Plywood: DHH Timber
Special Thanks: Alicia Arguelles Garcia, Liz Parr, Jonathan Cardy

Boano Prišmontas, the London-based studio of architects and makers, launched My Room in the Garden, an affordable prefab home office adaptable to almost anywhere in the UK. The low-cost solution is easy to assemble and it can be built in one day. The structure is made in London, and the modular design can fit a garden of any size. The project aims to address the need for affordable and remote working spaces.

My Room in the Garden, an answer to the future way of working, is a cozy prefab hideout for London gardens and courtyard spaces, perfect for those working from home or whoever is in need of a pocket space, tailored to their needs and comforts.

Boano Prišmontas has been working on this topic for several years, developing successful projects such as Minima Moralia (2016) and the Arches Project (2019). The need for a work-from-home solution became quite urgent lately when the COVID-19 pandemic required designers to come up with new solutions able to combine workspace with domesticity.

Despite the fact that the lockdown has ended in many countries around the world, an incredibly large number of people are still working from home, often without a clear date in mind of when their lives will be returning to normality. Normality is no longer there waiting; the pandemic brought radical changes that cannot be dismissed or ignored.

If on one side people working from home have to find their ways to integrate work equipment within their current home setting, on the other, companies have started seeing the renting of office space as an unnecessary and avoidable cost. The current live/work balance has been permanently disrupted and both the office and home design standards are now outdated and almost obsolete.

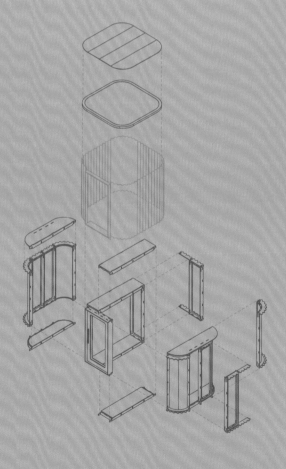

Exploded axonometric

Distanced desks and laptop stands have populated living rooms and saturated any shared space. London houses, whose space standards have been squeezed to the minimum, are struggling. That's why it is not fair that employees have to sacrifice and compromise their domestic environment any further. The solution is not to be found inside the houses, but outside. London houses are perfect to host home office pods in backyard gardens, courtyards, gated communities, rooftops, shared amenity spaces and pocket parks. Starting from £5,000 for the basic module, My Room in the Garden is a solution for both private homeowners and for companies that could reduce their rent cost for big offices in central London by instead purchasing home office pods for their employees.

The project seeks to find a balance between low-cost and cozy design. The structure is made of digitally fabricated birch plywood modules that can be customized according to each space and user's need.

Starting from a minimum of 1.8 x 2.4 m, the home office pods can grow infinitely, by just adding more modules. All modules come at a fixed height of 2.5 m, which is the max height that doesn't require planning permission in the UK.

The standard finish includes corrugated clear polycarbonate cladding that protects the interior space from the elements and allows for natural light to flood the internal space. The wall modules can host different finishes such as peg wall, mirror, plain or decorated wood. The user can compose the interiors to their taste and needs. The higher-spec version includes insulated wall/roof/floor panels and glass door/windows.

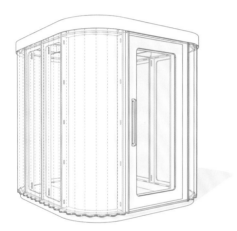

Perspective

Each component of the home-office pod is geometrically efficient and minimizes any material waste. The dimensioning of each component is based on human dimensions and standard material dimensions. The whole project is designed, manufactured and pre-assembled in the UK.

Like many other design businesses, Boano Prišmontas suffered the uncertainty brought by the COVID-19 pandemic. Instead of giving up working, waiting for the pandemic to pass, the firm invested time during lockdown to prototype and manufacture this project in our workshop. The designers always like to stress how important it is for architects and designers to mature adaptive skills and have in-depth know-how of manufacturing processes and materials.

The architecture profession is fragile, beautiful, and often deemed superfluous. The designers believe that the way out of any impasses relies on having an entrepreneurial attitude. Many practices are deeply suffering from the effects of the pandemic, but design can blur the boundaries of the profession and dare to envision a desired future.

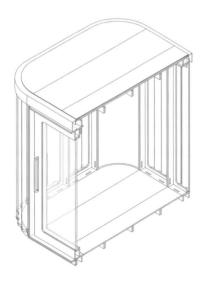

Section axonometric

TINI OFFICE /
tini

Design team: tini / tiniliving.com
Architects: delaVegaCanolasso
Location: Madrid, Spain
Year: 2020
Built area: 22 m²
Photography: Imagen Subliminal (Miguel de Guzmán, Rocío Romero)
Construction: tini / tiniliving.com

With a generous amount of glass that recalls great early-twentieth-century architecture, the Tini Office is a prefabricated modules made in Spain in 60 days and transported to any location. Each model comes ready-to-use and is fully furnished.

This featured module was for a garden office, fully custom-made for the client's needs. The module seamlessly blends into the trees and has magnificent views of the oak garden.

The module is made of a Corten Steel frame lined with OSB poplar wood, insulated with 12 cm of recycled cotton.

All kitchen furniture, cabinets and worktables are made of local wood, pine and poplar.

The chairs are custom made by Dr. Cato, and the remaining furnishings are midcentury.

The walls are decorated with works from delavegacanolas—so, antique fabrics sewn by machine with unique designs.

The space also features a collection of interior plants from Selvaviva.

The result is a space that maximizes every square meter, and provides a warm environment from which to work, rest and observe nature.

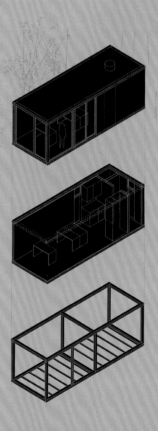

Exploded axonometric

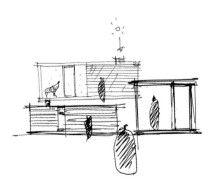

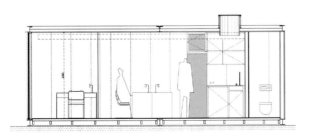

Detailed section

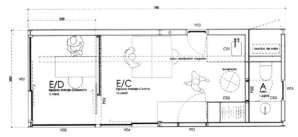

Detailed plan

SHADOW SHED /
Neil Dusheiko Architects

Architects: Neil Dusheiko Architects
Location: Belsize Park, London, United Kingdom
Year: 2015
Built area: 12 m²
Photography: Agnese Sanvito
Engineer: Momentum
Timber Cladding: Exterior Decking Company
Resin Floor: Sika
Glazing: EKS
Lighting: Mr. Resistor

A multipurpose garden pavilion designed to blend quietly into the back gardens in a conservation area to function as an ancillary space to the main dwelling—a dark jewel. It encompasses traditional Japanese building traditions and is designed as a small outdoor building within the rear garden of an existing Victorian house.

The back gardens are characterized by lush and verdant vegetation. The small garden building provides space for the client, to use as a consultation space during the day and for practicing yoga at night. The facade is made of heavily textured cedar, blackened using a traditional Japanese technique called Shou Sugi Ban.

The concept was for the pavilion to be a quiet, abstracted object in the landscape of the garden. The pavilion is conceived as an inhabited garden wall, the dark textured timber blending into the shadows of the trees and having a common language with shed architecture. The pavilion is sunken into the earth to reduce its scale within the garden with carefully managed excavations around existing tree roots. The garden facing elevation is raised above the ground forming an abstract pattern of dark timber and reflective glass creating glimpses into the structure—a play of solid and void.

The material palette is kept to three basic elements: a poured resin floor and recycled birch plywood skin internally with the charred blackened timber externally. Plywood is used to create joinery units inside. Lighting is provided by a collection of pinhole fiber optic points on the ceiling forming a constellation pattern and dimmable recessed LED lighting.

The ability to create a range of atmospheres within the small space allows it to be used in a multifunctional way during the day and night.

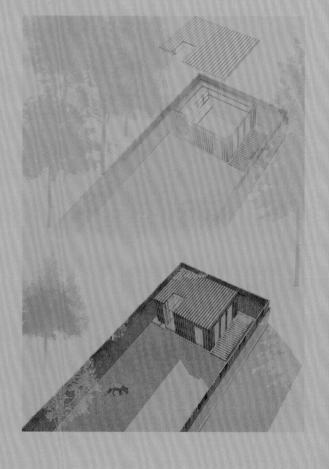

Project summary - Shadow Shed

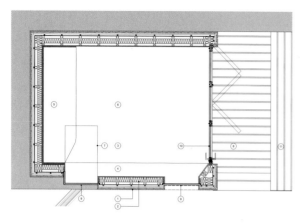

Floor plan

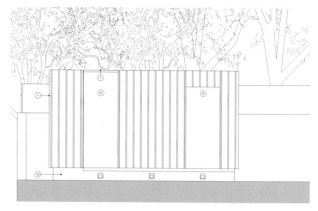

Elevation

1. Shou sugi ban cedar timber cladding
2. Timber stud walls with insulation
3. Birch plywood with acrylic finish
4. Birch plywood shelf
5. Birch plywood desk
6. Poured resin floor
7. Skylight over
8. Eco-decking on adjustable pads

9. Frameless glass window
10. Bi-folding double glazed doors
11. Storage bench with recessed lighting
12. Insitu concrete upstand
13. Recessed LED lighting
14. Eco-decking layer on GRP Roofing

Site - Proposed ground floor plan

Site - Proposed cross section

The choice of materials was a key factor in securing planning permission for this outdoor pavilion in a conservation area. The Conservation Department wanted something that would be quiet and ubiquitous in the back garden. The designers had an open dialogue with the Conservation Officer and suggested a burnt cedar cladding system, which they accepted.

We used Shou Sugi Ban, which is the traditional Japanese technique to burn Sugi timber to preserve the wood. By burning the wood one is able to provide a fireproof material that is low maintenance and resistant to rot and fire. We experimented with the process of creating the Shou Sugi Ban by burning the wood and cooling it down quickly with water allowing for an uneven textured surface. We used a range of different timbers before selecting cedar.

The process embodies the Japanese philosophy of Wabi-sabi. Wabi-sabi is a world view that is based on the acceptance of transience and imperfection. Beauty is seen as being "imperfect, impermanent and incomplete."

As the technique of burning is used on wood with differing age, water and sap content the results are not always controlled—this process allows for a richness of texture, color and grain that is at once beautiful and spontaneous.

Internally we chose a birch plywood finished with an acrylic coating to form a contrast to the highly textured external panels. The modular system of the birch is also contrasted with the thinner lengths of the dark planks.

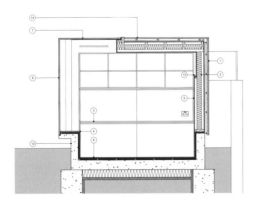

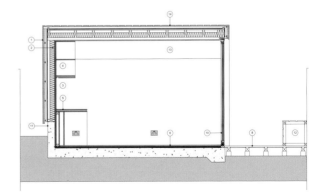

Short section

Long section

1. Shou sugi ban cedar timber cladding
2. Timber stud walls with insulation
3. Birch plywood with acrylic finish
4. Birch plywood shelf

5. Birch plywood desk
6. Poured resin floor
7. Skylight over
8. Eco-decking on adjustable pads

9. Frameless glass window
10. Bi-folding double glazed doors
11. Storage bench with recessed lighting

12. Insitu concrete upstand
13. Recessed LED lighting
14. Eco-decking layer on GRP Roofing

CUT & FRAME HOUSE /
Ashton Porter Architects

Architects: Ashton Porter Architects
Location: Grange Park, London, United Kingdom
Year: 2013
Built area: 178 m²
Photography: Andy Stagg
Structural Engineer: Constant Structural Design
Contractor: Allen Wilson Shopfitters & Builders

Cut and Frame House was driven by the requirement for both clients to work from home and both have separate spaces. The connection between the house and the garden writing hut was therefore a key element of the project. The existing house was internally remodeled, and a series of historical, somewhat ad hoc, compartmentalized additions and alterations were removed to provide improved interconnected living spaces.

The connection between hut and house is reinforced by framing elements. The main house has a floating seat of aluminum that becomes part of the internal seating of the house when the large glazed panels are slid away and a garden seat at other times. It is clad in highly contrasting anodized aluminum and hangs from a discreet steel frame cantilevering from within the existing house.

The reciprocal aluminum element to the writing hut can either be an elevated seat with access internally by steps or a display for artefacts and artwork.

One client is a children's book author, the other a therapist. The hut's facade that faces the main house is dominated by a large picture window framed in aluminum. It corresponds exactly, that is lines up with, a similar window in the main house. The interior is paneled in a light wood that lends it a Scandinavian flair. The cathedral ceiling ends in a skylight that floods the interior with natural light.

This site is landscaped in small terraces to compensate for the change in level. The large glazed panels enable the garden to become part of the living space and thus the writing hut, while providing privacy and tranquility, is still very connected to family life.

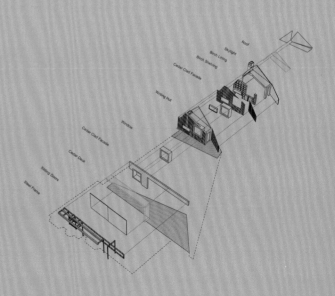

Exploded axonometric

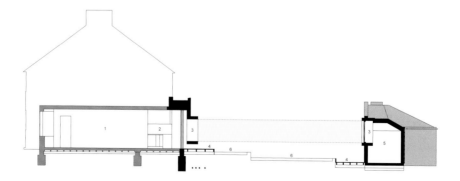

Section AA

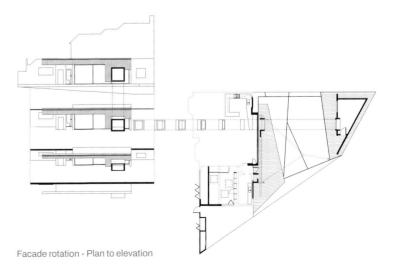

Facade rotation - Plan to elevation

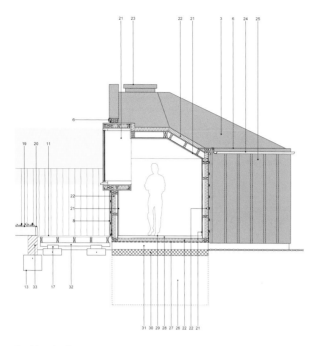

Working detail

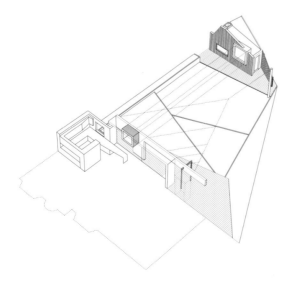

Axonometric

Appendix
Contributing Designers

Platform 5 Architects

Platform 5 Architects is an award-winning architectural practice founded by Patrick Michell in 2006 and was recently shortlisted for Building Design's Young Architect of the Year 2018. The firm has a diverse portfolio of projects in the residential, education, commercial and cultural sectors. Projects include a 63-unit housing scheme on the historic Toynbee Hall site which is currently on site, a major remodeling and new build project at Lewisham Southwark College in South London that won an AJ Retrofit Award in 2015, alongside smaller scale domestic works such as Facet House—a winner at the 2016 Don't Move Improve! Awards, and RIBA East Awards 2017 winner Backwater.

Feldman Architecture

Feldman Architecture is an innovative residential and commercial design practice recognized for creating warm, light-filled spaces that are site-sensitive and carefully detailed. Highly collaborative in nature, the firm approaches design as a dialogue between client, design team and site. Each project is an opportunity to create an innovative solution that is relevant to the project environs and tailored to clients' specific needs. The studio's culture is also informal and non-hierarchical; members of the small firm work with clients in an engaging, shared process to find smart and sustainable solutions. Closely guiding projects from design through construction, designers and project managers are deeply involved in research and probing the parameters of a project. Strong alliances with consultants, builders and artisans contribute to carefully informed design decisions and result in fully realized projects with conceptual clarity and precise detailing.

Almoznivila

Almoznivila is a small architecture studio that carries out small- and medium-scale works. Located in the Argentine Pampas plain, in Buenos Aires Province, it works in an integral and personalized way each project providing a creative response and solutions that are easy to build, minimizing the amount of materials to achieve a synthesis in the reading of the project. The firm's work is widely published in venues such as Archello, *ArchDaily*, *Dwell*, Four Square, Redditt, Contemporist, *Journal du Design*, among many others.

RISE Design Studio

RISE Design Studio is an innovative contemporary architecture practice based in London, making schools, restaurants and houses, dealing with England and Ireland's diffuse light and absolute materiality. Architecture is experienced emotionally, felt through the skin as much as viewed through the eyes. For this reason, since the studio was founded in 2011, there has been a strong focus equally on the physicality of their work as on its conception. The firm's work is informed by an awareness of place and context, craft and materiality, local climate, inclusion of sustainability, a consideration of form and an understanding of the simplicity and quality of well-made buildings. The studio approaches every project as a unique and singular opportunity. Through discussion, observation and research, informed by our considerable project experience, it engages in a critical investigation of each project's needs and constraints—with the objective of delivering the highest level of design quality, and buildings which are practical, inspiring and beautiful. The work is also characterized by a rigorous and analytical approach to function and planning, and a thorough process of refinement that is applied to every detail.

FLOAT architecture research and design

Erin E. Moore, AIA, is an architect who uses her design research practice FLOAT architecture research and design to explore and advance thought on ideas of nature in architectural design. She works with explicit intentions for material, ecological and multispecies life cycles. Recent work addresses the architectural space of fossil fuel consumption, biogenic carbon sequestration and climate change in the context of new materialisms, critical spatial practice, speculative design and the environmental humanities. Moore is a Professor in the Department of Architecture and in the Environmental Studies Program at the University of Oregon. She is a graduate of Smith College (BA) and University of California-Berkeley (MArch).

Studio Ben Allen

Studio Ben Allen is a multidisciplinary design practice. The firm operates at the intersection of architecture, design and art. It has a reputation for creating unique and engaging spaces using simple materials to striking effect. In order to create unique and engaging spatial sequences, each of the projects, from concept to production, has at its core an open collaborative dialogue between participants and disciplines. In 2017 the studio participated in the Folkestone Triennial and in 2018 it was listed as one of the top 20 emerging architects globally by *Dezeen*. Their workplace design for Cundall received the first European Well certification. The practice's project the House Recast was awarded the overall prize for the best London house in the 2021 the Don't Move Improve! awards and in 2022 the practice was awarded the Royal Scottish Academy Architecture Prize.

Serge Schoemaker Architects

Serge Schoemaker Architects is an award-winning multidisciplinary design studio founded in Amsterdam, the Netherlands in 2008. The practice works on carefully designed, bespoke buildings, interiors, landscape objects and art installations. Serge Schoemaker Architects designs buildings that last. That is why they put an emphasis on high quality materials, craft and taking the time to make sure the design is sustainable in its widest sense. The practice works on projects in the public domain, the cultural and private sector. They advise clients from initial concept—via feasibility studies and design sketches—to final completion. Special attention is given to the realization phase: through in-house project management during the construction process, they can ensure that the design will be executed with the quality that they envisioned. Their work has been frequently published and awarded. Serge Schoemaker Architects won the 2021 NRP Golden Phoenix Award and the 2021 Pieter van Vollenhoven Prize. Furthermore, they received an Honorable Mention in the 2021 BNA Best Building of the Year competition.

ANX / Aaron Neubert Architects

Founded in 2006, Aaron Neubert Architects is a design practice committed to orchestrating poetic relationships among landscape, light and materiality, resulting in beautifully crafted spaces that amplify the human experience and advance stewardship of the natural environment. Led by Aaron Neubert, FAIA, the Los Angeles based practice has produced a diverse portfolio of sustainable, site-specific work that spans private residences, housing, hotels, restaurants, commercial programs and institutional facilities. The practice's inventive formal and site resiliency strategies preserve delicate and complex ecologies

while improving the wellness of the community. The practice has been featured in a number of international publications including *Architecture*, *Architect*, *Interior Design*, *Metropolis*, the *New York Times*, the *Los Angeles Times*, the *Huffington Post*, *IFJ/India*, *Objekt International/Netherlands*, *Maisons & Bois International/France*, *Domus*, *Living Magazine/Brazil* and *Dwell*. This body of work has been recognized with awards from the Westside Urban Forum, AIA Los Angeles, AIA San Fernando Valley, AIA New York, Global Architecture & Design Awards, and the Van Alen Prize in Public Architecture. The projects have been exhibited and presented at the University of Southern California, Woodbury University and Dwell on Design in Los Angeles; the Royal Danish Academy of Fine Arts in Copenhagen, Denmark; Florida Atlantic University in Ft. Lauderdale, Florida; ARCHMARATHON in Miami Beach, Florida; and the Van Alen Institute in New York City.

Matt Gibson Architecture + Design

Matt Gibson Architecture + Design is a design-based practice located in Melbourne, Australia, that provides architectural, interior and furniture design services. MGA+D has produced numerous projects within the residential sector yet prides itself on being able to provide rigorously generated design solutions within a wide variety of project types and scales. The practice's growth has been based on promoting the principles of innovation and collaboration while truly fusing the disciplines of Architecture and Interior Design within a medium-sized practice. MGA+D is interested in spaces that address the primal experiential nature in people, through basic attractions to light, material and patterns of movement. This involves a commitment and close attention to the detailing of scale, surface, threshold and junction and the rigorous exploration of the zones between what has come before and what is new. MGA+D has received numerous local and international awards including most recently the AIA John George Knight award for Heritage Architecture in Victoria.

Richard John Andrews

Richard John Andrews was established in 2017 following the completion of a Cork House, a self-build home renovation and extension in East London. The studio has always been considered as an experimental testbed not only for materials, designs and details, but also company structure, business strategies and innovative schemes including a four-day working week with no loss in pay. Establishing a five-year plan early in its conception has laid out a clear set of milestones for the studio which included Conception, Expansion, Workplace and Holism. The Light Shed, featured within this publication, was a key element within the process of Expansion for the studio.

London Garden Studios

Cabinet maker Marc Salamon founded London Garden Studios in 2010, after building a workshop in his own garden a few years earlier as well as bespoke studios for friends. From the first, London Garden Studios has kept an all timber aesthetic, including doors and windows that are manufactured in the LGS workshop. In constant demand, the company has maintained a boutique profile, only working on one project at a time. Each studio is built on site by Marc and his assistant. This approach allows for close collaboration with the customer over the positioning of doors and windows and incorporation of personalised touches such as built-in furniture and landscaping around the studio.

Teresa Mascaro

Teresa Mascaro got her bachelor's degree in 2000 in architecture and urbanism from the University Mackenzie, São Paulo. From 2000 to 2006, she worked as a collaborating architect in a few different architecture offices. Teresa has had her own business since 2007, where she develops residential, corporate, commercial, institutional, cultural projects and manages the construction sites.

Panov-Scott

Panov-Scott is a practice with expertise in the fields of architecture and strategic and urban design, led by Anita Panov and Andrew Scott. The firm's practice has an ambition to engage meaningfully in the shaping of the physical and cultural world around us. In this sense we believe working with the everyday is the most profound offering of design, and our role is to recalibrate a new normal that enables joyful engagement with communities and environments, while retaining a position of empathetic sensitivity to the existing character of the places in which the studio works. The firm's practice and projects have been awarded in multiple forums for design excellence, and the practice has been commissioned for many projects via competitive design excellence processes. Those within the practice have been recognized as thought leaders within various disciplines as evidenced by regular and effective engagement in design review, teaching, advocacy, research and curation roles for different authorities, universities and other institutions.

Cutler Anderson Architects

Established in 1977, Cutler Anderson Architects' approach to design can be stated simply as an attempt to reveal the nature of every circumstance—the nature of the place in which it is located, the nature of the materials with which to build and the nature of the institution. Cutler Anderson projects span across three continents and include custom cabins, residences, libraries, resorts, churches and government ventures such as the Port of Entry between eastern Washington State and British Columbia, and most recently the modernization of the Edith Green Wendell Wyatt Federal Building in Portland, Oregon, a LEED Platinum high-rise. Dedicated to design excellence, Cutler Anderson Architects has received six National Honor Awards from the American Institute of Architects and over 50 other national and regional awards. The firm has been featured in numerous articles published in the *New York Times*, *Architectural Record*, *Elle Décor Italy*, *Häuser*, *Dwell* and *Seattle* magazine.

Franz&Sue

The five founders of Franz&Sue first met when they were studying architecture at the Vienna University of Technology and initially founded two independent architectural firms in Vienna, Franz and Sue. In the legendary Fight Club discussions, however, they discovered that they not only share an architectural approach, but also speak the same language in the culture of their companies

and in their commitment to building culture. In May 2017, they then grew together to form Franz&Sue. Since the "marriage" of Franz&Sue in May 2017, over 90 people from 18 nations have been working together. The founders and managing partners are Christian Ambos, Michael Anhammer, Robert Diem, Harald Höller and Erwin Stättner. Since the beginning of 2022, long-time employees Corinna Toell and Björn Haunschmid-Wakolbinger have been part of the management team as partners. We believe in relevance beyond fashion. That's why our architecture is clear, radical and sustainable. And made by people for people, not for prestige or trends. The neighborhood house and architecture cluster Stadtelefant is a project close to our hearts: an office building near Vienna's main railway station in the new Sonnwendviertel district, which we developed, financed, planned and built together with friendly architecture firms, industry-related companies and architectural institutions. The studio has been working here since the end of 2018, having lunch together in the in-house restaurant Mimi im Stadtelefant and exchanging ideas with people interested in architecture at events. However, as the firm has doubled in size in the past two years, the Stadtelefant became too small and we moved into new quarters 150 meters further east: the Franz&Sue Studio. This is where the competition team and other project groups work on two floors, where the staff tinker with new models in the workshop and enjoy their lunch in the adjoining courtyard.

Gluck+

At Gluck+, design matters and building matters. Better buildings result when architects take on the construction process. The firm's approach to Architect Led Design Build ensures that the built solution is done right. The evolution of the firm name from Peter Gluck and Partners Architects to Gluck+ recognizes that our practice has always been inclusive. From designer to builder to owner to developer, the firm does what it takes and cares how it's done. "Outside our scope" is not in the vocabulary. The work is diverse and recognized worldwide through national and international design awards and publications. The studio's range of projects—from houses, schools, religious buildings, community centers to hotels, university buildings, recreation centers and historic restorations—are all unique because each project is specific. Gluck+ is dedicated to advocating for the wants and needs of clients. It is their stories we want to tell.

Atelier Janda Vanderghote

A young agency from Ghent with a passion for craft and detail, Atelier Janda Vanderghote has built its knowledge and experience for a long time in leading agencies. The firm strives for sustainable projects that are subtly woven into their environment. It tries to achieve an ideal symbiosis of aesthetic design, a logical structure and a good landscape layout. The vision consists of a sustainable design of landscape, building and technology with an emphasis on optimal and ecological use. The designers strive for global sustainability, both in terms of design, choice of materials, integration into the environment and orientation. For example, the firm will opt for sustainable materials and materials with a limited environmental impact. Atelier Janda Vanderghote was founded by architects Indra Janda and Menno Vanderghote.

Podmakers

Podmakers Ltd was established through the union of high quality furniture design and a desire to engineer small spaces. Aspiring to create beautiful, unusual outdoor structures, Dominic Ash and Jeremy Fitter have collaborated to develop Podmakers. Dominic trained for six years with a Quaker furniture maker in Somerset before working on boat restoration in the Caribbean and going on to form his own company in 1994. Dominic Ash Ltd specializes in high-quality design in hardwood and contemporary materials. Podmakers benefits greatly from working closely with Dominic Ash Ltd and the 30 years of design experience Dominic brings to the team. After a master's in civil engineering, specializing in tree houses, Jeremy's design ideas were planted on more solid ground after working for Dominic Ash Ltd. His engineering background and passion for creating imaginative spaces, propelled Jeremy to co-found Podmakers.

Architensions

Architensions (ATE) is an international architectural design studio operating as an agency of research led by Alessandro Orsini and Nick Roseboro and based in New York and Rome. The studio was founded in 2010 as a vehicle to investigate the city and its spatial form and was re-founded in 2013 with Nick Roseboro. Diverse in backgrounds and creative experience, the studio looks at architecture, design and the city with a perspective rooted in site-specificity enabling us to explore new ways to connect history and culture.

LCAC Arquitetura

LCAC is an architectural firm based in São Paulo, and most of the firm's work is done in the capital and on the coast and mountains of São Paulo state. The office is coordinated by partners Luis Canepa and André Chukr with the collaboration of several professionals in the field of civil construction. The firm has the desire to produce good architecture for clients by building something special and unique with respect for the environment and the city.

FT Architects

FT Architects is a Tokyo-based architectural office founded by Katsuya Fukushima and Hiroko Tominaga in 2003. They both graduated from Tokyo National University of Fine Arts and Music in 1993. Katsuya worked for Toyo Ito & Associates, and Hiroko worked for Hisao Kohyama Atelier prior to founding their office. They have been involved in numerous projects in Japan and they have won the AIJ Award in 2015 with Timber Structure I and II. FT Architects have been interested in tectonics and aesthetics, being historical and being experimental. They have also been working on numerous research projects, and their book Holz Bau was awarded the DAM Architectural Book Award 2020. They have taught at a number of Japanese Universities; currently Katsuya is an Assistant Professor at Tokyo City University, and Hiroko is a Professor at Kogakuin University.

Boano Prišmontas

Tomaso Boano and Jonas Prišmontas are the co-founders and directors of the London-based architectural creative firm Boano Prišmontas Ltd. The studio works on architectural and modular design solutions, as well as urban regeneration schemes and design strategies. Tomaso Boano and Jonas Prišmontas have international experience within the areas of architecture and interiors, F&B and hospitality, retail, public realm, art, product design and digital manufacturing. The studio adopts a creative and hands-on approach as a strategic tool to propose design solutions to the contemporary world. Each project draws inspiration from, and combines, various aspects of art, architecture and technology. Boano and Prišmontas have been jurors for various architectural competitions, and lecturers at Manchester Metropolitan University (UK), Bilkent University (Turkey), FAL University (Germany), IUAV University (Italy), Architectural Foundation (UK) and FORMA (UK). Their projects have been published on many international blogs and magazines such as *Dezeen*, *DETAIL*, *ArchDaily*, *AR*, *DesignBoom*, *AJ*, *Area*, and *Domus*, among others. The arches project was finalist at the 2020 Building of the Year by *ArchDaily*. Our project Minima Moralia was also featured in several printed publications around the world including the book *Small Homes, Grand Living* by Gestalten.

tini

Created in 2020, tini started by offering a product, a small refuge in nature and we have evolved to encompass the entire process of having a custom home. The goal is to improve the experience through this process. With this system the firm can offer the client certainty in prices and deadlines, which the firm believes is crucial to start the adventure of building your own home. The question is, how would you like to live?

Neil Dusheiko Architects

Neil Dusheiko studied architecture at the University of Witwatersrand in Johannesburg graduating in 1994 with distinction. Following his studies, he worked for various practices in Sydney, Australia, until moving to London in 1998. Neil is passionate about designing homes. He is fascinated by the minutiae that make up people's lives and draws inspiration from his client's hopes and dreams for how they can live better lives by being in well-designed surroundings. Working with historic properties in London, Neil's work seeks to transform aged properties into light filled contemporary homes that enrich people's lives and create warm spaces they love to call home.

Ashton Porter Architects

Ashton Porter Architects is an award-winning RIBA Chartered Practice based in Enfield, London. The practice is led by partners Abigail Ashton and Andrew Porter, who both graduated from the Bartlett School of Architecture UCL in 1994. They were jointly awarded the Bannister Fletcher Prize and Medal for best graduating students. They also both jointly won the RIBA Silver Medal for best national diploma student in 1994. Their first project was in 1995 for the Petrie Museum Competition in Bloomsbury, London. They were awarded Second Prize by judges Richard Rogers, Enric Miralles and Itsuko Hasegawa. It was the first of many award-winning competitions. They have practiced in partnership ever since.

Book Credits
Edited by Oscar Riera Ojeda
Art direction by Oscar Riera Ojeda
Graphic Design by Lucía B. Bauzá

First published in the United States of America in 2024 by
RIZZOLI INTERNATIONAL PUBLICATIONS, INC.
300 Park Avenue South, New York, NY 10010
www.rizzoliusa.com

© 2024 Rizzoli International Publications, Inc. and Oscar Riera Ojeda
Publisher: Charles Miers
Editor for Rizzoli: Douglas Curran
Production Manager: Alyn Evans
Managing Editor: Lynn Scrabis
Design Manager: Olivia Russin
Proofreader: Sarah Stump

Front cover: The Light Shed (p. 114), by Richard John Andrews Architects; photograph by Chris Snook.
Back cover photos: Please see book interior for project and photo credits.
Introduction photos (pp. 10–11): all images courtesy iStock by Getty Images.

Printed and bound in China

2024 2025 2026 2027 2028/ 10 9 8 7 6 5 4 3 2 1
ISBN-13: 978-08478-7399-9
Library of Congress Control Number: 2023911318

Visit us online:
Facebook.com/RizzoliNewYork
Twitter: @Rizzoli_Books
Instagram.com/RizzoliBooks
Pinterest.com/RizzoliBooks
Youtube.com/user/RizzoliNY
Issuu.com/Rizzoli